PRACTICAL THEOLOGY

PRACTICAL THEOLOGY

Charismatic and Empirical Perspectives

MARK J. CARTLEDGE

STUDIES IN PENTECOSTAL
AND CHARISMATIC ISSUES

WIPF & STOCK · Eugene, Oregon

Wipf and Stock Publishers
199 W 8th Ave, Suite 3
Eugene, OR 97401

Practical Theology
Charismatic and Empirical Perspectives
By Cartledge, Mark J.
Copyright©2003 by Cartledge, Mark J.
ISBN 13: 978-1-62032-123-2
Publication date 4/1/2012
Previously published by Paternoster, 2003

To Joan and Rebekah

Contents

Acknowledgements

I would like to acknowledge, as ever, the support of my family throughout the process of writing this book. Joan, my wife, and Rebekah, my daughter, continue to be a great source of love and encouragement. A sabbatical study leave during the Epiphany term of 2002 enabled me to write the basic text of the book and I am grateful to St John's College Council for the opportunity to write in the course of my duties. This book is a sequel to my doctoral publication and develops some of my ideas contained there, especially in relation to methodology. My former doctoral supervisor, William Kay, continues to support my endeavours with his friendship and willingness to write a foreword to this book. I remain in his debt. It was a great joy to have our Canadian friend, Gloria Leahy, stay with us in Durham for three weeks in the summer of 2002. She read most the manuscript while on holiday and made invaluable suggestions for improvement. I am grateful to church friends Stuart Hutchinson and Andy Harris who read the manuscript and made helpful and insightful comments. Various academic colleagues have had occasion to read sections or drafts, including Walter Moberly, Paul Murray, Gavin Wakefield, Roger Walton, Jack Wisemore and Amos Yong. I am grateful to all of them for their feedback and advice. In addition, I have benefited from the statistical help offered by Leslie Francis and for which I am extremely grateful. While I have been the beneficiary of such assistance, none of these persons should be held responsible for any shortcomings in this study – these remain entirely my own!

I am pleased that Paternoster has launched the new monograph series, 'Studies in Pentecostal and Charismatic Issues', and that this book forms part of the initiative. I am appreciative of the editorial assistance of Jill Morris and others in the production of this book.

Finally, I wish to acknowledge permission for previously published material to be reproduced in this book. Permission has been
gratefully received from the named publishers for the following
material I have written:

To Sheffield Academic Press, Mansion House, 19 Kingfield Road,
  Sheffield S11 9AS, for: 'Interpreting Charismatic Experience:
  Hypnosis, Altered States of Consciousness and the Holy Spirit',
  Journal of Pentecostal Theology 12 (1998) pp. 117–32. 'Practical
  Theology and Charismatic Spirituality: Dialectics in the Spirit',
  Journal of Pentecostal Theology 10.2 (2002) pp. 93–109.

To Academic Press Ltd, 24–28 Oval Road, London NW1 7DX,
  for: 'The Future of Glossolalia: Fundamentalist or Experientialist?', *Religion* 28 (1998) pp. 233–44.

To Taylor & Francis Ltd, PO Box 25, Abingdon, Oxfordshire
  OX14 3UE, http://www.tandf.co.uk/journals, for: 'Empirical
  Theology: Inter- or Intra-disciplinary?', *Journal of Beliefs and Values*
  20.1 (1999) pp. 98–104.

To Continuum International Publishing Ltd, The Tower Building,
  11 York Road, London SE1 7NX, http://www.continuum
  books.com, for: 'The Socialization of Glossolalia' in Leslie J.
  Francis (ed.), *Sociology, Theology and Curriculum* (London: Cassell,
  1999) pp. 125–34.

To Gospel Theological Seminary, 143–31, Yongdu-dong, Jung-ku,
  Taejeon City, 301–110, South Korea, for: 'Charismatic Women
  and Prophetic Activity', *The Spirit and Church* 3.1 (2001) pp.
  97–111.

Anglicans Renewal Ministries, (no longer operational but previously
  based at) 4 Bramble Street, Derby DE1 1HU, for: 'The Role of
  Testimony in Worship', *Anglicans for Renewal – Skepsis* 87 (2001)
  pp. 27–31.

To Ashgate Publishing Ltd, Gower House, Croft Road, Aldershot,
  Hampshire GU11 3HR, http://www.ashgate.com, for: *Charismatic
  Glossolalia: An Empirical-Theological Study* (Aldershot: Ashgate,
  2002) pp. 29–30, 131–4, 138–9, 142–5.

To Grove Books Ltd, Ridley Hall Road, Cambridge CB3 9HU,
  http://www.grovebooks.co.uk, for: *Testimony: Its Importance, Place
  and Potential* (Cambridge: Grove, Renewal 9, 2002).

Preface

The Pentecostal Movement, whatever its precursors, only began at the beginning of the twentieth century and its overflow into historic denominations via the Charismatic Movement didn't even begin until the 1960s. Yet, in spite of its recent and humble origins, it is estimated that by the year 2000 Pentecostal and charismatic Christians numbered 543 million and on some projections will reach 811 million by 2020. It is hard to overestimate the significance of these streams within the contemporary church.

Although the Pentecostal and charismatic movements emphasize the priority of experiencing God, increasingly many such Christians are keen to reflect thoughtfully and academically on their particular strands of the Christian tradition. *Studies in Pentecostal and Charismatic Issues* aspires to create space for Pentecostal-Charismatic Christians to reflect in scholarly ways on their history, the nature of their experiences and the way in which they interpret biblical texts and themes. The focus will be upon studies of pneumatic Christianity in the contemporary world, historical studies on major figures and movements, and biblical and theological studies from Pentecostal–Charismatic perspectives. The series is about Pentecostal–Charismatic Christianity by Pentecostal–Charismatic Christians and sympathisers, but it will not shrink back from constructive criticism. The studies will range from very academic pieces of work through to thoughtful but more widely accessible texts.

If

→

If we are going to make
this work, we must begin
with a relational theology

Foreword

In an age of change research methods adjust to new philosophical and cultural realities. In an age of change theology is susceptible to regenerative impulses. In an age of change the church seeks new forms and expressions. This book gathers up these dissimilar strands of change and weaves them together into inventive new patterns.

Moreover, it does so at a time when higher education itself is well into the swing of the process of expansion and reconstruction. Not only are far more people than ever in Britain studying for degrees but these degrees, particularly at Master's level, are modular and interdisciplinary. The effect of this is to produce a highly educated professional population with a knowledge of many research techniques and fields of discourse. In the world of theology which has hitherto been dominated by academic theologians and clergy, these educational changes are played out in fresh ways. Those who have come to theology later in life may have brought with them the disciplines and skills of other academic fields. Those who have come to theology early in life may have moved beyond their original discipline into the multidisciplinary expertise of the reflective practitioner. In either case the synthesis between theology and practice informed by social science paradigms is likely to be apparent.

The result of this is to make the time ripe for the kind of book which Mark Cartledge has so skilfully given us. It is 'a textbook' and, like the best textbooks, allows readers to see worked examples of theory. This is a book which would benefit practitioners who want to understand how theology can be applied to particular church situations and, at the same time, allows those who have grown up only in the field of 'old-fashioned' theology – biblical studies, biblical languages, systematics, Reformation history, and the like – to extend their knowledge into the methods of social science, and to do so without having to embrace reductionist positivism or vastly complex mathematics. There is here a subtlety and suppleness of mind which will assure the suspicious theologian that reality has not simply been condensed to a row of numbers. The reader is offered an introduction to a range of theological and methodological literatures and an implicit encouragement to pick up the tools demonstrated in this book and to try to use them for him or herself.

Like all good books, this one speaks for itself. The introduction provides an overview of the journey to be taken and the subheadings within each chapter provides signposts to simplify the route. There is much here to enjoy and much insight to be gained by the exploration of real issues within real churches. The discussion of the role of women in pentecostalism is illuminating. The exploration of healing and faith is pastorally sensitive and methodologically sophisticated. In many instances the results these chapters provide could not have been obtained either by 'old-style' theology or by 'methodological atheistic' social science.

It is my hope that this book will enable practical theology to become more willing and able to be of service to the church. There is a case for saying that theology ought to be the handmaid of the church as much as it was once thought to be the Queen of Sciences, and this book strengthens that argument.

WILLIAM K. KAY

King's College, London, and the University of Wales, Bangor

Title Description

This book brings together the traditions of contemporary academic practical theology and Pentecostal and charismatic studies in a unique way. It provides a textbook introducing the reader to empirical research in theology while at the same time contributing to constructive charismatic theology. The book contains two parts. The first offers methodological chapters that consider the relationship of practical theology to social science and charismatic spirituality. Theories of truth and knowledge in relation to charismatic theology are discussed as well as the actual empirical research methods. Thus the two key perspectives of empirical research and charismatic theology are integrated in a mutually enriching manner. The second contains six individual studies that model the kinds of empirical research in Pentecostal and charismatic subjects. Two chapters use qualitative case study material and explore the topics of worship as a performance of spirituality and glossolalia in relation to postmodernity. Three chapters use quantitative data from a questionnaire survey in order to consider questions related to gender and prophecy, charismatic experience and the Toronto Blessing, and faith and healing. The final chapter uses both qualitative and quantitative data to explore glossolalia in relation to socialization theory. Thus the different types of material and data are used to explore the nature of contemporary theological praxis. At the end of each chapter there is a methodological reflection which aims to highlight what this process of empirically orientated practical theology has achieved. Each chapter concludes with suggestions for renewed theological praxis.

1

Introduction

It was in the process of writing this book that I read a collection of essays edited by John Goldingay.[1] One of those essays was written by Roger Cowley.[2] Roger was a staff member of the theological college at which I was a student preparing for ordained ministry in the Church of England (1986–8). At the time I was putting together a proposal for a research degree in theology on the subject of contemporary prophecy.[3] I knew that I was interested in practical theology and I was working through some of my interests related to the Charismatic Movement.[4] It was natural enough for me to want to bring the two together in some meaningful way. Roger had himself undergone an experience of charismatic renewal and exercised certain spiritual gifts regularly in his ministry. As he read my research proposal, he found my starting point to be strange, given the *contemporary* focus of the study. Looking at my proposed outline, he said, in his characteristic way, 'Mark, I understand that you want to research prophecy *today*, but as I look at your chapter headings I see New Testament, New Testament, New Testament. It is only at the end that I see anything related to today!' Of course, Roger was right. I had assumed that rigorous study of the New Testament would somehow enable me to 'read' the contemporary phenomenon without actually researching what it was that I wished to study. The sheer paucity of anything but popular literature on contemporary prophecy meant that I had to do some original empirical research if I was to understand the subject at all. That moment changed the project, my approach to theology, and the focus was developed to become a study of prophecy in the Church of England diocese of London. I subsequently brought my findings to be compared to Scripture.[5]

It was not until much later that I realized that the very same theological approach, which can still be seen across the theological colleges, was simply perpetuating a system that has its roots in the work of Friedrich Schleiermacher. For Schleiermacher, practical theology was the crown of theology, and came after all the real work had been done. Philosophical and systematic theology are the foundational sub-disciplines on which is built *practical application.*[6] The findings of the Bible mediated through the theological system, be it liberal Protestantism or Calvinism, are then applied in a way that pays very little attention to the contemporary context. Practical theology is thus allegedly determined by biblical and systematic theology. Of course, in hermeneutical terms, the picture was and is far more complex.[7] Biblical interpreters always bring with them a corporate worldview and personal mindset through which they 'read' the text.[8] This worldview is shaped by the language, values and culture of the interpreter, so it is arguable just how much of the interpretations on offer are actually biblical or indeed primarily theological. The view from nowhere does not exist.[9] All of us belong to a particular time, place and culture that inevitably influence our reading of reality, including biblical and theological texts. So the first aspect of practical theology that I wish to endorse is its *hermeneutical* nature. It is a discipline that is deliberately interpretative. Practitioners and researchers in practical theology are engaged in the reading of both the contemporary reality under study and the theological tradition from out of which they seek to operate. As a charismatic evangelical I regard Scripture as the normative principle in that hermeneutic, which, for me, is located within a charismatic spirituality. Charismatic spirituality provides the theological and spiritual milieux in which and from out of which it functions in a critical way. I would suggest that all theological perspectives function in a similar kind of way to a greater or lesser extent.

During my studies in the area of practical theology and the Charismatic Movement in the 1980s there was little substantial literature on the subject of methodology of which I was aware. As it turned out, the work of Don Browning and others in the USA,[10] Paul Ballard in the UK[11] and Johannes A. van der Ven in the Netherlands had begun to shape the landscape.[12] From the late 1980s through to the 1990s this was going to change. The

Discipleship: The Wrong Curriculum Transformation: Using the Right Curriculum

influence of liberation theology, with its rejection of the priority of Aristotelian abstract theory over action as ways of knowing, reprioritized the doing of truth through the emancipation of the oppressed.[13] The embracing of the social sciences by theology in continental Europe was also to prove significant. Van der Ven, Professor of Practical Theology at the Catholic University of Nijmegen, developed the Department of Empirical Theology, which from 1988 began to publish the *Journal of Empirical Theology*. The articles in the journal gave expression to empirically orientated research within theology. In Britain empirical perspectives have been used by Leslie J. Francis and William K. Kay as well as Robin Gill.[14] In addition, practical theology in the UK, through the influence of Paul Ballard, has explored the theological identity of this discipline by developing practical theology as an academic discipline.[15] The establishment of the British and Irish Association for Practical Theology offers some opportunity for debate within the usual constraints of a particular theological hegemony. The shift in postmodern consciousness by western theologians has also contributed to the diversity of practical theology today, most notably in the work of Elaine Graham from a feminist perspective.[16] This leads to my second point by way of introduction. Practical theology is a *diverse and fragmented* discipline. There are a variety of approaches that stress therapy, mission, liberation and pastoral practice.[17] Even the nomenclature of the discipline is hotly disputed! Should the discipline be practical theology or pastoral theology, or even empirical theology?[18] This diversity provides the context for practical theology that combines different perspectives in unusual ways. Evangelical theology has largely rejected the excessive therapeutic and liberationist models of practical and pastoral theology, and with good reason. However, the problem is that Evangelicalism, as a theological tradition, has put nothing in its place because it has not seen the need. It has virtually ignored the scholarly debate and very few evangelicals attend or are involved in national conferences, write in the journals or enter into dialogue with peers. However, the book by Ray Anderson, *The Shape of Practical Theology: Empowering Ministry with Theological Praxis*, looks set to begin to fill the void.[19] Unlike previous evangelical practical theology it does not buy into a Schleiermacherian theological methodology of applicationism, but takes seriously the work of

Browning and gives it an evangelical construction. This leads me to my third introductory point, namely that the diversity of practical theology provides opportunity for *confessional* theology. So far, evangelicals have basically failed to engage in confessional practical theology, to the detriment of theological education and the development of the broader tradition. This book aims to join in the work that Anderson has initiated by providing a different kind of practical theology book, that is, one from a different perspective.

These preliminary considerations indicate that I recognize the nature of the discipline, and its historical development, is at the present time somewhat fluid. This fluidity provides an opportunity to make a proposal from a particular viewpoint. So what I wish to undertake is a contribution to the field of practical theology from charismatic and empirical perspectives. This study builds on my earlier doctoral work,[20] as unpublished material from that research is integrated with some previously published work to make this book. My thinking has obviously developed as I have taught practical theology and continued to read the most recent Pentecostal and charismatic scholarship. In a sense, this book is a natural sequel to that earlier work, and is more of a programmatic proposal reflecting my current concerns. It does not attempt to give a state-of-the-art review of either practical theology or Pentecostal-Charismatic theology, although I was initially tempted to do so. Those tasks in themselves belong to full-scale books and this one is different in its scope and orientation.

The methodology section aims to offer a proposal for practical theology. Chapter 2 reviews the ways in which theology, and especially practical theology, has related to the social sciences. These concerns are linked to a reflection on the process of actually doing practical theology. I suggest a charismatic perspective that builds on the scholarship of practical theology and Pentecostal-Charismatic theology. Chapter 3 considers the important area of truth and epistemology. The debates in the social sciences regarding the use of empirical methods have often been dominated by questions around the kinds of knowledge that are thought to be generated by such research. This chapter reviews the question of epistemology in the light of recent philosophy and the nature of knowledge within Pentecostal and charismatic faith communities. Chapter 4 describes the different empirical methods used in the social sciences. Since the use of empirical methods for gathering data is essential to an empirically orientated discipline, the issues surrounding their use need to be considered before their transposition into a theological domain of use can be appreciated. A description of two examples of empirical research, one by qualitative methods and the other by quantitative methods, is also included in this chapter. The methodological chapters provide the basis for the empirical studies that follow; and the sequence of methodology followed by empirical studies is intended to be a progression. An understanding of my methodological proposal will assist the reading of the illustrative empirical chapters that follow. In case it could be suggested that the demarcation perhaps endorses a theory- or abstract-driven approach, I would counter that these chapters were not necessarily written in that order. For the most part, individual chapters started life as either conference papers or journal articles. In the writing of the book I tended to oscillate between empirical blocks of work followed by methodological sections. Thus the dialectic of engagement and reflection proposed in chapter 2 is also enacted in the writing of this book! However, it must be admitted that some readers may regard these methodological chapters as being demanding, especially if they are new to the academic literature in practical theology. In this case, the empirical chapters may be read first before referring back to the methodology.

Chapters 5 and 6 are based upon the case study example while chapters 7, 8 and 9 are based upon data gathered from a questionnaire survey. Chapter 10 is unique in that it combines both qualitative and quantitative research in the one essay by developing research from one to the other. It provides a useful example of how such research methods can be combined. I have attempted to offer methodological reflections on all the studies presented in order to help readers to appreciate the process through which I have gone to produce the text that I have. These chapters focus on concerns close to the hearts of Pentecostals and charismatics and are offered in a spirit of *critical solidarity*.

Finally, I should, perhaps, explain the denotation I am already using and will continue to use regarding the Pentecostal and charismatic movements. The relationship between 'Pentecostals' and 'charismatics' is ambiguous. The label 'Pentecostal' is often used by writers to include charismatic Christians from mainline denominations, the New/House Church movement and indigenous African churches.[21] Therefore there is increasing recognition of the diversity and fluidity within the denotation of 'Pentecostal-Charismatic'. While this is an important development that will eventually suggest various typologies, I shall use the word 'Pentecostal' to refer to the classical Pentecostal traditions. The label 'Charismatic Movement' will be used to denote the charismatic renewal of the mainline denominations from the 1960s, as well as the independent New/House Church and 'Third Wave' movements. The New Church movement is the successor to the House Church or independent charismatic church movement in the UK from the 1960s. The Third Wave movement has its origins in the ministry of John Wimber from California, and his influence in the UK from the mid–1980s, resulting in what became known as the Vineyard denomination. The influence of the Third Wave movement in the UK is seen most strongly in the New Wine network of churches and conferences, which are predominantly but not exclusively Anglican in leadership. In terms of theological denotation I shall use my preferred label 'charismatic' for both participants in the Pentecostal and charismatic movements and my own brand of 'Pentecostal-Charismatic' theology. That is, I am using the word 'charismatic' as a shorthand reference for the latter.

---

[1] J. Goldingay (ed.), *Signs, Wonders and Healing: Seven Prominent Christians Debate Today's Issues* (Leicester: Inter-Varsity Press, 1989).

[2] Roger was highly regarded for his pioneer work on biblical hermeneutics in the Coptic Orthodox Church of Ethiopia, where he was a missionary for many years. Roger tragically died from cancer, aged 48, while I was still a student at the college.

[3] M. J. Cartledge, 'Prophecy in the Contemporary Church: A Theological Examination' (Master of Philosophy dissertation, Council for National Academic Awards, 1989).

[4] The Charismatic Movement is a label given to the Pentecostal spiritual tradition as it is experienced and propagated in denominations other than classical Pentecostalism. For a good introduction to this spiritual

tradition, see H. Cox, *Fire from Heaven: The Rise of Pentecostal Spirituality and the Reshaping of Religion in the Twenty-first Century* (London: Cassell, 1996). For a history of its emergence in the UK, see P. Hocken, *Streams of Renewal: The Origins and Early Development of the Charismatic Movement in Great Britain* (Carlisle: Paternoster, 1986, 1997²).

5 M. J. Cartledge, 'New Testament Prophecy and Charismatic Prophecy', *Themelios* 17.1 (1991) pp. 17–19.

6 D. B. Forrester, *Truthful Action: Explorations in Practical Theology* (Edinburgh: T&T Clark, 2000) pp. 35–7.

7 A. C. Thiselton, *New Horizons in Hermeneutics: The Theory and Practice of Transforming Biblical Reading* (London: HarperCollins, 1992) illustrates just how complicated it can be!

8 N. T. Wright, *The New Testament and the People of God* (London: SPCK, 1993²) pp. 44–5.

9 T. Hart, *Faith Thinking* (London: SPCK, 1995) pp. 48–69.

10 D. Browning, *A Fundamental Practical Theology: Descriptive and Strategic Proposals* (Minneapolis: Fortress, 1991, 1996²); also see the contributions of J. W. Fowler, R. R. Osmer and J. E. Loder in F. Schweitzer and J. A. van der Ven (eds), *Practical Theology – International Perspectives* (Frankfurt am Main: Peter Lang, 1999).

11 P. Ballard (ed.), *The Foundations of Pastoral Studies and Practical Theology* (Cardiff: The Board of Studies for Pastoral Studies, The Faculty of Theology, University College, Cardiff, 1986); P. Ballard and J. Pritchard, *Practical Theology in Action: Christian Thinking in the Service of Church and Society* (London: SPCK, 1996).

12 J. A. van der Ven, *Practical Theology: An Empirical Approach* (Kampen: Kok Pharos, 1993).

13 See the discussion in Forrester, *Truthful Action*, pp. 23–31.

14 L. J. Francis and W. K. Kay, *Drift from the Churches: Attitude toward Christianity during Childhood and Adolescence* (Cardiff: University of Wales Press, 1996); R. Gill, *Church Going and Christian Ethics* (Cambridge: Cambridge University Press, 1999).

15 P. Ballard, 'Practical Theology as an Academic Discipline', *Theology* 782 (1995) pp. 112–22; P. Ballard, 'Where is British Practical Theology?', *International Journal of Practical Theology* 2 (1999) pp. 295–308.

16 E. Graham, *Transforming Practice: Pastoral Theology in an Age of Uncertainty* (London: Mowbray, 1996). See the response by N. Biggar, 'Should Pastoral Theology become Postmodern?', *Contact: The Interdisciplinary Journal of Pastoral Studies* 126 (1998) pp. 22–7.

17 E. Graham, 'Pastoral Theology: Therapy, Mission or Liberation?', *Scottish Journal of Theology* 52.4 (1999) pp. 430–54.

[18] The new series devoted to the subject by Ashgate hedges its bets – it is called Explorations in Practical, Pastoral and Empirical Theology!

[19] R. Anderson, *The Shape of Practical Theology: Empowering Ministry with Theological Praxis* (Downers Grove IL: Inter-Varsity Press, 2001).

[20] M. J. Cartledge, *Charismatic Glossolalia: An Empirical-Theological Study* (Aldershot: Ashgate, 2002).

[21] See the discussion by A. Anderson, 'Diversity in the Definition of "Pentecostal/Charismatic" and its Ecumenical Implications', paper presented at the 31st Annual Meeting of the Society for Pentecostal Studies (SPS), Southeastern College, Lakeland, Florida, March 2002, pp. 731–47.

PART ONE
METHODOLOGY

2

Practical Theology, Social Science and Charismatic Spirituality

1. Introduction[1]

The idea that theology could have a relationship with the social sciences has had a mixed reception, partly due to the naturalistic reductionism associated with the social sciences. As a reaction John Milbank in his *magnum opus* argued that theology was wrong to allow secular reason, in the form of sociological construction, to determine our understanding of social theory.[2] In its place he argued for a postmodern Augustinian model of society that is fundamentally a theological model. While I have a great deal of admiration both for the scope of Milbank's work and his critique of the social sciences from a theological perspective, I am not sure that postmodern Augustinianism is the theological vision I wish to embrace! Nevertheless, it gives other theologians reasons for dismissing an engagement with the social sciences in preference for other dialogue partners, such as the natural sciences.[3] Such dialogues should be welcomed and embraced, but for practical theology, with its orientation of engagement with real people in real social contexts, the need to use empirical approaches is fundamental to the discipline. Theoretical and abstract discussions also remain essential but they are used primarily in relation to empirical and concrete studies of people. In this chapter I aim to introduce the discussion of practical theology in relation to the social sciences and situate it as a research discipline within Christian spirituality, in particular charismatic spirituality.

2. Theology and Social Science

The empirical approach to theology as an area of practical theology is beginning to be recognized in Britain largely due to the influence of Professor Johannes van der Ven and the model of empirical theology proposed in his book.[4] The question of disciplinary boundaries is still a matter of concern among practitioners of practical theology and those intending to do empirical theology. The idea of empirical theology is a cause of excitement mingled with caution. This is because practical and pastoral theology in Britain is still in the process of definition. Practitioners acknowledge the need to engage with the social and medical sciences in order to explore the nature of contemporary religious experience, but the exact relationship that theology should have to these other disciplines is unclear, so very often the term 'inter-disciplinary' is used to describe the relationship. For some this has been described as 'pragmatic syncretism',[5] or auxiliary usage,[6] or balanced dialogue which avoids the confusion of discourses and any kind of imperialism,[7] while others repudiate dilettante eclecticism.[8] Before considering the work of van der Ven directly it is perhaps useful to consider how theology has been seen to relate to the area of sociology and how religious educationalists have defined disciplinary boundaries.[9]

Sociology and Theology

Peter Berger coined the phrase 'methodological atheism' when researching religion within the discipline of sociology;[10] that is, from a strictly methodological perspective, reality is viewed in empirical terms. Later he was to talk about 'signals of transcendence' whilst still retaining his methodological stance.[11] Given such a methodological commitment, he was able to say that: 'An "empirical theology" is, of course, methodologically impossible. But a theology that proceeds in a step-by-step correlation with what can be said about man empirically is well worth a serious try.'[12] In this case, God a priori could not act as an independent variable within the given social context.[13] Critical correlation, however, is an approach which is now accepted in practical theological circles, notwithstanding such origins.[14]

The sociologist and theologian Robin Gill has provided a different approach to the problem, which may be termed 'methodological

fiction'.[15] He rejects the use of the term 'atheism' as being unfortun-
ate and misleading. Instead he posits an 'as if' methodology, that is,
within the sociological sphere, to work 'as if' there were social
determinants of all human interactions. He recognizes the need
for irreducible symbols and beliefs that are not explained away
and thereby aims to offer a more generalized theory than Berger.
Sociology and theology are regarded as distinct if complementary.
Thus the sociologist views the world 'as if' it is socially determined,
while the theologian views the world 'as if' there are transcendent
determinants of it.

The example of religious sociology is often used to illustrate
how academic sociology can be corrupted by a pragmatic approach.
Religious sociologists such as Ferdinand Boulard and Gabriel Le
Bras have been considered by some practical theologians to have
misused sociology for church-related ends.[16] In contrast to this,
Robin Gill explains that sociology of religion is not without its
values, which influence the sociological interpretation of data.[17]
The era of value-free sociology is now almost terminated and
'reflexivity' on the part of the sociologist is advocated.[18] In addition, Gill notes how sociology is now often used not for purely
academic purposes but can influence policy and practice as a result.
Such sociological work is commissioned in order to inform
operational decisions in industry, education and race relations.[19] In
that case it is highly practical in its orientation. Therefore the
clear distinction between the sociology of religion and religious
sociology cannot be sustained in contemporary scholarship. The
categorization of van der Ven's work as belonging to religious
sociology is consequently unhelpful and outdated.[20]

Religious Education

Religious educationalists Leslie J. Francis and William K. Kay
likewise regard their approach as being inter-disciplinary.[21] Each
discipline requires 'an agreed terminology, publicly testable
concepts, standard procedures, notional boundaries, and so on, and
these are most clearly mapped out by philosophical techniques'.[22]
Inter-disciplinary enquiry can form one of four alternatives. (a) A
reassessment of the content of one discipline in the light of another.
(b) The amalgamation of two separate disciplines according to a
completely new set of criteria, as in the case of social-psychology,

thus creating a new and separate discipline. (c) The concept of a discipline may be questioned in the usual sense of the term and an *ad hoc* approach used depending on the problem investigated. (d) An approach is taken which seeks to satisfy the practitioners of both disciplines in terms of the nature of the discipline and the criteria appropriate to it. Kay and Francis argue that (d) is the only really satisfactory option. They recognize that this is the most stringent approach, needing to pass two sets of criteria for it to be acceptable to two sets of practitioners. Education itself is a composite discipline that includes psychology, sociology and philosophy, while religion is also wide ranging and includes morals, aesthetics, beliefs and behaviour, history and philosophy. Therefore religious education requires itself to be located 'at the heart of interdisciplinary enquiry'.[23]

The approach of Kay and Francis is one possible approach, but it raises a couple of issues. First, the definition of the interdisciplinary approach is based on the *competence* of the practitioner, not necessarily on the nature of the discipline. Indeed, since both religion and education as categories of subject areas are themselves composite, their boundaries are not as tightly defined as Kay and Francis seem to indicate. Second, if the definition of what is to be considered 'religion' or 'education' is set by practitioners, what happens to the practitioner who is *innovative* and steps outside the boundaries of convention? In practice, academic peers do regulate what is included and what is excluded, but the innovative scholar is likely to be at the forefront of such developments. Johannes van der Ven is one such person.

Practical Theology as Empirical Theology

Van der Ven argues that theology should be conceived as an empirical discipline in the sense that it would aim to explore, describe and test theological ideas contained within a specific context. The direct object of empirical theology therefore is the faith and practice of people concerned. The social sciences are used to further this enterprise and theology is dependent upon these disciplines within practical theology. He argues that theology gathers into itself the appropriate techniques and methods to facilitate this development. That is, the overall framework of thought is theology and the hypotheses to be tested are theological.

Van der Ven considers whether practical theology should be viewed as mono-disciplinary, that is, the application of theology to situations in church and society. In this approach, ideas drawn from historical or systematic theology are applied to a concrete situation. However, there is no standard approach as to how theological insights might be applied in practice. The multi-disciplinary model is one which is also used today, that is, a two-phase approach, where an empirical description by a social scientist is followed by theological reflection. This means that the theological enterprise is highly dependent upon the social science analysis of the present situation. Alternatively, some have suggested an inter-disciplinary model, that is, an interactive model between the social sciences and theology that stresses reciprocity. If a multi-disciplinary model is viewed sequentially as a series of monologues, then an inter-disciplinary model is seen as a number of co-operative parallel dialogues.

In terms of an inter-disciplinary approach by a single practical theologian a great deal of pressure is put upon the individual 'because it requires legitimation by both theology and the social sciences, something that is generally difficult to attain for the practical theologian who as a rule hold degrees only in theology'.[24] But, in that case, what are the criteria by which the practical theological hypotheses are evaluated? Are they social science or theological criteria? And how do these relate to one another? Alternatively, inter-disciplinary work may be carried out as a dialogue between several people. However:

> [r]egardless of how one feels about it, in establishing a dialogue with the present-day social sciences, theology is entering into an unequal balance of power. The reason is that the social sciences do not need theology in order to practice their discipline, whereas for practical theology, at least the inter-disciplinary version, this cooperation with the social sciences is essential.[25]

Finally, van der Ven opts for an intra-disciplinary model. He argues that such a model requires that 'theology itself become[s] empirical, that is, that it expands its traditional range of instruments, consisting of literary-historical and systematic methods and techniques, in the direction of an empirical methodology'.[26] The term intra-disciplinary refers to the idea of borrowing concepts, methods and techniques from other disciplines and integrating these into another science.[27]

> Such intra-disciplinarity processes occur in all scientific fields: in the natural sciences, in the linguistic, historical and social sciences, in the philosophical and theological sciences. Intra-disciplinarity encourages innovation in these sciences. By way of example, one need only look at the relationship between biology and chemistry (biochemistry), physiology and psychology (physiological psychology), linguistics and sociology (sociolinguistics), linguistics and psychology (psycho-linguistics), history and psychology (psychohistory), the linguistic sciences and philosophy (philosophy of language), and so on.[28]

Theology likewise has integrated aspects of other disciplines, including philosophy (Aquinas), psychology and philosophy (Tillich) and sociology (Metz).

As I have already noted, practical theology as an empirical discipline is under development. Van der Ven recognizes that theologians will want to use the tools of the social sciences without claiming to do social science. No doubt this approach will cause social scientists to question such innovation. However, it is the practical theological community as practitioners in the field who are perhaps the most suitable judges of such innovation. It is they who live and work on the edge of theology and who are best positioned to evaluate these developments. The approach of Francis and Kay, whilst being the most rigorous, is not without difficulty, as mentioned above. It may commend itself to the religious educational community of scholars, but practical theologians, who see themselves primarily as theologians rather than social-psychologists, will be drawn more to the model of van der Ven. It is in light of van der Ven's argument that the problem over inter-disciplinarity comes into focus. It is fundamentally about the preference of a person doing the research in terms of theoretical frameworks, concepts and methods. Such preferences inevitably empower one of the disciplines over and against the others used. In practical theology, there should be no doubt as to which is the dominant discourse, however sympathetically and critically other discourses are used.[29]

3. Practical Theology and Charismatic Spirituality[30]

The older model of practical theology as the application of the fruits of biblical and systematic theology is now something that has been challenged significantly. The challenge has come from the perspective of Liberation Theology but also from the context of cultural transition: the move from modernity to postmodernity. The liberation theologians have stressed that truth is not something that is abstract and remote: orthodoxy. Rather, the truth is some-thing that is done, it is truth in action: orthopraxy.[31] This shift to praxis or action arises out of the concrete realities of poverty and oppression in the Third World countries of Latin America, Africa and Asia. In the West the move to a praxis orientation is also derivative of the liberationist awakening. However, the postmodern shift in culture must also go part way in explaining the change. In postmodernity experience as the prime mediator of truth and reality is preferred. There is a suspicion of overarching theories that do not allow the freedom to pick and mix according to taste. In postmodern discourse, truth is not primarily a matter of revelation, since that can always be manipulated ideologically – truth is about what works for you. This is a shift from epistemological realism (positivism) to constructivism or theological pragmatism (see chapter 3 for a discussion of these perspectives). Therefore the accent is upon the local narrative rather than universality. In this regard, contemporary British practical theology appears to be largely postmodern.

In this section I aim to articulate an approach to practical theology which takes seriously, if critically, the postmodern turn, but also wishes to consider the liberationist emphasis of orthopraxis. While the notion of praxis is not without its difficulties,[32] it will be used to denote *theological and value-laden* actions, habits and practices.[33] In this sense, praxis denotes a way-of-being-in-the-world that is part and parcel of someone's worldview, beliefs and values.[34] In order to open out the discussion I shall use the word 'lifeworld' to denote the particular concrete setting of a circumstance under study. This is one pole of the dialogue with which I believe practical theology is engaged. The other pole is the theological structures within the 'system' of the individual or group engaged in the exercise of practical theology. While the word 'system' is not altogether adequate it refers to the constellation of beliefs and values which constitute a theological position.[35] This is consciously (if not strictly denominationally) confessional. It belongs to a particular tradition that is historically and culturally mediated. It also engages with the social sciences at theoretical and practical levels. These two poles are mediated by the practical theologian as a person belonging to an ecclesial community of a particular spiritual tradition. At times the ecclesial tradition and system will overlap and at other times they will be in tension. In every event the system as a 'trans-contextual' system has the capacity to critique both the theologian and the spiritual tradition and thus offer a corrective to both. (This feature is expanded upon below.)

The word 'spirituality' is used commonly today and is something of a slippery term. From a Christian perspective it concerns the spiritual life of faith which contains devotional practices and concrete behaviour. Alister E. McGrath defines Christian spirituality in the following way:

> Christian spirituality concerns the quest for a fulfilled and authentic Christian existence, involving the bringing together of the fundamental ideas of Christianity and the whole experience of living on the basis of and within the scope of the Christian faith.[36]

The main components can be seen to comprise a search for the God who is revealed in Christ, and an encounter with this same God by means of the Holy Spirit, which consequently effects change or transformation.[37] In other respects it can be understood to contain the elements of narrative, symbols and praxis. I shall return to the *process* of spirituality (search-encounter-transformation) later in relation to the process of practical theology, as well as defining charismatic spirituality more *structurally* by means of narrative, symbols and praxis, which are integrated within Christian affections.[38] For practical theology the *process* is the movement between two poles often conceived in a circular fashion, while the two poles themselves provide the *foci* around which there is purposeful movement.

The charismatic perspective consciously brings to this exercise a commitment to perceive and understand theology and the life of the church as a gift from God. This gracious gift is bestowed by means of the Holy Spirit. Theological understanding and engagement with the world is itself part of the *missio Dei*, God's own mission in the world. Theological argumentation, construction and prayer belong together within the community of faith. The charismatic approach to theology wants to emphasize that God himself, by his Spirit, is involved and active in the process. The church thus seeks to draw people into a relationship with the Triune God: Father, Son and Holy Spirit. The means of such a relationship is by the Spirit of God. Therefore a charismatic perspective is primarily *Trinitarian and doxological* as well as being missiological.[39] Its contribution to theological truth is the rediscovery that knowledge of God is holistic. Truth is not simply doxological and theological (orthodoxy), nor simply action based (orthopraxy), but it is affective (orthopathy).[40]

The call to a relationship is by means of a dialectic between the God who is transcendent and who is immanent.[41] This God is revealed and is known in worship as glory is given to him, and through our appropriation of right affections towards him.[42] This, however, is not simply an emotional turn. It is not a legitimation of the excesses of experiential emotionalism because the affections are ways of 'seeing' that grow out of Christian concern, which when mature is a passion for the kingdom of God.[43] Affections are at the heart of the gospel: to love God with one's heart, mind, soul and strength, and to love one's neighbour as oneself (Mark 12:28–34). This is the central thesis of Steven Land, who states that:

> Christian affections are objective, relational and dispositional. To say that Christian affections are objective means that affections take an object. In this case the object is also the subject: God is the source and object of Christian affections. The God who proves righteous, commands righteousness. The God who is love and has 'so loved' evokes love. The God who has acted powerfully to deliver, gives power and strength. What God has said and done, is saying and doing, will say and do is the source and *telos* of the affections.
>
> God's righteousness, love and power are the source of correlative affections in the believer. The narratives describing these attributes of God evoke, limit and direct the affections of the believer. God as righteous, loving and powerful is also the *telos* of Christian existence and thus of the affections. To believe God is to receive the kingdom

of righteousness, peace and joy in the Holy Spirit and to await its coming consummation.[44]

Land elucidates these 'apocalyptic' affections with particular reference to gratitude (praise, thanksgiving), compassion (love, longing) and courage (confidence, hope). It is these affections which are expressed in the *process* of search-encounter-transformation, as well as the structure of narrative, symbols and praxis.

From Action-Reflection to Dialectics

Practical theologians, taking their cue from their liberationist colleagues, have focused on experience of the situation or concrete reality that moves subsequently to theological reflection.[45] In these approaches often the emphasis is put upon the process of practical theology. This process is usually viewed as a sequence of stages within a circular or spiral movement.[46] That is, one consciously starts with experience (1); which is then explored (2); and reflected upon (3); before a response being advocated (4). Alternatively, a particular praxis is named (1), that is, focused upon. This in turn is reflected upon critically (2) before being brought to the Christian story (3). There is subsequently a dialectical hermeneutic as both praxis and the Christian story engage one another (4). As a consequence, there emerges an invitation to new praxis (5).[47]

Emmanuel Larty, while retaining an interest in the process of practical theology, wishes to suggest a 'way of being and doing' approach. This model is concerned with asking questions about the content of faith and practice believing that tradition; context and experience are shaping factors. It is therefore praxis orientated but also asks questions about those engaged in the task of practical theology. Thus the context of the theologians involved is examined and a hermeneutic of suspicion operates whereby the question as to who benefits from the exercise is asked. Therefore Larty starts with concrete experience (1); and moves to a situational analysis of experience by means of sociological and psychological analysis that is multi-perspectival (2). This is followed by theological analysis where faith perspectives are allowed to question the encounter (3). These faith perspectives are themselves the subject of questioning of the encounter in the situational analysis of theology (4). Finally, a response is offered by the theologian and the group in which this process is set (5).[48]

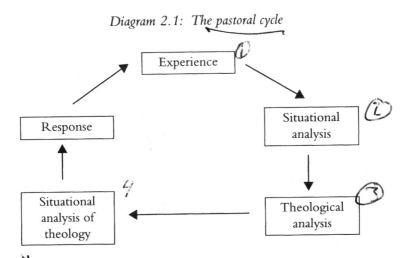

Diagram 2.1: The pastoral cycle

This pastoral cycle could be augmented by reference to the empirical-theological cycle of van der Ven. This cycle is consciously a research tool which is used to pursue practical theology at an academic level.[49] It contains five phases. The problem of the subject under investigation is chosen (1). This subject is investigated inductively by empirical research, either qualitative or quantitative methods. This is followed by the formulation of the research question and the design of the next phase (2). The theoretical and empirical concepts previously gathered are quantitatively modelled and operationalized if a questionnaire survey method is used. This is the method preferred by van der Ven and others, but a subsequent qualitative approach is also possible (3). A second engagement with a different empirical reality results in a new set of information about the area of study. This is subsequently analysed (4). The resultant material is interpreted and reflected upon theologically before recommendations are made (5).

Both models are action-reflection models in essence and both models start with the concrete reality of a particular setting. However, with the research model of van der Ven, the subjects of the research tend to be chosen by the researcher. It tends to use the quantitative methods of the social sciences and it analyses data rigorously. These circles or spirals of process are heuristic tools.

Diagram 2.2: The empirical–theological cycle

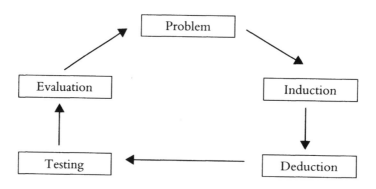

Time and again the empirical reality of the concrete setting under investigation and the involvement of the researcher intertwine. Just as belief and practice are intertwined in theological praxis, so the researcher(s) or investigator(s) are intertwined with the reality they wish to explore. The methodology provides a distancing mechanism to help guide the process. It is not something that should be used slavishly, but with discernment. It is a conceptual tool that is important but it cannot guarantee any quality of engagement or theological reflection. That depends upon the researcher(s). However, I believe that underlying the action-reflection model, and even the theory-to-action model, there is an important philosophical and theological concept. It is the concept of dialectic.[50]

The concept of dialectic is based on the notion of dialogue. However, instead of the position which sees the dialogue move from thesis to antithesis and finally to synthesis (Aristotle and Hegel), I aim to suggest that the dialogue between polar opposites is to be held together in the response of faith (Barth).[51] Theological dialectics are based upon the dialogue between the creature (in the context of the created order) and its Creator, between those 'being saved' and the Saviour. It is theology that takes seriously the revelation of God through creation and through the person and work of Jesus Christ. Pentecostals are already exploring what a dialectic of Word and Spirit might mean in terms of their spirituality.[52] In the following, I wish to articulate a model of practical theology that is based on the notion of dialectic.

The language that will be used to describe this dialectic is borrowed from Jürgen Habermas via the pastoral theological hermeneutic of Anthony Thiselton.[53] I accept that practical theologians have focused upon the concrete reality of interest at the expense of the larger system of thought. Thiselton argues that the two poles of practical theology should be conceptualized in terms of 'lifeworld' and 'transcontextual system'. Following Habermas, Thiselton understands that lifeworld:

> belongs to the *hermeneutical level of inter-personal understanding and co-operative behaviour* . . . But the hermeneutical dimension cannot operate at the level of *psycho-social critique:* for this, a standpoint is demanded in which *contextual-behavioural features are transcended in a larger system.* System provides a frame or *dimension for ideological and social critique.*[54]

If we confuse the system with the lifeworld or simply remain within the horizons of the lifeworld then, according to Habermas, 'fictions' cannot be detected. For Thiselton, the system is the expression of the love of God demonstrated in the cross and resurrection of Christ. As he states:

> [T]he cross and the resurrection stand not only as a critique of human self-affirmation and power, but also as a *meta-critique which assesses other criteria, and which transforms the very concept of power.* The power of the cross lies *precisely not in rhetorical self-assertion or manipulation* (1 Cor. 2.1–5) . . . The power of the cross does *not lie in what merely overwhelms us as impressive* (2 Cor. 8 through to 13). It is *power-in-weakness* (1 Cor. 1.23–25) because it is derived from 'a Christ crucified' (1 Cor. 1.23). *It revaluates self-affirming, manipulative, dominating power as self-destructive.*[55]

The context of this critical criterion is the past, present and future of the Bible and eschatology.[56] It is this criterion which, according to Thiselton, enables a transformation of particular lifeworlds. The purpose of such a dialectic is ultimately to integrate system and lifeworld in a new and transformed whole (2 Corinthians 5:17; Galatians 3:28).[57]

Of course, this kind of construction flies in the face of the postmodern critique, which argues that metatheories or metanarratives do not exist but are only ideological constructs serving special interests. However, does not any philosophical position that purports to offer a universal proposition, for example, the assertion that *all* theology is contextual, approximate in the end to some form of metanarrative claim?

Dialectics in the Spirit (1): Charismatic Spirituality and the Practical Theologian

The starting point for the practical theological investigation is the person as the agent of investigation. This may be as an individual or with others in a research group. The person, or persons, involved in the study has a particular spirituality arising from a specific worldview and belongs to a particular ecclesial tradition. Indeed there may be a tension between the spirituality and the ecclesial tradition, for example, as seen in how charismatics relate to the Church of England.[58] For the purposes of this chapter, I shall attempt to define charismatic spirituality in terms of basic worldview categories. This construction contains three features.[59]

A spirituality defined in this way contains (1) stories through which humans view reality. Narrative is the most characteristic expression of one's spirituality. (2) In addition, symbols express the stories and the answers to basic existential questions. These can be artifacts such as buildings, or they can be events such as festivals. Symbols tend to function as boundary markers. They are actions and visible objects that express spirituality at the deepest level. (3) Finally, spirituality contains praxis, that is, a way-of-being-in-the-world. The real shape of a person's spirituality can be seen in the actions he or she performs, especially from behaviour that is habitual. Thus a spirituality literally gives a lens through which the world is viewed and gives to people a sense of identity and place which enables them to be the people that they are. As noted earlier these components are integrated within Pentecostal and charismatic spirituality by means of the 'apocalyptic' affections of gratitude, compassion and courage.

Charismatic spirituality belongs to a variety of ecclesial traditions. Classical Pentecostalism and the New Church movement are very different expressions of Christianity from Anglicanism or Roman Catholicism.[60] Yet charismatics are just as likely to be seen in these churches as anywhere else. There is a commonality at the level of spirituality that transcends ecclesial boundaries. The narrative structure is similar to those found in other expressions of Christianity. Yet the difference lies in pneumatology and participation. There is an expectation and experience that suggests that the God of the Bible is at work in a similar kind of way today.[61] 'The point of Pentecostal spirituality . . . [is] to experience life as part of a biblical drama of participation in God's history.'[62] This obedient participation is a *via salutis*.[63] Historically, this has derived from the locus of Pentecostal experience, namely 'baptism in Spirit', as a second crisis spiritual experience subsequent to conversion–initiation. Later charismatics relativized this by speaking of more frequent 'encounters' with the Holy Spirit as part of the ongoing life of the believer. Therefore charismatics expect God to reveal his glory in worship, to answer prayer, to perform miracles, to speak directly by means of dreams and visions and prophecy. It is a presupposition of the charismatic narrative. God is not absent but deeply present.[64] Even if the end of worship is the worship of God, charismatics expect to experience 'something' of the divine life in the church because of the sheer graciousness of God.[65]

The symbolic world of the charismatic is shaped by the narrative. Until the late twentieth century Pentecostals have been the poor relations in the church. This is still the case in most parts of the world. As such they could not afford to build enormous edifices that showed how powerful God is. Instead, they had a 'baptism in the Spirit' (an overwhelming and dramatic experience of grace), and spoke in tongues, otherwise know as glossolalia.[66] Speaking in tongues is a key symbol for charismatics because it is the 'cathedral of the poor'.[67] You can speak in tongues anywhere. It does not locate you. Indeed, it becomes a kind of universal language that is not tied to privilege, power and status. It demonstrates the power of God in the weakness of humanity. It enables a person to identify with a particular group and yet to retain individuality. There are other embodied symbols, often embedded in rituals, such as falling over under the power of the Holy Spirit, or crying or laughing in worship.[68] Indeed, these symbols give expression to one of the deepest domains of person knowledge, the human emotions. The Pentecostal and charismatic emphasis upon right affections before God and one's neighbour are expressed by means of these key symbols as well as social justice issues.[69]

The praxis of charismatics can be seen in an enthusiasm for prayer with others. It is the primary theological activity of Pentecostals and charismatics.[70] It appeals to the intuitive and extrovert, prayer is something to be encountered with others.[71] The way of being in the world is prayer-centred. Life is so imbued with the presence of God that prayer becomes a habit. This is a habit formed 'in the Spirit' and received 'through the Spirit'. Praying in tongues is as natural to many charismatic Christians as any other kinds of prayer. In the various ecclesial traditions the evidence of prayer ministry teams displays this concern for prayer that is expectant of transformation.[72] People express care for one another by praying for each other. The expectation is that God answers prayer in the lives of believers and the world in which we all live. The kingdom of God has broken into this present age with the coming of Christ and the foretaste of this kingdom is opened up by the eschatological Spirit. Eschatological orientation and personal knowledge of God through the Holy Spirit, therefore, influence this primary theological activity.

The person in the theological tradition is also a member of a doxological and missiological community: the local church. It is this community of faith which supports and facilitates charismatic spirituality because it is 'a public, social and therefore int[er]-subjective reality'.[73] The theologian as investigator is in a dialectic with that community of faith.[74] The research findings and theological reflection that are descriptive, critical and constructive contribute to the life of the ecclesial community to which the person belongs. The contribution is at the level of understanding in terms of its worship and mission. At the same time the community of faith as the bearer of charismatic spirituality is able to interrogate the findings, suggestions and theological constructs of the practical theologian. Through such critical solidarity the life of the community and the person as researcher is renewed. Thus the process of practical theology becomes itself a mechanism for transformation within the kingdom of God. Practical theology viewed in this light is theology in the service of the church for the world. This means that critical questions can be raised by theologians for the communities sustaining charismatic spirituality.[75] It also means that academic theology is critiqued by a particular spiritual tradition. The *critical participation* required of the practical theologian within a

lebab – heart

particular spiritual tradition is therefore dialectical. In practical theology, academic and the popular theologies are in dialogue.

Dialectics in the Spirit (2): The Methodology of Practical Theology

It is, perhaps, easiest to begin this section by referring to the dialectical approach by means of the common spirituality process of search–encounter–tranformation.[76] Spirituality defined in this way is expressed clearly by Mark McIntosh when he states that spirituality is:

> [A] discovery of the true 'self' precisely in *encountering* the divine and human other – who allow one neither to rest in a reassuring self-image nor to languish in the prison of a false social construction of oneself . . . [S]pirituality so conceived is inherently oriented towards discovery, towards new perceptions and new understandings of reality, and hence is intimately related to theology. Perhaps one might think initially in terms of encounter with God as the common ground of spirituality and theology: spirituality being the impression that this encounter makes in the transforming life of people, and theology being the expression that this encounter calls forth as people attempt to understand and speak of the encounter.[77]

It is this dimension of exploration and discovery that correlates with the process of practical theology. In practical theology, as in other branches of theology, the concept of dialectic provides a way of expressing the nature of this engagement and reflection (see Diagram 2.3 below).

The starting point for the process of practical theology as dialectics is the theologian(s) as they engage with the twin poles of the 'lifeworld', the concrete reality, and the 'system', or theological identity. For the purposes of this proposal, I shall assume that the system contains a metanarrative, that is, an overarching theological narrative that stands outside of the concrete reality. This also contains a theological critical theory, such as a theology of the cross. Such a critical theory guards against the domestication and manipulation of the metanarrative by the theologian(s).[78] This system, as an open system, contains relations with other disciplines from the natural, medical and social sciences. While the theological system is dominant, contemporary human experience can be described in complementary terms. In this regard, the intra-disciplinary approach of van der Ven is preferred, because priority in the relations is given to theology. As I have already stated, this is entirely appropriate in the context of a discourse that claims to be practical theology.

Diagram 2.3: Dialectics in the Spirit

(1) Questions from the lifeworld (search)
(3) Engagement with ecclesial belief and practice in the lifeworld (encounter)
(5) Re-engagement with ecclesial belief and practice in the lifeworld (encounter)
(7) Recommendations for renewed ecclesial belief and practice (transformation)

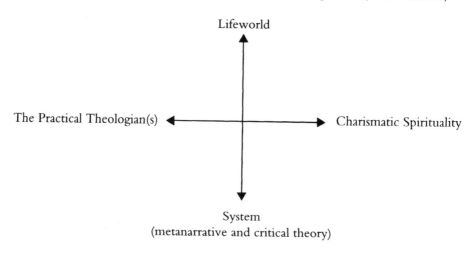

(2) Questions from the system: articulation of issues and project (search)
(4) Analysis of data, literature review, engagement of theology with social science, hypotheses (encounter)
(6) Analysis of data, recommendations for renewed understanding, critical and constructive theology (encounter)

Questions for investigation can emerge from either the lifeworld (1) or from the metanarrative (2). The Bible itself can suggest issues as the person engages with it in the routine of the spiritual discipline of reading. A routine or habitual concern may suggest itself or, alternatively, a crisis event or situation may demand serious theological and pastoral attention. The dialectic approach to the initial starting point means that either pole can suggest preliminary questions. In a sense this phase belongs to the search phase in spirituality. It belongs to the seeking after meaning, purpose and truth.

A praxis-orientated approach to practical theology will now start at the lifeworld end of the dialectic (3). The concern of practical theology with human beings in real-life human experiential reality is presuppositional. At this point the concern is engaged with by means of a variety of methods. The concern is the beliefs and practices of the subjects under study within a particular lifeworld. The obvious focus of practical theology is the life of the church in the world. This includes the internal life of the church in its worship and ministry, but also its life of witness and involvement in the world. Such an engagement will take seriously the concerns, perceptions and expressions of belief and practice as demonstrated by the people themselves. Primacy will be given to their stories, symbols and praxis.

This information is constantly in a dialogue with more theoretical literature (4). This literature gives perspectives from the social sciences that are global and local. Cultural analysis in terms of postmodernity and psychologically in terms of personality theory are just two examples of the kinds of insights that can be found. The data from the empirical encounter is investigated and mapped. The major themes and interests are highlighted. This leads to a very creative part in the process as the oscillation between praxis and theory generates insights. This phase is an encounter phase. The experience of the people in the concrete reality is brought into fruitful encounter with the academic literature on the subject. This encounter primarily includes theology. The beliefs and practices found in the lifeworld are made to encounter the beliefs and practices of the metanarrative. While the insights of experience can open up the horizons of Scripture, Scripture gives insight and meaning to experiential reality. Theological normativity is located in Scripture and can challenge and modify the values embedded in the theological praxis.[79]

The dialectic continues at this point by proceeding via the research mode of van der Ven (5). Alternatively, it can come to the point of recommendation for renewed theological praxis (7). In the research paradigm of van der Ven, the dialectic produces a further set of questions, which are tested on another set of empirical

realities before being interpreted and reflected upon theologically.
From a research perspective, empirical reality is encountered both
in an inductive and deductive stage. However, from the less rigorous
perspective of the pastoral cycle or the action-reflection model,
the dialectic will conclude at an earlier stage or perhaps continue
in other less-formal ways. The point is that at the end of each
encounter there is either an articulation of further questions or
hypotheses (6), or there is a proposed transformation of theological
praxis. This is achieved by means of specific recommendations for
change (7). The changes may be at the level of orthodoxy,
orthopraxis or orthopathy.[80] These recommendations for change
are offered in love and truth. They can never be imposed. They
reflect the nature of grace, not law. Of course, true change always
comes from God, and it is a work of grace. Charismatic theology
invites change at the levels of affection, attitude and behaviour.
However, it is always the Holy Spirit who is the agent of such
transformation.

The charismatic dialectic of practical theology also asks the
questions: (1) what is the Holy Spirit doing in this context?; (2)
how does this activity relate to the work of the Holy Spirit revealed
in Scripture?; and (3) what is the Spirit saying to the church
(Revelation 2:11)? The process of research and discernment reflects
the spirituality process of search-encounter-transformation. That
is, it begins with a search for the divine, which is encountered in
the experiential reality of human existence, often through the
symbols associated with the spirituality. This encounter occurs
within the doxological-missiological community of the church. As
a consequence, the person participates in the divine life of the
Triune God, and is (re)empowered to enter once again into the
missio Dei, the mission of God in the world. The transformation
has a divine purpose. It enables the person so transformed to serve
the work of God through the church for the sake of the world, so
the world may be transformed according to the purposes of God.
Therefore transformation is not self-serving but God serving. A
theology of the cross, as a critical theory, functions to keep the
focus of the spirituality Christological and Trinitarian by means of
the Spirit, since the Spirit points to Christ and the cross as the
locus of redemptive history.[81] Christ himself points to the Father
(John 6:43–46, 10:30, 14:6,9).

4. Conclusion

The aim of this chapter has been to bring together the concerns of the practical theological academy in its attempts to articulate an understanding of its methodology, that is, its process of doing practical theology and being practical theologians within a charismatic spirituality. This charismatic spirituality is informed not only by my own experiences but also by the Pentecostal and charismatic traditions upon which I draw and use. I stand as a person within a number of theologian traditions. I could say that there is a series of internal dialectics at work even as I write. Two of these dialectics I believe have wider import for the church and for scholarship. That is why I have attempted to bring these two elements together in this way. I shall endeavour to make this methodology visible in the empirical studies that follow.

Each empirical study will conclude with a methodological reflection. This reflection will assist the reader to appreciate the process of research and writing. It is inevitably schematized and in reality the process of research and indeed the writing are less orderly. It is a heuristic tool. However, it is hoped that the reflection will illustrate the process that I have discussed in this chapter. The outcome of this process is either suggestions for renewed theological praxis, where the 'lifeworld' side of the pole has priority, or suggestions for renewed understanding, where the 'system' has priority. Practical theologians should endeavour to make recommendations for renewed theological praxis wherever possible. This requires a particular context into which practical theological recommendations can be made. I have made some recommendations in these studies, but these recommendations are at their most concrete and specific when they are targeted at the case study context rather than the survey. Some studies emanate from more theoretical considerations and it is sometimes necessary for the outcome to be renewed understanding at the level of theological conceptualization. Since this is also integral to the exercise of practical theology it is an important and legitimate outcome. As practical theological research grows so these conceptualizations will contribute to the research process of others in the field.

[1] Part of this section originally appeared in M. J. Cartledge, 'Empirical Theology: Inter- or Intra-disciplinary?', *Journal of Beliefs and Values* 20.1 (1999) pp. 98–104.

[2] J. Milbank, *Theology and Social Theory: Beyond Secular Reason* (Oxford: Blackwell, 1990, 1993²). See the assessments by F. Kerr, R. Williams, A. Nichols and K. Flanagan together with a response from Milbank in R. Gill (ed.), *Theology and Sociology: A Reader* (London: Cassell, 1996). Cf. J. A. Coleman, 'Every Theology Implies a Sociology and Vice Versa' in M. H. Barnes (ed.), *Theology and the Social Sciences* (Maryknoll NY: Orbis, 2001) pp. 12–33 and a defence of Milbank by M. J. Baxter, 'Whose Theology? Which Sociology? A Response to John Coleman' in Barnes (ed.), *Theology and the Social Sciences*, pp. 34–42.

[3] A. E. McGrath, *A Scientific Theology Volume 1: Nature* (Edinburgh: T&T Clark, 2001) pp. 15–18. He builds upon the work of T. F. Torrance, *Theological Science* (Edinburgh: T&T Clark, 1969, 1996²).

[4] J. A. van der Ven, *Practical Theology: An Empirical Approach* (Kampen: Kok Pharos, 1993).

[5] P. Ballard, 'The Challenge of Sociology' in P. Ballard (ed.), *The Foundations of Pastoral Studies and Practical Theology* (Cardiff: The Board of Studies for Pastoral Studies, The Faculty of Theology, University College, Cardiff, 1986) pp. 86–94 (p. 92).

[6] D. Lyall, 'Psychiatry in Pastoral Studies: An Interprofessional Encounter' in Ballard (ed.), *The Foundations of Pastoral Studies*, pp. 102–9 (p. 106).

[7] P. Ballard and J. Pritchard, *Practical Theology in Action: Christian Thinking in the Service of Church and Society* (London: SPCK, 1996) pp. 108–10.

[8] S. Pattison, 'The Use of Behavioural Sciences in Pastoral Studies' in Ballard (ed.), *The Foundations of Pastoral Studies*, pp. 79–85 (p. 82).

[9] An alternative typology can be seen in the work of R. H. Roberts, *Religion, Theology and the Human Sciences* (Cambridge: Cambridge University Press, 2002) pp. 192–207 where he suggests the types: (1) theology repels the social sciences: fundamentalism; (2) Ernst Troeltsch: sociology overcomes theology; (3) Dietrich Bonhoeffer: theology recruits sociology; (4) Edward Farley: theology and social science mutually merged?; and (5) postmodern quasi-fundamentalist: John Milbank.

[10] P. Berger, *The Social Reality of Religion* (London: Penguin, 1967, 1973²) p. 182.

[11] P. Berger, *A Rumour of Angels* (London: Penguin, 1970) p. 70.

12 Berger, *The Social Reality of Religion*, p. 189; D. Martin, *Reflections on Sociology and Theology* (Oxford: Clarendon Press, 1997) p. 73. An example of this kind of model in relation to Pentecostalism is provided by R. Shaull and W. Cesar, *Pentecostalism and the Future of the Christian Church: Promises, Limitations, Challenges* (Grand Rapids MI: Eerdmans, 2000) especially pp. 108–11.

13 R. Gill, *The Social Context of Theology* (London: Mowbray, 1975) p. 29.

14 Ballard and Pritchard, *Practical Theology in Action*, pp. 47–50; actually it was Paul Tillich who first used the phrase in relation to analysis of the human situation. See P. Tillich, *Systematic Theology* (Chicago: University of Chicago Press, 3 vols, 1951, 1957, 1963).

15 Gill, *The Social Context of Theology*, pp. 37–40.

16 F. Boulard, *An Introduction to Religious Sociology* (London: Darton, Longman & Todd, 1960); G. Le Bras, 'Religious Sociology and Science of Religions' in J. Brothers (ed.), *Readings in the Sociology of Religion* (London: Pergamon, 1967) pp. 129–49.

17 Gill, *The Social Context of Theology*, pp. 21–5.

18 See for example E. Baker, 'The Scientific Study of Religion? You must be Joking!', *Journal for the Scientific Study of Religion* 34.3 (1995) pp. 287–310; K. Flanagan, *The Enchantment of Sociology* (London: Macmillan, 1996).

19 Gill, *The Social Context of Theology*, p. 24.

20 Ballard and Pritchard, *Practical Theology in Action*, p. 25.

21 W. K. Kay and L. J. Francis, 'The Seamless Robe: Interdisciplinary Enquiry in Religious Education', *British Journal of Religious Education* 7.2 (1985) pp. 64–7; L. J. Francis and W. K. Kay, *Drift from the Churches: Attitude toward Christianity during Childhood and Adolescence* (Cardiff: University of Wales Press, 1996).

22 Kay and Francis, 'The Seamless Robe', p. 64.

23 Ibid. p. 66.

24 van der Ven, *Practical Theology*, p. 98.

25 Ibid. p. 101.

26 Ibid.

27 Coleman, 'Every Theology Implies a Sociology', pp. 14–15 states that 'no method is unique to theology. It draws on literary studies, history, the historical-critical method, philosophy, ethics and . . . also on social science.'

28 van der Ven, *Practical Theology*, p. 101.

29 Coleman, 'Every Theology Implies a Sociology', p. 28 opposes any form of theological imperialism, for example by Milbank or Browning. It runs the danger of taming the autonomous voice and critique of

sociology to theology. This may be the case, but I would suggest that most correlation or inter-disciplinary proponents *de facto* privilege the social sciences and undermine the identity of theology. I wish to affirm the identity of practical theological discourse by privileging theology a priori.

[30] This section was first prepared as a paper for the British and Irish Association for Practical Theology Conference, July 2001, Oxford. It was subsequently published in the *Journal of Pentecostal Theology* 10.2 (2002) pp. 93–109.

[31] P. C. Phan, 'Method in Liberation Theologies', *Theological Studies* 61.1 (2000) pp. 40–63.

[32] For a Pentecostal critique of the concept of praxis, see C. B. Johns, *Pentecostal Formation: A Pedagogy among the Oppressed* (Sheffield: Sheffield Academic Press, JPTS 2, 1993) pp. 37–41. She states that 'Praxis is, therefore, an insufficient means of knowing God and achieving human transformation. Human reflection–action, while important, is distorted and may become self-serving, thereby hindering true knowledge of God. Without an authority beyond the self that transcends and even negates reflection–action, we are left, in spite of our worthy intentions for the transformation of society, with sinful praxis' (pp. 38–9).

[33] For a useful historical summary of praxis in the thought of Aristotle and Marx, see J. W. Fowler, 'The Emerging New Shape of Practical Theology' in F. Schweitzer and J. A. van der Ven (eds), *Practical Theology – International Perspectives* (Frankfurt am Main: Peter Lang, 1999) pp. 75–92, especially pp. 78–80; D. B. Forrester, *Truthful Action: Explorations in Practical Theology* (Edinburgh: T&T Clark, 2000) ch. 2.

[34] N. T. Wright, *The New Testament and the People of God* (London: SPCK, 1993[2]) p. 124.

[35] Although see D. B. Forrester, 'Theology in Fragments: Practical Theology and the Challenge of Post-modernity' in P. Ballard and P. Couture (eds), *Globalisation and Difference: Practical Theology in a World Context* (Cardiff: Cardiff Academic Press, 1999) pp. 129–33. Forrester offers the advice that 'the gospels and even the epistles do not present a system. Rather they are full of parables, stories, epigrams, injunctions, songs; fragments, in short. The system-building came far later, and it is still not easy to co-ordinate the material into a coherent consistent system. Perhaps theologians – particularly practical theologians – should sympathise with the postmodernists' suspicion of systems and system building!'

[36] A. E. McGrath, *Christian Spirituality* (Oxford: Blackwell, 1999) p. 2.

37 See M. A. McIntosh, *Mystical Theology* (Oxford: Blackwell, 1998) pp. 3–34.

38 J. D. Johns, 'Pentecostalism and the Postmodern Worldview', *Journal of Pentecostal Theology* 7 (1995) pp. 73–96, who says: 'At the core of the Pentecostal worldview is affective experience of God which generates an apocalyptic horizon for reading reality. In this apocalyptic horizon the experience of God is fused to all other perceptions in the space-time continuum. The fusion holds all things in a dialectical tension between the already and the not yet' (p. 87).

39 See also A. Purves, 'The Trinitarian Basis for a Christian Practical Theology', *International Journal of Practical Theology* 2.2 (1998) pp. 222–39.

40 S. J. Land, *Pentecostal Spirituality: A Passion for the Kingdom* (Sheffield: Sheffield Academic Press, JPTS 1, 1993) p. 41. S. Solivan, *The Spirit, Pathos and Liberation: Toward an Hispanic Pentecostal Theology* (Sheffield: Sheffield Academic Press, JPTS 14, 1998) develops the similar word 'orthopathos' by which he means a critical and personal first-hand engagement with the biblical, theological and social reality of suffering and marginalized communities.

41 M. Bonnington, 'Patterns in Charismatic Spirituality: Worship as Dialectic, Sacrament and Story', *Anglicans for Renewal – Skepsis* 83 (2000) pp. 29–35 (p. 32).

42 Johns, 'Pentecostalism and the Postmodern Worldview', pp. 92–3 says: 'Pentecostals are concerned with truth, but not just propositional truth. In their paradigm orthodoxy, orthopraxy and orthopathy form the purpose, function and structure/essence of truth. Orthodoxy, in both the sense of giving glory to God and in the sense of correct belief, is the purpose of knowledge. It is that toward which the church must always be moving. Glory will be given to God most purely when we are finally transformed in entirety so that our being, behaviour and beliefs conform fully to the truth intended for us.'

43 R. C. Roberts, *Spirituality and Human Emotion* (Grand Rapids MI: Eerdmans, 1982) p. 11.

44 Land, *Pentecostal Spirituality*, pp. 134–5.

45 The notion of 'theological reflection' is not altogether agreed within practical theology. At the very least it means engaging with the theological structures in some meaningful way. See, for example, P. O'Connell Killen and J. der Beer, *The Art of Theological Reflection* (New York: Crossroad, 2000).

46 The pastoral cycle is clearly related to the educational theories of experiential learning, although I am unaware of the origins of such a

connection. See D. A. Kolb, *Experiential Learning: Experience as the Source of Learning and Development* (Englewood Cliffs NJ: Prentice Hall, 1984) especially pp. 20–38.

47 E. Larty, 'Practical Theology as a Theological Form' in D. Willows and J. Swinton (eds), *Spiritual Dimensions of Pastoral Care: Practical Theology in a Multidisciplinary Context* (London: Jessica Kingsley, 2000) pp. 72–7 (pp. 73–4).

48 Ibid. pp. 74–7.

49 van der Ven, *Practical Theology*, pp. 113–56. For an accessible summary of his approach see J. A. van der Ven, 'An Empirical Approach in Practical Theology' in Schweitzer and van der Ven (eds), *Practical Theology – International Perspectives*, pp. 323–39. For a comparison of his methodology with the pastoral cycle also see M. J. Cartledge, 'Practical Theology and Empirical Identity', *European Journal of Theology* 7.1 (1998) pp. 37–44.

50 This concept also stands behind the 'critical conversation' or 'revised critical correlation' model approach. See D. Browning, *A Fundamental Practical Theology: Descriptive and Strategic Proposals* (Minneapolis: Fortress, 1991, 1996²) pp. 44–7. Also see D. Browning, 'Toward a Fundamental and Strategic Practical Theology' in Schweitzer and van der Ven (eds), *Practical Theology – International Perspectives*, pp. 53–74 (p. 26).

51 D. G. Bloesch, *A Theology of Word and Spirit: Authority and Method in Theology* (Downers Grove IL: Inter-Varsity Press, 1992) pp. 76–9.

52 See A. Yong, ' "Life in the Spirit": Pentecostal-Charismatic Life and the Dialectic of the Pentecostal Imagination', unpublished paper, 30th Meeting of Society for Pentecostal Studies, 16–18 March 2000, Northwest College, Kirkland, Washington, USA. I am grateful to the author for this item.

53 A. Thiselton, *New Horizons in Hermeneutics: The Theory and Practice of Transforming Biblical Reading* (London: HarperCollins, 1992) pp. 388, 608–14.

54 Ibid. p. 388.

55 Ibid. p. 615.

56 See M. J. Cartledge, 'Empirical Theology: Towards an Evangelical-Charismatic Hermeneutic', *Journal of Pentecostal Theology* 9 (1996) pp. 115–26.

57 Thiselton, *New Horizons in Hermeneutics*, p. 393.

58 See M. J. Cartledge, 'A New *Via Media*: Charismatics and the Church of England in the Twenty-first Century', *Anvil* 17.4 (2000) pp. 271–83.

59 Wright, *The New Testament and the People of God*, pp. 122–39 uses
    four categories: narrative, questions, symbols and praxis. For the
    purpose of this discussion I have omitted the category of questions
    since the whole practical theological enterprise is based upon the
    notion of question raising.

60 See W. J. Hollenweger, *Pentecostalism: Origins and Developments
    Worldwide* (Peabody MA: Hendrickson, 1997) chs 13, 25, 26.

61 Johns, 'Pentecostalism and the Postmodern Worldview', p. 90 suggests
    that, for Pentecostals, Scripture is a living book in which the Holy
    Spirit is active and through which God is encountered. Therefore
    Scripture functions (1) as a primary reference point for communion
    with God; (2) as a template for reading the world; and (3) as a link to
    God's people and God's presence in the world and throughout the
    ages.

62 Land, *Pentecostal Spirituality*, pp. 74–5.

63 Ibid. p. 75.

64 J. Goldingay, 'Charismatic Spirituality: Some Theological Reflections',
    Theology 789 (1996) pp. 178–87, especially pp. 181–2, offers a typology
    from a charismatic perspective which sees God's action in the world
    in terms of (1) the miraculous, (2) interaction, (3) cause and effect,
    and (4) human decisions. I think that categories (3) and (4) could also
    be defined in terms of interaction. See my categorization in M. J.
    Cartledge, 'A Spur to Holistic Discipleship' in D. Hilborn (ed.),
    *'Toronto' in Perspective: Papers on the New Charismatic Wave of the
    Mid 1990s* (Carlisle: Evangelical Alliance/Paternoster, 2001) pp. 64–
    71.

65 S. Chan, *Pentecostal Theology and the Christian Spiritual Tradition*
    (Sheffield: Sheffield Academic Press, JPTS 21, 2000) p. 118 under-
    standably criticizes the pragmatic reason for worship which is so
    prevalent in charismatic thinking. But this need not be the case.

66 For a review of recent scholarship on the subject, plus my own
    perspective, see M. J. Cartledge, *Charismatic Glossolalia: An Empirical-
    Theological Study* (Aldershot: Ashgate, 2002).

67 W. J. Hollenweger, *Geist und Materie* (München: Chr. Kaiser Verlag,
    1988, Interkulturelle Theologie 3) pp. 314–15, cited by F. D. Macchia,
    'Tongues as a Sign: Toward a Sacramental Understanding of
    Pentecostal Experience', *PNEUMA: The Journal of the Society for
    Pentecostal Studies* 15.1 (1993) pp. 61–76 (p. 61).

68 D. E. Albrecht, *Rites in the Spirit: A Ritual Approach to Pentecostal/
    Charismatic Spirituality* (Sheffield Academic Press, JPTS 17, 1999)
    p. 216 writes: 'The desire for transformation drives nearly all Pent/
    Char ritual. This desire appears in the language and other symbols of

Pentecostal ritual. Transformation symbols that permeate the rites, the testimonies, the songs, the sermonic illustrations and the altar calls, to name a few, express the language of transformation.'

[69] One person who has argued that speaking in tongues should be linked to issues of social change from a black Pentecostal liberationist perspective is R. Beckford, 'Back to my Roots: Speaking in Tongues for a New *Ecclesia*', *TransMission* (Bible Society, Summer 2000) pp. 12–13. See also R. Beckford, *Dread and Pentecostal: A Political Theology for the Black Church in Britain* (London: SPCK, 2000).

[70] Land, *Pentecostal Spirituality*, p. 166.

[71] My research has suggested that extrovert women more than men are attracted by charismatic spirituality. See my *Charismatic Glossolalia*, pp. 163, 167–9, 176, 180–82. For a review of women's ministry in terms of prophecy see chapter 7.

[72] It is interesting to note that the first booklet in the new Grove Renewal series is on this subject because of its importance. See J. Leach, *Developing Prayer Ministry: A New Introduction for Churches* (Cambridge: Grove, Renewal 1, 2000).

[73] Bonnington, 'Patterns in Charismatic Spirituality', p. 30.

[74] See J. C. Thomas, 'Pentecostal Theology in the Twenty-first Century', *PNEUMA: The Journal of the Society for Pentecostal Studies* 20.1 (1998) pp. 3–19, especially pp. 7–12, who proposes that Pentecostal theologians should be willing to characterize their theology in relation to (1) the worshipping Pentecostal community, (2) the integration of theology (heart and head, through dialogue with other ecclesial traditions, and through intra-Pentecostal inter-disciplinary work), (3) accountability to the wider church, (4) attention to the context, and (5) commitment to theology as confessional in nature.

[75] For example, in relation to demonology, see Goldingay, 'Charismatic Spirituality', pp. 186–7; A. Walker, 'The Devil you Think you Know: Demonology and the Charismatic Movement' in T. Smail, A. Walker and N. Wright, *Charismatic Renewal: The Search for a Theology* (London: SPCK, 1993) pp. 86–105; N. Wright, 'Charismatic Interpretations of the Demonic' in A. N. S. Lane (ed.), *The Unseen World: Christian Reflections on Angels, Demons and the Heavenly* (Carlisle: Paternoster, 1996) pp. 33–64.

[76] I have developed this model of spirituality by drawing upon McIntosh, *Mystical Theology*, pp. 5–6. In relation to the symbolic configuration of speaking in tongues, see Cartledge, *Charismatic Glossolalia*, pp. 190–9. The encounter-transformation feature of Pentecostal worship and ritual is clearly described by R. J. Boone, 'Community and Worship: The Key Components of Pentecostal Christian Formation',

Journal of Pentecostal Theology 8 (1996) pp. 129–42 and includes congregational singing, prayer, testimony, preaching and response (via altar calls).

77 McIntosh, *Mystical Theology*, pp. 5–6.

78 See, for example, Cartledge, *Charismatic Glossolalia*, pp. 200–3. Indeed, C. B. Johns argues that praxis must be relativized epistemologically by its incorporation into the Pentecostal faith tradition. She states that 'God must be understood to be the ultimate source and judge of all truth. Knowledge of God involves encounter with and participation in the divine nature which results in the transformation of the knower. The praxis that would flow out of such encounter would generate a fresh vision of the kingdom of God, a vision that incorporates an ethic that is consistent with an epistemology which joins knowing and loving' (*Pentecostal Formation*, p. 40). This praxis is both judged and transformed by its engagement with Scripture.

79 I have previously made use of the biblical authority model of Wright, *The New Testament and the People of God*, pp. 139–43, which has a narrative structure. See Cartledge, 'Empirical Theology: Towards an Evangelical-Charismatic Hermeneutic', pp. 119–21 and Cartledge, 'A New *Via Media*', pp. 278–80. See also M. Hargreaves, 'Telling Stories: The Concept of Narrative and Biblical Authority', *Anvil* 13.2 (1996) pp. 127–39.

80 I shall use these categories in a looser way than Land, *Pentecostal Spirituality*, p. 41 and *passim*.

81 T. Smail, 'The Cross and the Spirit: Towards a Theology of Renewal' in Smail, Walker and Wright (eds), *Charismatic Renewal*, pp. 49–70.

3

Truth and Epistemology: A Charismatic Perspective[1]

1. Introduction

The question as to how we may know what we know is an old philosophical one. How we may justify what we believe to others is concomitant to it. Both of these aspects are based upon questions about the nature of truth and reality. These questions recur throughout the history of ideas and in particular the history of philosophical thought. Historically, this area is not one that many Pentecostals and charismatics have engaged with in an overt way. However, recent Pentecostal writers have begun to address the concerns of human knowledge from a distinctly Pentecostal perspective. This, in part, has arisen because of a greater awareness of the hermeneutical task of theology and, in part, because of the awareness of postmodern discourse, which has given a greater voice to previously marginalized theological traditions, including the Pentecostal and charismatic traditions.

This chapter therefore proposes to do four interconnecting tasks. First, I shall introduce three well-known theoretical frameworks for understanding the nature of truth in relation to claims of human knowledge. Second, I shall describe three Pentecostal writers who have made reference to questions of epistemology and truth in an attempt to clarify in what ways these theories are located in Pentecostal scholarship. Third, I shall aim to integrate the previously outlined theoretical framework within the Pentecostal and charismatic traditions by considering the sources of knowledge and the nature of testimony. This is achieved by drawing upon the work of the epistemologists Robert Audi and C. A. J. Coady. In so doing, my intention is to suggest an integrated framework that may be of value for Pentecostals and charismatics wishing to extend their theologically reflective tools in relation to philosophy. Fourth, and finally, the nature of truth and testimony in Pentecostal scholarship is reflected upon in the light of biblical material before the contribution of this approach to the empirical studies that follow is suggested.

2. Theories of Truth

There are commonly three well-known theories of truth. These are known as the correspondence, coherence and pragmatic theories.[2] In this section I aim to give a brief outline of these theories. I am interested primarily in describing theories of truth rather than theories of justification, although they can easily be confused. In this book a theory of truth is concerned with whether a belief or proposition is either: (a) in correspondence with reality; or (b) in coherence with other beliefs or propositions; or (c) useful to humans – as a necessary and/or sufficient condition for it being true.[3] Theories of justification, on the other hand, aim to discover what sort of evidence or warrant is available to determine whether a given belief or proposition is true.[4] Epistemology, in the stricter sense of the word, is concerned with justification rather than truth. However, it is impossible to understand the nature of justification unless one has appreciated the prior nature of truth upon which it is based.[5]

Correspondence Theory
The correspondence theory of truth is universally recognized as a 'common-sense' approach to truth. Basically, the theory contends that what is said about the world as true depends on how the world is. Sometimes it is phrased in terms of propositions being true if and only if they correspond to the facts.[6] Of course, this raises questions regarding the nature of 'facts'.[7] Nevertheless, the theory states that the association of a true proposition with an external and objective reality independent of the knower is an association of words with world.[8] Truth therefore relates to propositions that are asserted in relation to external reality. These propositions may be controversial, trivial or little known, but their

FACTS

significance does not affect their truth-value.[9] True propositions 'correspond' with reality and they are true in virtue of that correspondence.[10] Some theorists would wish to clarify this relationship by terms such as 'correlation' or 'congruence'.[11] In this model, minds are either knowing or ignorant, propositions are either true or false, and objects are either real or imaginary. Beliefs may depend on minds for their existence but the content of a belief is not dependent on minds believing it to be true. Truth is mind-independent.[12] However, to some extent, the relations of propositions to reality has a mysterious quality which the word 'correspondence' does not do full justice to.[13] It is because of difficulties associated with the relationship of language to reality that some philosophers consider other theories of truth.[14]

Coherence Theory

The coherence theory of truth regards a statement to be true if it coheres with other statements of truth.[15] Any statement that does not cohere with other statements is regarded as false. A true proposition is justified by its coherence with every other justified proposition.[16] The use of the term cohere has been regarded as problematic by some. Does it mean 'is consistent with' or 'entails and is entailed by'?[17] Within the network of statements that constitute the web of beliefs, some statements must be assigned a greater weight. This problem raises the question about how such a set of beliefs is constructed in the first place. How does the first proposition ever get selected and by what criteria?[18] Nevertheless, proponents of this theory argue that there are several sets of cohering statements that need to be held together in order to describe the world correctly.[19] This theory is often linked to linguistics and culture. Truth in this sense is simply a contingent creation of language expressed in a culturally mediated way. It represents beliefs and values but cannot be said to represent or mirror reality itself. It simply functions as a kind of map, but we have no way of checking the map with the territory itself since nothing can be known outside the language.[20] Verification, as it exists, is by consistency and harmony with existing beliefs only.[21] Indeed, this reason gives rise to the potential problem that there could exist more than one distinct coherent systems of belief but which are *inconsistent* with each other. Two or more of these systems could not be true since the criterion of coherence is ultimately breached.[22]

Pragmatic Theory

The pragmatic theory of truth contends that truth must be understood in terms of practice.[23] The notion that truth corresponds between belief and reality is not rejected but clarified by reference to actions. True propositions are also those that work by being successful in practice.[24] Truth is understood by Charles Sanders Peirce as 'settled' habits of action by the community of enquirers. This community of enquirers, it is hoped, will converge on truth in the infinite long run. The mechanism for this convergence is the scientific method since this method alone is constrained by reality which is independent of belief and can therefore lead to consensus among scholars.[25] In the meantime all beliefs and truth claims are considered to be fallible and criticizable.[26] The only propositions upon which everyone would be expected to agree are those which reflect objective reality. Hence Peirce's pragmatic theory is based upon a correspondence theory.[27] William James thought that truth should lead to consistency, stability and the growing of human discourse.[28] James' pragmatism is a kind of instrumentalism. He says, for example, 'The possession of true thoughts means everywhere the possession of invaluable instruments of action.'[29] Beliefs are therefore true in so far as they are useful in manipulating objects of the world, allowing successful communication, accurate predictions and explanations of other occurrences.[30] In postmodern discourse truth is often seen in terms of its function: it is a tool for achieving certain ends.[31] Truth is what gets things done and is therefore instrumental.[32] Indeed, true assumptions provoke actions that lead to desirable results.[33]

It seems reasonable to argue that each of these theories has something of value. The correspondence theory appears to be the most basic theory which emphasizes the objectivity of reality independent of human knowing and which can influence and impact the conceptual frameworks we use. The coherence theory emphasizes the use of language in the articulation of knowledge that is culturally mediated. It highlights that the minds of the knowers and the context of knowing are located within social contexts. If these emphases are combined we can suggest a *critical realist* epistemology which understands that knowledge is partial and limited and may need to be revised in the light of external reality and acknowledged incoherence. In the meantime, it is held as true knowledge, however, partially. N. T. Wright suggests that critical realism is a relational epistemology, as opposed to a detached one, that functions within a narrative-laden world. Thus it contains both personal and propositional knowledge.[34] The pragmatist theory adds to this perspective the emphasis that knowledge progresses through revision, but also that true knowledge makes a difference at very practical levels because it also works. In other words, it has a transforming influence upon the knowers. While theories of truth are distinct from actual epistemologies they underpin such positions functioning in an implicit but nevertheless significant way. It is important as well as useful, therefore, to make these assumptions as explicit as possible for greater understanding to be appreciated.

3. Pentecostal Epistemology

The Yada and Praxis Approach

Cheryl Bridges Johns in her book on Pentecostal formation outlines a biblical epistemology in the context of a discussion of Paulo Freire's educational paradigm.[35] She starts from the Old Testament word for knowledge, that is, *yada*, which includes heart and participatory knowledge that is experiential as opposed to mental knowledge that is remote and distant from that which is known.[36] She contrasts this experiential and relational knowledge with the Greek approach to knowledge characterized by the word *ginoskein*, which means to know something by looking at a distance. She states that:

> Within the understanding of *yada*, if a person knows God, she or he is encountered by the one who lives in the midst of history and who initiates covenant relationships. Knowledge of God, therefore, is measured not by the information one possesses but by how one is living in response to God. A person is ignorant or foolish not because of the lack of awareness of facts of God but rather because of a failure to the do will of God.[37]

Therefore knowledge contains an acknowledgement of God and emotion and will which honours and obeys his will. She suggests that the Hebrew way of knowing is present in and through the Greek language of the New Testament.[38] This means that knowledge of God is grounded in loving relationship (1 John 4:7–8,16,20) and is manifest through obedience to the known will of God (1 John 2:3–5, 5:1–5). Jesus Christ is Lord of life (1 John 5:6–12) and knowledge of the Lord comes through keeping his commands (1 John 2:3).

Johns also wishes to ground such epistemology within the covenant people of God. Therefore she states:

> Covenant community forms the context for an encounter with God and for an interpretation of the resulting transformation. The covenant God offers to people is a covenant to be the people of God. He dwells in the midst of his people so that the church, being grounded in covenant relations, operates within an epistemology not of detachment and manipulation (which is a result of operating only with facts and principles) but rather of participation and accountability. There is, therefore, the avoidance of privatized subjectivism on the one hand and totalitarian objectivism on the other.[39]

Johns then compares this biblical understanding with Freire's praxis epistemology.

Freire, according to Johns, understands praxis as 'reflective engagement in history which transforms the world'.[40] Praxis overcomes the dichotomy of theory and practice by uniting them dialectically as twin moments of the same activity. Freire takes his understanding of praxis from Karl Marx. For Marx, praxis was an activity which humans were engaged in so that economic and social structures could be transformed and liberated. This means that people are active subjects rather than passive objects caught up in a world beyond their control. For Freire, praxis is a human responsibility, and God is a 'subjective presence in the historical process'.[41]

Johns contends that there are a number of problems with praxis as a source of epistemology. In and of itself, praxis is an insufficient basis upon which to know God and achieve human transformation. Any action-reflection may become distorted and

praxis – living in the world

self-serving. There needs to be an authority beyond the self that transcends and even negates such action-reflection. Any knowledge that comes through praxis is effected by sin and in order for transformation to occur it must begin with the knower before the person can effect transformation in the world. It is at this point that Johns suggests that, while Pentecostals have understood themselves to be objects of transforming grace, they have neglected the idea that they are partners with God in the redemptive process.

Johns aims to integrate praxis into *yada* by refining the former by the latter. This is essential in order to incorporate such a concept into the Pentecostal theological tradition. In this tradition God is the ultimate source and judge of truth and knowledge of God 'involves encounter with and participation in the divine nature which results in the transformation of the knower'.[42] This knowledge and praxis would be based upon a vision of the kingdom of God and would integrate knowing and loving. This knowledge being experiential and relational is compatible with human praxis that is judged and transformed by the word of God; that is an encounter with God through personal *yada*.

In terms of the theories of truth outlined above, it would seem that Johns assumes the correspondence view, while offering a pragmatic view in terms of encounter and transformation. It can be argued that the dominance of the *yada* way of knowing assumes a degree of correspondence between the language and categories of the biblical revelation and the reality encountered and to which they refer. While Pentecostals and charismatics may be less happy with the language of propositional revelation than evangelicals,[43] they often function in their epistemology by assuming both a correspondence view of truth and its propositional basis. Pentecostals and charismatics as well as evangelicals use this theoretical structure, even if Pentecostals and charismatics wish to emphasize the experiential and relational dimensions to biblical knowledge which leads them to use the notion of *yada* as personal, encountered knowledge of God.

The Cultural-Linguistic Approach
Joel Shuman has attempted to move the debate concerning baptism of the Holy Spirit and the doctrine of initial evidence forward by

locating it within the cultural-linguistic framework borrowed from George A. Lindbeck.[44] The impact of this upon the doctrine of initial evidence, while important and interesting, is not the focus of this discussion. Rather, I am interested in describing the manner in which this particular epistemological approach has been utilized within Pentecostal theology.[45]

Shuman initially bases his thinking in this regard on the work of Geoffrey Wainwright, who suggests a fundamental link between liturgical practices in a broad sense and formally expressed doctrines as a way of seeing the world. Based upon the ancient maxim *lex orandi, lex credendi* (the law of prayer is the law of faith) cited by Wainwright, Shuman contends that the 'material interplay' between doctrine and worship has significant epistemological implications.[46] The Christian vision of reality is only really understood 'from within' the community of faith by means of participation. The truth of what is experienced in worship is subsequently altered by means of theological reflection. This points to an interrelationship between worship and doctrine, praxis and reality. It is in this context of liturgical practices of the Pentecostal community that Shuman locates baptism in the Holy Spirit.

Following the work of Hans-Georg Gadamer, Shuman writes:

> Particular languages are the products and possessions of particular, historically traditioned communities which teach their members to see and describe the world in a particular way. One can only understand and describe what is taking place in one's world by virtue of one's participation in a tradition.[47]

A person, therefore, understands not as an isolated individual but as a participant in a tradition. All knowledge is therefore situated within a tradition and from a particular perspective. The language that is used is inextricably tied to a specific tradition by its vocabulary and it is used to express the beliefs and values of that tradition. In this sense it is embedded in a religious culture. Consequently, Shuman states that 'Theological doctrine may best be seen as a tradition-dependent cultural-linguistic phenomenon of a liturgical community.'[48] Following Lindbeck, religion is understood as an interpretive scheme that embodies myths, narratives and rituals, giving structure to human experience and understanding of the world. It is analogous to Wittgenstein's 'language game', where language corresponds to a particular way of life.

Shuman argues that such an understanding of doctrine and knowledge does not exclude the notion of truth. Experience and indeed experience of God is important. They are, however, embedded in the narratives, symbols and practices of our Christian communities. This means that such religious traditions invite participation in certain practices. This knowledge is therefore not abstract but concrete and real within the framework of practices demonstrated in the community of faith.[49]

Embedded in these practices are beliefs and values which doctrine seeks to articulate and defend against contesting claims. When communities do this they affirm their own identity over and against others. The Bible, often used in this context, is the 'property' of the Christian community that offers interpretations not in abstract but based upon practice. This scriptural world creates an interpretive framework and a basis from which and upon which believers can understand reality. In that sense it absorbs and recreates the world in which believers live. Believers therefore make the story of the Bible to be their story.

When we attempt to place this particular model within the theories of truth outlined above, the dominant model is clearly a coherence model, although the emphasis on practice resonates with pragmatism. Language games only make sense within their own worlds of meaning. In that sense they are self-referential. The practices and rituals that inform the interpretive framework are regulated by a bounded group of people who form a Christian community with common beliefs and values.[50] This community functions in this sense to define acceptable practice, experience and doctrine. This is based upon its coherence with the community's linguistic-cultural usage of Scripture to legitimate and resource contemporary religious praxis.

The Carry-over of Value Approach

Amos Yong has written a fascinating account of glossolalia in terms of the question of truth.[51] By drawing upon Robert Cummings Neville's theory of religious symbolism, Yong introduces us to a significant truth theory in relation to Pentecostal and charismatic experience. Neville defines truth in terms of the 'carry-over of value' from the object into the person's experience by means of signs. It is this emphasis on the carry-over of value that indicates its pragmatic nature in relation to truth.[52] However, while emphasizing the pragmatic nature of truth in this way, he also wishes to retain the correspondence and coherence models.[53] In this approach, religious experience is made sense of by means of its signs or symbols, their referents, meanings and interpretations. In this sense, Yong uses the metaphor 'Tongues of Fire' as symbolic of a believer's experience of God. It is through the use of the imagination that such interpretations are suggested. The imagination, interpretation, theory and practice combine in what Neville called 'engagement'.[54] It is through this engagement that the process of transformation must be understood. Yong says:

> Transformation thus refers to the ongoing progress toward spiritual maturity and is the most important effect produced by a genuine encounter with the divine. In other words, genuine 'tongues of fire' are transformative; without the latter, the former may just be gibberish.[55]

Yong suggests that such transformation occurs at the individual level and that praxis is defined in relation to the religious community. It is the individual transformations that allow people to participate in the transformation of the community. The religious symbols shape the imagination with respect to the divine and, according to Lindbeck's cultural-linguistic theory, interpret the worldview of the religious community and enable responses to be made.

Following Neville, Yong argues that the divine is mediated via symbols that contrast the finite and the infinite. Interpretation is understood both 'extentionally' and 'intentionally'. By extentionally is meant the overlapping network of symbols that refer one to another. Intentionally, however, is the effort to understand the real religious object. Thus Yong argues '[i]ntentionality produces "content meaning" which internalises network meaning and by which "the network meaning as an actual experiential symbol [is] actually disclosive"'.[56] Therefore the symbol 'Tongues of Fire' both refers extentionally to networks of meaning within the Judaeo-

Christian tradition and intentionally to the Holy Spirit in Pentecostal experience. This means that truth is also devotional and practical, not simply theological. He summarizes Neville's pragmatic theory of truth by saying that 'religious symbols "might be here referential, there not, here meaningful, there not, here interpreted, there not, here true, there not ..... That is, they are true but broken"'.[57]   *esoteric settlement*

Yong contends that glossolalia is devotionally true in so far as the Pentecostal soul is transformed to be more like the Spirit; practically true in so far as Pentecostal practices embody the Spirit; and theologically true in so far as the understanding of the mind is attuned to the Spirit. In each of these features truth is regarded as that value which is carried over from the object to the knower(s).[58] He summarizes the truth of glossolalia when he states:

> [T]he truth of glossolalia can thus be said to lie, on the one hand, in its symbolic function which allows the tongues-speaker both to experience and correctly to understand the divine in a unique way, and on the other hand, in its power of spiritual transformation, which carries the divine reality over into the life and community of the glossolalist. At the same time, because the divine infinitude can never be completely experienced, the meaning and truth of glossolalia will continue to take on new forms.[59]

The truth of glossolalia can therefore only be partially experienced. It continues to require ongoing interpretation. As a broken symbol, glossolalia remains true provisionally and never absolutely.

Yong concludes by considering some critical questions in relation to this pragmatic theory of truth and glossolalia. We may paraphrase some of the questions as follows: If truth is restricted to pragmatic considerations, how do we break out of the network of symbols? We cannot. Are we not locked into some form of hermeneutical circularity? How do we know that the divine is indeed carried over by means of these symbols? Who says so? Which traits are actually divine and not idolatrous or demonic? Such questions, Yong suggests, are mistakenly based upon a 'correspondence-of-form' view of truth. They are misplaced in relation to the thesis of Yong's article. He does not reject a correspondence view of truth *per se*. Rather, 'glossolalia is true in so far as the divine freedom, the divine speech and the unity of the divine life are all carried over into the tongues-speaker and the glossolalic community. Truth is that which sets us free (John 8:36) – that which is properly transforming, both spiritually, historically, and existentially.'[60] Such an approach to truth, Yong contends, is congenial to Pentecostal sensibilities that are concerned with stories and experiences rather than argumentation and treaties. Pentecostal resources are to be found within its linguistic-cultural framework and engagement with the world.[61]

These three approaches utilize the theories of truth outlined above in either explicit (Yong) or implicit (Johns and Shuman) ways. Is there any way of combining them within a charismatic perspective? I want to suggest that there is at least one possible way in which this might be done.

4. Testimony to the Truth of Encounter: The Integrating Centre of Pentecostal and Charismatic Epistemology

In an attempt to integrate theories of truth, Pentecostal scholarship and epistemology together I shall draw broadly upon the work of the epistemologists Robert Audi and C. A. J. Coady.[62] In Audi's key text on the subject of epistemology he outlines five sources for our knowledge of ourselves and the world around us. Although Audi does not argue for a theological understanding of these sources, I suggest that they can be readily transposed into theological discourse.

The first source is *perception*: through our fives senses we perceive the world around us. The reality of the external world is mediated to us by means of our senses. If our senses are open to the world around, then it is perceived, and we tend to form beliefs about it. These perceptions are indeed fallible, but nevertheless real. The second source is *memory*. Memory does not produce beliefs but it preserves what is known. It is often a basic source of the justification of belief, for example, when we remember our experience of conversion or 'baptism in the Spirit' and use that memory to explain such a belief to others. The third source is our inner perception or *consciousness*. 'When we look into our own consciousness, we find beliefs also arising in the same natural, seemingly irresistible way in which they arise from outer perception. We have, however, far more control over the scenes and events that we experience only inwardly.'[63] The inner and outer world both produce beliefs that are direct and irresistible. The fourth source is *reason*. Reason enables us to turn our attention to abstract matters while being bombarded by sensory information. It enables us to makes inferences from information known to us and extends our use of categories and relations. It enables us to cohere what we sense, remember and imagine into a framework. The fifth source is *testimony*. There is so much that we cannot possibly know without relying on others. Beliefs and knowledge are significantly grounded in social reality. This social dimension is often informal, through casual conversations, but also through literature and the media, now including the Internet.

Audi summarizes these sources and how they function in terms of epistemology when he says:

> Perception looks outward, and through it we see the physical world. Memory looks backward, and through it we see the past, or at least some of our own past. Introspection looks inward, and through it we see the stream of our own consciousness. Reason looks beyond experience of the world of space and time, and through it we see concepts and their relations. Testimony draws on all these sources. It enables others to see – though at one remove, through the attester's eyes – virtually anything that an accurate and credible person attests to.[64]

Thus the individual aspects of knowing are integrated socially by the notion of testimony. It is the social mechanism of testimony that is of supreme importance to Pentecostal and charismatic understanding of our knowledge of God. We do not believe and know God in isolation; rather, we are part of a worshipping and witnessing community of faith.

These features can be integrated within the theological structures by prioritizing the testimony of Scripture above other aspects. The Bible as the book of the church, read within the covenant of faith, provides a unique testimony to the purposes of God for the salvation of his creation. As Scripture is read and expounded within the community of the church, so God's testimony through the writings of his servants is heard. It constantly refreshes the corporate memory of individual congregations and gives a strong basis for hope of future blessings. The correspondence view of truth in relation to Scripture has a high regard for the testimony of Scripture as accurate and truthful in what it testifies to. In other words, there is positive correlation between the biblical accounts and the realities to which they testify. However, 'for Pentecostals . . . belief in the authority of scripture is not determined by cognitive constructs alone, rather it is greatly determined by the Pentecostal's immediate experiences of God in, and through the text . . . Pentecostal experience informs one's understanding of the text; yet the text *testifies* of the same experiences among the early church and the apostles'.[65] This understanding is based upon a correspondence theory of truth and assumes that the experience of today *corresponds* with the experience of the early church. A critical realist adoption of this position, as opposed to a naïve realist or positivist position, suggests that its correspondence is always part of a hermeneutical process from *within* a worldview and that it is under continual, sometimes slight and sometimes significant, adjustment.[66]

Testimony is therefore an important constituent of the Pentecostal and charismatic traditions.[67] While tradition may have a negative connotation, it is now widely accepted that we all do our theology from some kind of position or tradition, that is a linguistic-cultural context. Tradition, which is living, is open to change and trans-formation, nevertheless provides a platform from which to speak, act and judge. All three Pentecostal scholars cited above have a positive view of the testimony of tradition. In this sense, they embrace, if not exclusively, the positive features of the cultural-linguistic theory of truth. Of course, with a living tradition, it merges into the contemporary and experiential side of faith and practice. It is here that testimony is perhaps most obvious.[68] The occasion for someone to testify to what God has done and is doing, within the context of worship, provides the key to understanding testimony in its cohering function of the other sources of Christian and general knowledge. Indeed, it is interest-ing to observe that the sequence of stages in Pentecostal worship and formation noted by R. Jerome Boone include at its heart the opportunity for testimony.[69] It is also the first movement in the Bible study approach proposed by Jackie David Johns and Cheryl Bridges Johns under the title 'Sharing our Testimony – *Yada* of Life in the Community'.[70]

The pragmatist approach, as illustrated by Yong, uses the insights of both the correspondence and coherence theories and 'cashes them out' in terms of pragmatism. Here, the perception, memory, consciousness and imagination cohere as someone gives a reasoned account of the transformation done by God. All three Pentecostal writers clearly give importance to the pragmatic approach to truth.[71] The reality of changed lives gives meaning not only to the individuals concerned but also to the congregation as a whole. The narrative structure of Pentecostal and charismatic spirituality gives the best possible framework for such testimony as people simply tell and retell their stories about life with, through and in God.

C. A. J. Coady considers testimony to be a speech act performed under certain conditions and with certain intentions.[72] The contexts for such speech acts are defined in terms of the formal setting, the informal context and the extended sense.[73] By *formal testimony*, he refers to the kind of testimony that is offered in a court of law, commission or enquiry that is provided by persons who are regarded as witnesses. *Informal testimony* refers to the natural testimony of everyday life. It includes such things as giving geographical directions, reporting an incident that has happened and giving a football score. *Extended testimony* refers to the practice of reporting information based on sources other than firsthand experience. For example, historians refer to documents such as private diaries, confidential minutes of meetings and newspaper reports as testimony. In a church context, formal testimony would correspond to the kind used in a worship service when a leader interviews someone or creates space for testimony from the congregation.[74] Informal testimony happens within casual conversation especially in small group settings. Extended testimony can be found in popular magazines or church newsletters and bulletins. In order to appreciate the nature of formal testimony, which can be seen for example in the formal testimonies produced by churches and Christian organizations, it is useful to note the characteristics set out by Coady. He defines the marks of formal testimony in the following way:

(a) It is a form of evidence.

(b) It is constituted by person *A* offering their remarks *as* evidence so that we are invited to accept *p* because *A* says *p*.[75]

(c) The person offering the remarks is in a position to do so, i.e. he has the relevant authority, competence, or credentials.

(d) The testifier has been given a certain status in the enquiry by being formally acknowledged as a witness and by giving his evidence with due ceremony.

(e) As a specification of (c) within English law and proceedings influenced by it, the testimony is normally required to be firsthand (i.e. not hearsay).

(f) As a corollary of (a) the testifier's remarks should be relevant to a disputed or unresolved question and should be directed to those who are in need of evidence on the matter.[76]

He proposes that some of these characteristics are to be located within natural testimony (a, b, and f), although other characteristics are less obvious (c, d, and e). Most of the reports accepted as testimony are not first hand; there is much less scepticism towards hearsay in this context (as indeed is the case of formal legal testimony within Scottish and much of Continental law).[77] The different context of natural testimony means that it should be considered more akin to promising than giving evidence. There is acceptance of a clear connection between how a person says things are with how they actually are.[78] Having said that, natural testimony is often believed because of the relevant competence, authority or credentials of the person testifying, even though such credentials are not formalized in an institutional manner.

Coady argues that fundamentally we believe the testimony of an individual because we trust the witness. The witness has a particular kind of authority to speak on the matter in question. The attitude of trust is fundamental but not blind. He states that:

What happens characteristically in the reception of testimony is that the audience operates a sort of learning mechanism which has certain critical capacities built into it. The mechanism may be thought of as partly innate, though modified by experience, especially in the matter of critical capacities. It is useful to invoke the model of a mechanism here since the reception of testimony is normally unreflective but it is not thereby uncritical. We may have 'no reason to doubt' another's communication even where there is no question of our being gullible; we may simply recognise that the standard warning signs of deceit, confusion, or mistake are not present.[79]

He suggests that we naturally begin with an inevitable commitment to some degree of reliability.[80] This is enforced when we find cohesion and coherence with our expectations. It is here that local and cultural factors play their part in determining what is and what is not believable. Indeed, 'we require a conceptual apparatus and related beliefs in order to construe our experience at all'.[81] When this is related to Pentecostal and charismatic epistemology we can see that the testimony of Scripture as reliable and its ongoing narrative power to form the cultural-linguistic context provide the crucial matrix from within which to benefit from and appreciate the role of testimony.[82] When we turn to Scripture we find that testimony is a central feature as the biblical writers give testimony to God's purposes through the two testaments of Old and New.

5. Testimony in the Bible

In order to close this particular discussion on the subject of epistemology and the importance of testimony to it, I shall describe briefly the biblical material on the subject of testimony and the knowledge of God before offering some concluding reflections.[83]

Walter Brueggemann, in his *Theology of the Old Testament*, uses the concept of testimony and the metaphor of trial as co-ordinating ideas through which to structure an approach to Old Testament study.[84] This reflects the importance of the concept in the Old Testament and therefore for Christian theology.[85] In the Old Testament the notion of testimony is based upon an act of encounter between the person and God to which the person gives testimony, for example Moses and the burning bush (Exodus 3).[86] This is also seen in Moses' encounter with Yahweh at Sinai. As a consequence, 'testimony' in the Pentateuch often refers to the decalogue, or the tent of meeting (Exodus 29:4), or the ark of the covenant (Exodus 40:3). That is, these things function as evidence that calls to mind particular events of encounter between God and his people. This evidence becomes a basis of revelation in terms of the Torah. The idea of testimony is further developed in the sense of a legal setting through the Old Testament (see, for example, Numbers 35:50; Deuteronomy 19:15,18). In the book of the prophet Isaiah (43:10,12; 44:8) the nation of Israel is ordered to come forward as a witness to the other nations regarding the unique righteousness of Yahweh. The scene is one of bringing a case against the nations as a final judgment on the world.

Paul Ricoeur, in an important essay on the hermeneutics of testimony, comments on the Isaiah 43:8–13 passage:

> The irruption of meaning is fourfold. At first the witness is not just anyone who comes forward and gives testimony, but the one who is sent in order to testify. Originally, testimony comes from somewhere else. Next, the witness does not testify about isolated and contingent fact but about radical, global meaning of human experience. It is Yahweh himself who is witnessed to in the testimony. Moreover, the testimony is orientated toward proclamation, divulging, propagation: it is for all peoples that one people witness. Finally, this profession implies a total engagement not only of words but of acts and, in the extreme, in the sacrifice of life. What separates this new meaning of testimony from all its uses in ordinary language is that the testimony does not belong to the witness. It proceeds from an absolute initiative as to its origin and its content.[87]

In the New Testament there is evidence of a legal framework within the Synoptic Gospels (for example, Mark 14:55,56,59; Luke 22:71); future legal testimony of the disciples is anticipated as public witness to Jesus in the hostile environment of persecution (Mark 10:18). Luke, in the Acts of the Apostles, uses the concept of testimony in the general sense of attestation to good conduct (Acts 16:2, 22:5,12) or a good name (Acts 6:3) as well as in reference to false witnesses (Acts 6:13, 7:58). However, in Acts 23:11 the verb 'to bear witness' means to proclaim Christ and is associated with the apostolic testimony of the gospel (Acts 4:33).

As L. Coenen states:

For Luke it is the apostles, the disciples, who have been commissioned by Jesus with the proclamation of the message of the kingdom, who are witnesses. They are more precisely defined in Acts 1:22 as witnesses of the resurrection of Jesus (cf. Acts 2:32; 3:15; 13:31; 26:16 – Paul, because the risen Lord met him) and of his deeds (also predicted in Acts 22:15 of Paul).[88]

For Paul too the concept of testimony usually refers to the proclamation of the gospel (1 Corinthians 1:6, 2:1; 2 Thessalonians 1:10).

The concept of witness has a more central role in the Johannine material.[89] Although John in his Gospel is aware of the classical sense of testimony as human attestation (John 2:25, 18:23, 12:17, 3:28, 8:17), testimony chiefly concerns testimony to or of Christ. Therefore, John the Baptist testifies to Jesus (John 1:7,8,15,32, 3:26,31). Jesus testifies to the truth concerning himself (John 8:13,14 – in tension with 5:31). He also states that his works (John 5:36, 10:25), his Father (John 5:32,37, 6:65) and the Scriptures (John 5:39) all bear witness to him. Jesus himself witnesses to the truth (John 18:37) because of what he has known and seen (John 3:11). In John's Gospel, therefore, Jesus, like Moses, is a mediator of the testimony, or revelation of God to the world (John 3:31–34, 7:16, 12:48–50). The world rejects his testimony (John 8:14) and is judged by the witness who is also the judge.

The Johannine material also contains references to the confirmation of God's truth through the testimony of believers. Thus, the Samaritans believe in Jesus on account of the Samaritan woman encountered by Jesus at the well (John 4:29). In addition to the witness of the Spirit of truth, the Paraclete (John 15:26), the disciples of Jesus are also expected to testify to Jesus (John 15:27). The epistles especially stress the role of testimony in the proclamation of the gospel (1 John 1:2, 4:14). This is again witnessed to by the Spirit (1 John 5:6) and is carried by the believer (1 John 5:10). Thus testimony is something which is experienced by faith and known through faith in the context of a believing community.

This is stated well by Andrew T. Lincoln in the context of the lawsuit motif in John's Gospel:

Just as Jesus' witness to truth is self-authenticating, so the community's witness to Jesus in its written testimony is self-authenticating. In an inevitable circularity, the community claims that its own witness is true. In the end, in knowing where truth lies in the cosmic lawsuit, there can be no going behind the witness. This would be to assume that there is some superior vantage point from which to make a judgment; if, as the narrative claims, the truth of the lawsuit is about God, then by definition there can be no such vantage point. In line with such a perspective, the response the narrative calls for is acceptance of its witness or belief. The only way to discover its truth for oneself, to align oneself with true judgment in the world, is to participate in it by believing. Hence Jesus' words to Pilate, 'Everyone who belongs to the truth listens to my voice' (18.37). The attitude that correlates to this narrative's notion of truth is faith seeking understanding, or as Jesus puts it earlier: 'Anyone who resolves to do the will of God will know whether the teaching is from God or whether I am speaking on my own' (7.17) and 'believe . . . so that you may know and understand that the Father is in me and I am in the Father' (10.38).[90]

The Revelation of John refers to the testimony of Jesus Christ as the word of God (Revelation 1:2,9, 12:11). Testimony is the 'spirit of prophecy' (19:10). To be touched by the testimony of Jesus Christ places the recipient in the service of the witness. This also means sharing in the persecution and suffering of Christ (Revelation 12:11). Since Jesus is the faithful witness *par excellence* (Revelation 1:5), it is anticipated that those in Christ will also be faithful witnesses to the gospel (Revelation 2:13) and hold firmly to the hope that is set before them.

6. Conclusion

This chapter has developed a dialogue between the discourse of contemporary philosophy on the one hand (via theories of truth, sources of knowledge and an analysis of the epistemology of testimony) and Pentecostal scholarship on the other. In the light of the biblical material described above, the following observations can be made in order to conclude.

The notion of testimony is basic to the biblical revelation. Indeed, the personal encounter of God with Moses provides the backdrop to the language of testimony in the Old Testament. The forensic language of testimony continues throughout the Bible. The New Testament makes clears that testimony of encounter with God is inextricably tied to the person of Jesus Christ: his life and ministry, death and resurrection, especially his resurrection. All testimony, if it is to continue in this respect, should have a Christological focus. Moreover, such a Christological focus needs to be situated within a Trinitarian context. This is what Jesus does with respect to his own testimony. He testifies on behalf of the Father and says that the Paraclete will continue to testify about him after he has returned to the Father (John 14 – 16). Given the concern of Pentecostals and charismatics to integrate their epistemology by means of community testimony, the biblical survey demonstrates just what a sound basis they have chosen. John's Gospel states that the Paraclete will help the disciples in the testifying to the truth of encounter (John 15:26–27). Yet the biblical material, especially in John's Gospel, also indicates that such testimony is discerned spiritually through the eyes of faith. The testimony of the faithful will be rejected by the world, as then, so now. So long as Pentecostals and charismatics continue to use such a Christological focus within a Trinitarian context as the standard by which they judge such testimonies, then testimonies can continue to be regarded as authentically Christian. Therefore the testimony of Scripture as the supreme witness to the purposes of God in Christ functions in a critical way even as the testimony of the church as community functions in a cohering sense.

From the perspectives of empirical studies that acknowledge a realist ontology it would seem that the other sources which Audi uses are also important and deserve to be acknowledged as having a significant role in the project. In particular, our perceptions of present reality and memories of past experience will continue to be sought in order to provide data upon which to make informed judgments. The role of consciousness and reason provide sources for frameworks and concepts that are tested via the empirical data collected. While testimony provides a cohering function at popular levels it also functions in an academic context as the community of scholars share their own stories of reality. Their interpretations of theological praxis found within the communities of faith enable them to make recommendations for its renewal. Therefore the empirical studies aim to engage with theological praxis in specific ways and they are intended to illustrate the kind of knowledge that is possible within the enterprise of practical theology from charismatic and empirical perspectives joined in a creative and mutually critically manner. It is my intention that these studies will contribute to our understanding of the truth in ways in which it corresponds to reality (what people really believe and practice). Truth that is coherent and yet challenges what we already understand (is consonant with the discipline of critical and constructive theology). And more: that it transforms our knowing with purposeful activity for the sake of the kingdom of God (worship and mission).

---

[1] An earlier version of this chapter was presented as a paper entitled 'Testimony to the Truth of Encounter: A Study of Pentecostal-Charismatic Epistemology' at the 31st Annual Meeting of the Society for Pentecostal Studies (SPS), Southeastern College, Lakeland, Florida, March 2002. Sections of the paper have also appeared in M. J. Cartledge, 'The Role of Testimony in Worship', *Anglicans for Renewal – Skepsis* 87 (2001) pp. 27–31 and M. J. Cartledge, *Testimony: Its Importance, Place and Potential* (Grove, Renewal 9, 2002). I am grateful to Paul D. Murray for his insightful comments on theories of truth.

[2] It is interesting to note that even in standard introductions to social research these theories are described as the main contenders for discussion. See, for example, M. Williams and T. May, *Introduction to the Philosophy of Social Research* (London: University College London Press, 1996) pp. 36–9, 94–103.

[3] R. L. Kirkham, *Theories of Truth: A Critical Introduction* (Cambridge MA: Massachusetts Institute of Technology, 1992, 1995^2) p. 22; cf. A. I. Goldman, *Knowledge in a Social World* (Oxford: Clarendon Press, 1999) pp. 41–68.

[4] Kirkham, *Theories of Truth*, p. 24.

[5] Ibid. p. 42; see ch. 7 for a discussion of foundationalism, instrumentalism and coherence as theories of justification.

[6] See S. Haack, *Philosophy and Logics* (Cambridge: Cambridge University Press, 1978, 1995) pp. 91–2.

[7] See the discussion in Kirkham, *Theories of Truth*, pp. 138–9.

[8] T. Honderich (ed.), *The Oxford Companion to Philosophy* (Oxford: Oxford University Press, 1995) pp. 166–7.

9 D. Groothius, *Truth Decay: Defending Christianity against the Challenge of Postmodernism* (Leicester: Inter-Varsity Press, 2000) p. 89.

10 R. Audi, *Epistemology: A Contemporary Introduction to the Theory of Knowledge* (London: Routledge, 1998, 2000²) p. 239.

11 Kirkham, *Theories of Truth*, pp. 120–30.

12 Groothius, *Truth Decay*, p. 89.

13 Kirkham, *Theories of Truth*, pp. 135–6 defends the use of the word 'correspondence' as a handy 'summing up' phrase.

14 P. Horwich, 'Truth, theories of' in J. Dancy and E. Sosa (eds), *A Companion to Epistemology* (Oxford: Blackwell, 1992, 1993²) pp. 509–15 (p. 511).

15 Haack, *Philosophy and Logics*, p. 95.

16 Audi, *Epistemology*, p. 241.

17 The problem of defining the meaning of the term 'coherence' is noted by Kirkham, *Theories of Truth*, p. 104.

18 Some philosophers marry a correspondence/realist theory at this point with a coherence/idealist theory in order to overcome the problem of regress. See ibid. pp. 105, 114–16.

19 Honderich (ed.), *The Oxford Companion to Philosophy*, p. 140.

20 Groothius, *Truth Decay*, p. 93.

21 Horwich, 'Truth, theories of', p. 511.

22 Kirkham, *Theories of Truth*, pp. 106, 108, 111.

23 Actually, pragmatism is pluralistic and contains a number of perspectives like a family resemblance. This section offers a sketch of classical pragmatism for the sake of analysis.

24 Audi, *Epistemology*, p. 242.

25 Haack, *Philosophy and Logics*, p. 97; Kirkham, *Theories of Truth*, p. 80.

26 N. Frankenberry, 'American Pragmatism' in P. L. Quinn and C. Taliaferro (eds), *A Companion to Philosophy of Religion* (Oxford: Blackwell, 1997, 2000) pp. 121–8 (p.122).

27 Kirkham, *Theories of Truth*, p. 83. Kirkham also suggests that, for Peirce, while reality may be independent of one mind, and a subset of minds, it is not independent of all minds (p. 84). He regards this position as quasi-realist since agreement is given priority over the notion of mind-independence (p. 87).

28 Honderich (ed.), *The Oxford Companion to Philosophy*, pp. 709–10.

29 Cited by Kirkham, *Theories of Truth*, p. 92.

30 Ibid. p. 93.

31 Even that instrumentalism can be reduced to what may be 'helpful'. The later pragmatism of R. Rorty, *Philosophy and the Mirror of Nature* (Oxford: Blackwell, 1980, 1989) pp. 371–2, eschews correspondence theory altogether in the relation of sentences or thoughts to reality.

The language of 'correspondence' is a rhetorical device that enables successful normal discourses to be complimented or honoured. He proposes that 'edifying philosophy' does not seek to discover truth but simply continues the conversation (pp. 373, 377).

[32] Groothius, *Truth Decay*, p. 104.

[33] Horwich, 'Truth, theories of', p. 511.

[34] N. T. Wright, *The New Testament and the People of God* (London: SPCK, 1993²) pp. 32–46. Jack Wisemore's response to my SPS paper drew attention to the notion of person-centred knowledge. Wright's relational epistemology would certainly affirm such a perspective while at the same time containing a propositional component which expects the possibility and actuality of truth being spoken about in relation to external reality, both personal and non-personal. Such a person-centred and relational epistemology ultimately has its basis in the persons of the Triune God and the notion of perichoresis, although this is a theological implication not developed by Wright. However, see S. Patterson, *Realist Christian Theology in a Postmodern Age* (Cambridge: Cambridge University Press, 1999) pp. 103–6, 114–36; cf. B. D. Marshall, *Trinity and Truth* (Cambridge: Cambridge University Press, 2000).

[35] C. B. Johns, *Pentecostal Formation: A Pedagogy among the Oppressed* (Sheffield: Sheffield Academic Press, JPTS 2, 1993).

[36] Ibid. p. 35.

[37] Ibid.

[38] This is also the argument of R. Nicole, 'The Biblical Concept of Truth' in D. A. Carson and J. D. Woodbridge (eds), *Scripture and Truth* (Leicester: Inter-Varsity Press, 1983) pp. 287–98, but he focuses on the words *'emet* and *aletheia*, and defines their meaning as involving factuality, faithfulness and completeness (p. 296).

[39] Johns, *Pentecostal Formation*, p. 36. J. D. Johns, 'Pentecostalism and the Postmodern Worldview', *Journal of Pentecostal Theology* 7 (1995) pp. 73–96 says: 'A Pentecostal paradigm must find its structure, function and purpose in the knowledge of God. This knowledge is the knowledge of encounter and relationship, *yada*. To begin at this point is to build on an epistemology which is based upon personal revelation and response. All knowledge is covenantal in nature. The knower and the known must experience, honour and respond to each other according to the true nature of each. Truth is an expression of being and since God is the ground of all that is, he is the ground of all truth. God is thus the witness and guarantor of all knowledge' (pp. 91–2). Johns continues by elucidating truth in terms of orthodoxy, orthopraxy and orthopathy (pp. 92–4).

40 Johns, *Pentecostal Formation*, p. 37.

41 Ibid. p. 38.

42 Ibid. p. 40.

43 For a standard evangelical argument that the biblical view of truth is the correspondence view, see Groothius, *Truth Decay*, chs 3 and 4.

44 J. Shuman, 'Toward a Cultural-Linguistic Account of the Pentecostal Doctrine of the Baptism in the Spirit', *PNEUMA: The Journal of the Society for Pentecostal Studies* 19.2 (1997) pp. 207–23. Cf. G. A. Lindbeck, *The Nature of Doctrine: Religion and Theology in a Postliberal Age* (London: SPCK, 1984).

45 I note the reservation in terms of epistemology expressed by P. W. Lewis, 'Towards a Pentecostal Epistemology: The Role of Experience in Pentecostal Hermeneutics', *The Spirit and Church* 2.1 (2000) pp. 95–125 (p. 100). This is because, as a Pentecostal, he expects God to be able to impact individuals apart from their cultural-linguistic group.

46 Shuman, 'Toward a Cultural-Linguistic Account', p. 213.

47 Ibid. p. 214.

48 Ibid. p. 215.

49 Ibid. pp. 216–17.

50 See R. J. Boone, 'Community and Worship: The Key Components of Pentecostal Christian Formation', *Journal of Pentecostal Theology* 8 (1996) pp. 129–42.

51 A. Yong, '"Tongues of Fire" in the Pentecostal Imagination: The Truth of Glossolalia in Light of R. C. Neville's Theory of Religious Symbolism', *Journal of Pentecostal Theology* 12 (1998) pp. 39–65.

52 Ibid. p. 44.

53 This is more fully developed in A. Yong, 'The Demise of Foundationalism and the Retention of Truth: What Evangelicals can Learn from C. S. Peirce', *Christian's Scholar's Review* 29.3 (2000) pp. 563–88. I am grateful to the author for a copy of this and other papers on this subject.

54 Yong, 'Tongues of Fire', p. 46.

55 Ibid. p. 47.

56 Ibid. p. 48.

57 Ibid. p. 49.

58 Ibid. pp. 50–62 proceeds to define glossolalia's networks of meaning in relation to the three concepts of innocence, growth and adept. I have commented on some aspects of this approach in relation to charismatic glossolalia: see M. J. Cartledge, *Charismatic Glossolalia: An Empirical-Theological Study* (Aldershot: Ashgate, 2002) p. 207.

59 Yong, 'Tongues of Fire', p. 62.

60 Ibid. p. 64.

[61] The whole area is developed more fully from a pragmatic perspective in A. Yong, *Spirit-Word-Community: Theological Hermeneutics in Trinitarian Perspective* (Aldershot: Ashgate, 2002) ch. 5.

[62] Audi, *Epistemology, passim*; C. A. J. Coady, *Testimony: A Philosophical Study* (Oxford: Clarendon Press, 1992, 2000²).

[63] Audi, *Epistemology*, p. 318.

[64] Ibid. p. 320.

[65] Lewis, 'Towards a Pentecostal Epistemology', pp. 110–11 (my emphasis). See also the work of J. K. A. Smith, 'The Closing of the Book: Pentecostals, Evangelicals, and the Sacred Writings', *Journal of Pentecostal Theology* 11 (1997) pp. 49–71, who uses the category of testimony to emphasize a postliberal community epistemology, justified on oral-cultural grounds. However, see S. A. Ellington, 'History, Story, and Testimony: Locating Truth in a Pentecostal Hermeneutic', *PNEUMA: The Journal of the Society for Pentecostal Studies* 23.2 (2001) pp. 245–63 (p. 245), who gives the Bible a functional and absolute authority because of inspiration but maintains that for Pentecostals biblical truth claims have been both conceptual and experiential.

[66] Ellington, 'History, Story, and Testimony', p. 257 suggests that 'a process of testing the stories of the text against lived experienced is essential to a Pentecostal community's appropriation of the truth-claims of Scripture'.

[67] K. J. Archer, 'Pentecostal Hermeneutics: Retrospect and Prospect', *Journal of Pentecostal Theology* 8 (1996) pp. 63–81 suggests that this testimony can be encapsulated by the idea that God is breaking into the everyday lives of believers (p. 69).

[68] Lewis, 'Towards a Pentecostal Epistemology', p. 99.

[69] Boone, 'Community and Worship', pp. 129–42. The stages are: congregational singing, prayer, testimony, sermon and response (altar services).

[70] J. D. Johns and C. B. Johns, 'Yielding to the Spirit: A Pentecostal Approach to Group Bible Study', *Journal of Pentecostal Theology* 1 (1992) pp. 109–34 (pp. 125–7). The subsequent movements are: searching the Scriptures, yielding to the Spirit, and responding to the call.

[71] This emphasis as a holistic and relational approach is also noted by Lewis, 'Towards a Pentecostal Epistemology', pp. 123–4.

[72] Coady, *Testimony*, p. 25. Goldman, *Knowledge in a Social World*, pp. 103–30 suggests that testimony-related activity produces socially distributed knowledge through: (1) discovery, (2) production and transmission of messages, (3) message reception, and (4) message acceptance (p. 104).

[73] Coady, *Testimony*, pp. 27–53.

[74] S. A. Ellington, 'The Costly Loss of Testimony', *Journal of Pentecostal Theology* 16 (2000) pp. 48–59, following the work of M. Poloma, notes how the control from the pulpit is a form of institutionalization (p. 53). What could be suggested here is that it is congruent with a move from informal to formal modes of testimony.

[75] The denotation *p* refers to a given proposition.

[76] Coady, *Testimony*, p. 33.

[77] Ibid. p. 39.

[78] Ibid. p. 43.

[79] Ibid. p. 47.

[80] C. F. Davis, *The Evidential Force of Religious Experience* (Oxford: Oxford University Press, 1989, 1999²) pp. 96–105 discusses the principle of credulity as an initial presupposition, as does K. J. Vanhoozer, *Is there a Meaning in this Text? The Bible, the Reader and the Morality of Literary Knowledge* (Leicester: Inter-Varsity Press, 1998) pp. 290–1. This is reversed by D. Middlemiss, *Interpreting Charismatic Experience* (London: SCM, 1996), who posits an initial approach of incredulity: see my review of his book in *Evangelical Quarterly* 71.1 (1999) pp. 85–8.

[81] Coady, *Testimony*, p. 196.

[82] Vanhoozer's proposal of a canonical-linguistic approach has much to commend itself as an evangelical modification of the postliberal paradigm. See K. J. Vanhoozer, 'The Voice and the Actor: A Dramatic Proposal about the Ministry and Minstrelsy of Theology' in J. G. Stackhouse (ed.), *Evangelical Futures: A Conversation on Theological Method* (Grand Rapids: Baker, Leicester: Inter-Varsity Press and Vancouver: Regent College, 2000) pp. 61–106.

[83] For a discussion of the scriptural narrative as primarily a 'witnessing tradition' see J. Goldingay, *Models for Scripture* (Grand Rapids MI: Eerdmans, 1994) pp. 77–82.

[84] W. Brueggemann, *Theology of the Old Testament: Testimony, Dispute, Advocacy* (Minneapolis: Fortress, 1997). For a critique of his use of testimony and trial, see A. T. Lincoln, *Truth on Trial: The Lawsuit Motif in the Fourth Gospel* (Peabody MA: Hendrickson, 2000) pp. 364–7.

[85] Although, arguably, a key epistemological principle in the Old Testament is expressed in Proverbs 1:7: 'The fear of Yahweh is the beginning of knowledge' (Proverbs 9:10, 15:33; Psalms 111:10; Job 28:28). See G. von Rad, *Wisdom in Israel* (London: SCM, 1972) pp. 65–8. I am grateful to Walter Moberly for reminding me of this.

[86] This section draws from the article by L. Coenen, 'Witness' in C. Brown (ed.), *The New International Dictionary of the New Testament* Vol. 3 (Exeter: Paternoster, 1978) pp. 1038–47.

87 P. Ricoeur, 'The Hermeneutics of Testimony' in P. Ricoeur, *Essays on Biblical Interpretations* (London: SPCK, 1981) pp. 119–54 (p. 131). Lincoln, *Truth on Trial*, p. 344 observes that the last point is not to be found in the passage, but regards it as strange that Ricoeur is reluctant to make any connection to the Suffering Servant of Isaiah.

88 Coenen, 'Witness', p. 1044.

89 Lincoln, *Truth on Trial* explains how the lawsuit motif contains the major themes of witness, interrogation, trial and judgment – *passim*.

90 Ibid. p. 230.

4

Empirical Research Methods

1. Introduction

In the discussion so far the nature of practical and empirical theology has been described in relation to the social sciences. A charismatic approach to the nature of truth and epistemology within theological research has been proposed. It now remains for a description of the actual empirical research methods themselves to be given and their philosophical bases elucidated. Together with the previous methodological chapters, this will give a framework for understanding the nature of empirical research in theology, and guide the reader in the process of actually doing such research. I shall first describe qualitative and quantitative methods and their philosophical traditions before giving two worked examples of how I have conducted research using these respective traditions.

2. Qualitative Research Methods

According to Alan Bryman, qualitative research has a number of characteristics.[1] These include a commitment to 'viewing events, actions, norms, values, etc. from the perspective of the people who are being studied'.[2] Typically this means a commitment to sustained involvement with the group over a period of time and being prepared to engage with a variety of worldviews and perspectives. However, it is usual for the researcher to function with a focus or set of foci, and these inevitably form part of the negotiation process of field research. The intention of such research is to provide detailed description of the social contexts under investigation.

Inevitably researchers move beyond mere description and begin to offer analysis and explanations for the phenomena they describe. Such understanding is offered by elucidating the contexts of certain beliefs, values and behaviour. It is the meanings that are ascribed by the people under study that are conveyed by such analyses. Thus the whole of the social and historical situation is taken into account when seeking to appreciate what individuals within that context communicate when they speak and act in specific ways.

The social context of research is also viewed in terms of a procession of interconnected events since the situation is usually, if not always, engaged over a period of time. In terms of an analogy, it is not so much a camera snapshot, but a video clip that enables the sequence of events to be understood chronologically. Qualitative researchers, wishing to focus on the worldviews of the subjects under study, tend to operate with an open and flexible research strategy rather than one which is overly prescriptive from the start. This means that research problems tend to be organized around more general and open questions rather than tightly defined and theory-driven questions. Qualitative researchers tend to favour a process that formulates and tests theories and concepts as they arise from within the data under collection.

Participant observation

This usually entails the immersion of the researcher in and among those whom he or she seeks to study in order to generate an in-depth understanding of the group and its organization. This has its origin in social anthropology and is often associated with 'ethnography', that is, the detailed investigation of specific groups, societies and cultures. Participant observation has been used by sociologists to study young people, ethnic communities, management and industrial workers. By means of observation, with varying degrees of participation or non-participation, the researcher aims to describe and analyse the beliefs and behaviour of a group of people within a particular time, place and culture. It does so from the perspectives of those under investigation. Participant observers will often interview people in an *ad hoc* manner, as the opportunity arises, examine documents relating to the group in question, life histories and biographies of key individuals, and even use the postal survey method.[3] This means that ideas generated from one source of material can be checked by reference to other sources. This is often called 'triangulation' and enhances the reliability of the results of the research. They also use other methods, especially interviews, because participant observation has its limitations. There are certain locations that are 'out of bounds'. This means that other mechanisms for gleaning information must be used in an auxiliary way. Indeed, participant observation is not a single method, but can and does embrace different methods within it. That is why some writers prefer to describe it as field research. It is often regarded as the main method within the discipline of ethnography.

The participant observer, as part of the design of the study and as part of the gaining access to the group in question, needs to decide at some point whether he or she will function in the role of researcher, or researcher participant, or participant.[4] The role of 'researcher' obviously means that the researcher is present but that he or she does not speak or interrupt the social processes being observed. This role can be associated with covert research approaches. The researcher as 'researcher participant' takes part in a social setting while at the same time engaging in positive social interaction. For example, when I conducted case study research, I joined in the worship of the churches I was studying and therefore participated with them. This role can be associated with overt research approaches. The researcher as 'participant' is involved in a situation already, but takes time to step back and analyse what is happening from a research perspective. For example, clergy in the habit of taking funerals may from time to time decide to record the process of bereavement visiting, sermon preparation, preaching and leading a funeral service, and follow-up visiting. These reflections can be analysed and form the basis of research in pastoral theology. However, all researchers, whatever degree of participation they adopt, need to be aware that their presence will have some influence on the social dynamics of their study.

Interviews

Interviews are also used within field research and complement participant observation.[5] Interviews can take a variety of formats, but unstructured interviewing is most associated with participant observation. In this kind of interview the researcher provides a minimal amount of guidance to the interviewee and allows the conversation to develop naturally. Some researchers may use a group of themes and ideas to guide such an unstructured interview. Structured interviews contain questions as part of an interview protocol that the interviewer uses to guide the interview. In a strictly administered structured interview, the interviewer follows the procedure exactly every time, thus producing similar interview transcripts each time. A semi-structured interview will have set questions but allow for the opportunity of new questions to emerge during the conversation. If something interesting and relevant arises during the interview, then the researcher is prepared and able to follow a new line of enquiry. In the qualitative mode, attention is paid to the quality of the interaction between the interviewer and the interviewee as a proper conversation. In survey research, an interview protocol may be used, but it will typically have standardized questions and seek to interview as many people as possible in order to quantify the answers given.

Focus Groups or Group Interviews

This method of the group interview, often called a 'focus group', uses a group dynamic to uncover information about a particular group or sub-group of people.[6] It builds on the unstructured interview technique but extends it beyond one person to a group. The discussion is guided by means of a number of themes or topics.[7] The discussion enables different perspectives to be highlighted and contradictions to be noted. These different perspectives can be pursued by the researcher and a greater depth of information obtained.

Life Histories

This method entails the construction of the lives of key individuals in the group under investigation.[8] The sources for such life histories can include diaries, autobiographies, personal historically orientated interviews, and conversations with acquaintances and colleagues of the person. 'The life history document is typically a full-length book giving the account of one person's life in his or her own words.'[9]

Oral History

Oral history is similar to life history, although it is from the perspective of a social group rather than an individual. Information from members of a group about the past enables a people's history to be told. It can be used both to illustrate the theoretical concerns of the researcher as well as benefiting the people who share their memories and stories.[10]

Documentary Analysis

There is much that can be learnt from groups through the literature that they produce themselves. This may be diaries, as used in life histories, but more typically refers to books, magazines, newspapers, notices and letters. It can also include photographs, pictures and drawings. For example, for researchers engaged in Church of England studies, there is a wealth of material ranging from parish records, church biographies, parish and diocesan magazines, as well as national church newspapers and parachurch publications.

Combinations of Methods

All of these individual methods can be used in distinct qualitative approaches. For example, *grounded theory* develops theory from data in the field and typically uses 20–30 interviews in order to 'saturate' descriptive and explanatory categories. *Ethnography* describes and interprets cultural and social settings primarily using participant observation, informal interviews and extended time in the field. *Case study* research develops an in-depth analysis of a single or multiple cases using multiple sources.[11] A case study is illustrated later in this chapter and forms the basis of material discussed in chapters 5 and 6.

The data that is produced by qualitative procedures are usually word (and image) based, through field notes, interview transcripts (from tapes) and memos that enable ongoing reflections to be recorded in the process of research. There are now qualitative computer software packages available to enable a rigorous approach to data analysis to be performed.[12] Essentially, this process facilitates analytic categories to be created, in which there are sub-categories. Links can be made between categories to enable relationships to be mapped. In this way the key themes and relationships can be described. This analysis always requires a great familiarity by the researcher with the data, but can enable a more sophisticated exploration to be made possible. Appendix 1 illustrates how an interview protocol can be modified through research and chapter 6 illustrates how an interview transcript can be used within a written report.[13]

3. Quantitative Research Methods

Quantitative research contains much that is similar to research in the natural sciences. Researchers in the natural sciences include within their discourses the concepts of variables, control, measurement and experiment. Quantitative research also uses these terms but, of course, applies them to social reality rather than the physical world. There has been an ongoing debate as to how similar social science should be understood in relation to the sciences in epistemology and methodology of research. It has been usual to regard quantitative researchers as embracing the more scientific or factual approach, while qualitative researchers are regarded as embracing approaches that are more person-centred and have more in common with the arts. There are, of course, many contemporary social scientists using both kinds of research traditions and rejecting the polarized views of the past as being both philosophically weak and practically unhelpful. Indeed, both traditions have strengths and weaknesses that are inherent, and this is increasingly being realized by a new generation of social scientists wishing to use both traditions of research. I shall review the philosophy of social science below as a preliminary exercise before suggesting in subsequent chapters how an empirical-orientated practical theology can use all the methods on offer within a *theological* framework.

Surveys

Survey questionnaires are used to acquire research data collected from a cross-section of people at a single point in time in order to understand the ways in which certain variables relate to one another. Each question contains at least one variable, and sometimes more, depending upon how it is constructed. Information is collected for the same variables from a number of cases (that is, respondents).[14] Appendix 2 gives an example of a questionnaire in an edited form. The large social survey, for example the national census, is probably the best-known kind of survey used by sociologists. It provides a snapshot of a large number of people at a given moment in time regarding a broad range of issues.[15] There are a variety of sample strategies for the purpose of gathering data from particular groups of people. These include both random and non-random sampling techniques.[16]

Experiments

In social psychology experiments are often used in which at least two groups, comprising people who have been randomly allocated, are tested in relation to a particular theory. One group is the experimental group and the other is the control group. The experimental group is exposed to an experimental stimulus of some kind (often called an independent variable) but the control group is not. Any difference between the two groups is understood to be due to the independent variable, since all other factors are deemed to be equal.[17]

Data Mining

Quantitative research will also seek to use other previously gathered data that is publicly available.[18] Often if questions are replicated by subsequent studies, then a comparison can be made with earlier studies. In other cases new hypotheses can be generated from newer theory development that had not previously been tested in relation to the older data. Obviously care needs to be taken that the integrity of the data is respected and that all data are used appropriately.

Structured Observation and Interviews

The quantitative approach to the collection of data can also be applied to more qualitative methods. A structured design with a clear and predetermined list of items can be used in order to structure the process of observation. In structured interviews a predetermined set of questions is used with no attention given to the interaction between interviewer and interviewee.[19] Such data are often presented in a quantitative manner with numbers and tables rather than narrative and interview extracts.

The data produced by experimental and survey questionnaires are usually coded and entered into a computer statistical package. The most commonly used package is *Statistical Package for the Social Sciences*.[20] Data from questionnaires are reduced to individual variables, the answer options of which are coded within the database. For example, the gender question, with two possible options, could be coded male = 1, female = 2 or vice versa; or yes/no answers to questions could be coded no = 1, yes = 2. Thus all the questions from the questionnaire are entered into the database and statistical tests can be used to establish the kinds of relationships between the variables that are possible within the sample. An example of a survey is given later in this chapter and chapters 7, 8, 9 and 10 all contain results based upon statistical analysis from that survey data.

4. Philosophical Traditions in Social Science Research

It is inevitable that methods in the social sciences belong to a particular history and tradition. These traditions have been forged to give an account of the process of research in order to guide the researcher and to defend the findings to the scholarly guild. Therefore, as part of understanding how these methods have been used, and with what presuppositions, it is important to describe the two main philosophical traditions that have been articulated, although there are important sub-traditions.

Positivism

Positivism is associated with the belief that the methods and processes of the natural sciences are appropriate to the social sciences.[21] The appreciation that people are different from objects and things in the physical world because they can have feelings, communicate, create meaning and are uniquely different from one another is not regarded as an obstacle to the use of the scientific methods. It advocates that only those phenomena that are observable to the senses can validly be regarded as knowledge. Therefore phenomena must either be experienced or observed directly, or measured with the assistance of instruments. The metaphysical is excluded a priori as having no place in the enterprise. It is suggested that scientific knowledge proceeds by means of accumulated verified facts, which in turn feed into a particular domain of knowledge. Science is deductive in the sense that theories generate hypotheses, that is, conjectures regarding causal relationships that are then tested empirically.[22] If the hypotheses are rejected then the theory is revised. Research in the positivist tradition aims to be value-free and objective, so anything that might impair the objectivity of the research exercise must be removed. This leads to a sharp distinction being drawn between scientific issues and normative issues. Normative issues cannot be verified in relation to experience and therefore are beyond the remit of science.[23]

Quantitative research is believed to be positivist in its conception and orientation. Practitioners tend to conceptualize research in terms of a logical structure, in which theories determine the problems to which researchers address themselves in the form of hypotheses derived from general theories. These hypotheses tend to be causal connections between concepts. Data collection is usually by means of social survey or experiment. Once collected the data are analysed for the verification or falsification of the hypotheses in question. These findings are absorbed back into the theory that set the whole process going in the first place. Thus quantitative research is conceived as a rational and linear process. But this description overstates the role of theory in the process, since not all quantitative research is theory driven in this way. There are different levels of theory from grand theories (for example Marxism) to mid-range or low-level theories (for example glossolalia as a prayer language). Research in all forms is much more complex and certainly not as orderly and as linear in execution as some proponents would have us believe. It involves the imagination and hunches much more than is realized.[24] It is often the idealized model that is presented in reports. These reports usually contain the sequence: theory (deduction) → hypotheses (operationalization) → observations/ data collection (data processing) → data analysis (interpretation) → findings (induction).[25] Report writing is rationalized and constructed in a way that conforms to the scholarly conventions.

Non-Positivistic Approaches

Qualitative research belongs to a different intellectual paradigm. Bryman's discussion includes the perspectives of phenomenology, symbolic interactionism, *Verstehen* and naturalism.[26] As traditions within qualitative research, they overlap to some extent. They have emerged as a critical alternative to positivism by rejecting scientific methods believing that people are not objects.[27] Rather, they are 'conscious, purposive actors who have ideas about their world and attach meaning to what is going on around them' that influences their behaviour.[28] In other words, they construct a social world of meaning that they inhabit. Qualitative research does not present its findings as 'true' but as an invitation to view things from a particular perspective.[29] It aims to enable the search for meaning in a complex social world.[30]

Alfred Schutz (1899–1959), drawing upon the work of Edmund Husserl (1859–1938), argued that a *phenomenological*-grounded social science is concerned to understand the constructs that people use in order to make the world in which they live both meaningful and intelligible.[31] This means that the subject of social science, namely people in their social reality, is fundamentally different from the subject matter of the natural sciences. It also means that investigations that aim to understand social reality must be grounded in people's experience of that social reality.[32] The people under investigation are the primary interpreters of social reality and researchers must seek to understand this interpretation. This is achieved by the researcher denying any prior understanding in order to grasp the experience of others in a pure form.[33] The social scientist by seeking to understand such everyday constructs of the subjects creates 'second order constructs'. These intellectual constructs must, however, retain a basic coherence with the subjects' own comprehension of social reality. In effect, allegiance to a phenomenological stance quite often means nothing more than an attendance to the subjects' point of view. The main qualitative approach that has used this philosophical undergirding is *ethnomethodology*, which takes as its central focus the subject's own perspective and reasoning of the social world.[34]

Ethnomethodologists essentially make use of participant observation and unstructured interviews in order to gather data. These provide the basis for ethnographic studies of groups and communities, sometimes supplemented with conversational analysis in which conversations in natural settings are recorded and analysed.

'*Symbolic interactionists* view social life as an unfolding process in which the individual interprets his or her environment and acts on the basis of that interpretation.'[35] This interaction is on the basis of meanings that are assigned to the world. Social life is expressed primarily through symbols with language being the most important symbol system.[36] There is always a stage of examination and deliberation prior to action. The self, according to George H. Mead (1863–1931), has two facets, the 'I' and the 'Me'. The 'Me' contains the views of ourselves as others see us, while the 'I' refers the individual urges. It is the 'Me' that is the reflective part of the person and enables reflection on action according to how it will be perceived socially. The self is seen as a process, an outcome of the dialectic between the 'I' and the 'Me', and action is viewed as part of this process. Therefore we do not simply act, rather, we act according to how we define the situation and how we think others will view our actions. Herbert Blumer, a student of Mead's, suggested that symbolic interactionism rests on three premises: (1) that human beings act towards things on the basis of the meanings the things have for them; (2) that the meaning of such things is derived from the social interaction that one has with others; and (3) that the meanings are handled and modified through an interpretative process.[37] The third premise is influential because it directs attention to examining the subjects' interpretations. Meaning is thus established through the process of social interaction as a hermeneutical activity. This need to focus on meanings has tended to imply the automatic use of the method of participant observation as a crucial strategy, although other methods are also used.

The idea of *Verstehen* originates with Max Weber (1864–1920) and means 'to understand' in German. Weber viewed the primary objective of sociology as being 'understanding'.[38] This is because human action is a combination of both behaviour and meaning assigned to it.[39] He wrote: 'Sociology . . . is a science which attempts the interpretive understanding of social action in order to arrive at a causal explanation of its course and effects.'[40] Weber considered two forms of understanding: (1) direct observational understanding of the subjective meaning of a given act; and (2) explanatory or motivational understanding which has set a particular act or action within a sequence of activity such that an explanation is facilitated.[41]

Naturalism, in a qualitative research sense, reflects the view that research should remain true to the phenomenon under study.[42] All phenomena being studied should be considered as naturally as possible. Therefore, it rejects artificial methods of research which provide distorted pictures of social reality, and seeks to describe the social world in a way that is consistent with the picture that the subjects carry. This means that researchers, instead of using distance as a research tool, should get close to the subjects under study and certainly not impose quantitative techniques upon them.

Colin Robson has suggested that with the demise of positivism a number of perspectives are attracting attention.[43] These include (1) post-positivism, which accepts the influence of the researcher's values on the project but nevertheless maintains a commitment to objectivity and the ontological independence of social reality. It can be known but imperfectly and probabilistically. (2) Constructivism maintains that social reality is constructed, although it is also called 'interpretive' and 'naturalistic'. For constructivists, objective reality cannot be known, rather the task is to understand the multiple social constructions of meaning. (3) Feminist and emancipatory approaches are referred to as critical approaches. They critique other research by arguing that it is done by powerful experts researching powerless people (for example ethnic minorities and disabled people). Feminists focus on the gender imbalance in such relationships and the oppression experienced by women in contemporary society. Feminist research raises the questions and concerns of women rather than supporting and continuing in the support of the male-dominated agenda. Its purpose is to facilitate female emancipation and a renewed understanding of women's worldviews. Robson himself argues for a form of realism that can mediate between positivism on the one hand and relativism or constructivism on the other. Realism maintains a scientific attitude to research with an interest in explanatory mechanisms but it can also incorporate emancipatory concerns. This combination he labels critical realism because it has potential to fulfil emancipatory concerns.[44]

5. Epistemology or Technique?

Quantitative research has been traditionally understood to view its perspective as from the outside looking in, with detached scientific objectivity. It starts with theories and concepts that are formulated as hypotheses and tested through reliable instruments of measurement. Its procedures are logical, structured and replicable, giving rise to law-like findings. Consequently it tends to have a rather static view of social reality, regarding the individuals as external to it and constrained by it. But it regards its data as hard, rigorous and reliable.

Qualitative research, by contrast, does not have a fleeting or non-existent contact with the people under study, but a sustained engagement. It seeks to get close to the data and engages with the subjects as an insider. Initial theories are rejected as restrictive and a commitment to develop theories as the research proceeds or at the end of the study is proposed. As such, qualitative approaches aim to be flexible and more responsive to the subjects' perspectives. Instead of seeking to discover laws it locates findings in specific time periods and locales and concerns itself with the processes of social life. Good and varied data can be shown to provide insights that are rich, deep and meaningful.

In the past, these two traditions have been entrenched positions.[45] However, it is widely recognized that qualitative research is not a second-rate approach, only useful in the exploratory phase. Rather, it can be done rigorously both to explore relatively unclear situations and in order to test more specific theories and concepts generated from either literature or quantitative data. Indeed, survey data can be a source of surprise, not simply providing answers to previously formulated questions.

Bryman raises the question as to whether the philosophical traditions underlying these methods need be determinative for their usage.[46] Do we have to assume that because we use a particular method we automatically accept the philosophical 'baggage' which it carries? The question, therefore, resolves around whether we can unhitch them: is it a choice between epistemology and technique? To clarify, Bryman asks: 'What is to pass as warrantable and hence acceptable knowledge?'[47] Traditionally, quantitative researchers would respond by saying that only research that conforms to the canons of scientific method could be treated as knowledge, while qualitative researchers simply rejected this in favour of the subjects' interpretations. These answers are also rejected by those who regard the respective methods in question as techniques. They contend that the problem or situation under investigation determines the approach that is required. Therefore they may be combined if the research design requires that different kinds of data are desirable.[48] This position, therefore, rejects the idea that methods are inextricably linked to different epistemological paradigms which are in turn mutually exclusive.[49]

Certainly anyone wishing to use the various methods in the social sciences should be aware of the debates of the past. But the question is, should they determine how these methods are used in the present? It could be argued that even the philosophers of science and scientists have moved away from a strictly positivist position to critical realism,[50] while some qualitative researchers are clearly realists not only in terms of epistemology but also social ontology.[51] From a more theological perspective, which views the whole of creation as God-given and able to be known in a variety of ways, knowledge need not be polarized in an 'either/or' fashion. Surely a 'both/and' solution is better, even if we may acknowledge personal preferences for one over the other? Practical theologians in their use of social science methods and techniques will bring a distinctly *theological* epistemology that is influenced by a Christian worldview and spirituality. This epistemological approach will recognize the value of engagement with the lifeworld of the people under study as well as the value of a more detached and structured approach that uses mechanisms of distance. Therefore, knowledge is to be gained both by participation and by reflection, by engagement and detachment.[52] They are, in effect, two sides of the same coin, or twin moments in time. This means that they can be usefully employed together in order to understand the theological praxis of groups.

6. Examples of Case Study and Survey Research

In order to provide a context for the individual studies that follow, this chapter offers a description of two types of research. The first approach is in the qualitative tradition of a case study. The second is a quantitative survey. I conducted both of these research projects as part of a larger project. Although they may appear to be discrete research exercises, in fact they were part of a much larger process. Chapters 5 and 6 are related to empirical material generated from the case study, while chapters 7, 8 and 9 are studies arising from analysis of survey data. Chapter 10 illustrates how both qualitative and quantitative studies can be combined. In order to assist the non–specialist reader to understand the statistics used in the quantitative results, I have also included an explanation of key terms at the end of this chapter.

A Case Study

To enable an understanding of glossolalia within the New Church movement, it was decided to begin, within the inductive phase of the empirical-theological cycle, by using an explorative case study. A pilot case study was chosen for reasons of accessibility and geographical convenience. As a study it helped to develop questions and conceptual clarification as well as enabling practice of the procedures involved.[53] In this particular case initial contact was made with the church by a member of staff at the university, whom I knew through my work there. I subsequently discussed with her my interest in carrying out a case study of the church that she attended and she prepared the way by approaching the church leaders on my behalf. I was then able to meet with one of the church leaders, explain my research interest into glossolalia, and gain permission to proceed with the enquiry. I attended Sunday worship services, was given access to some church documents, and conducted interviews. Thus an overt approach was adopted. I was subsequently able to give feedback regarding my research to those in the church that were interested. Participant observation was the main approach to gaining information from the Sunday worship.

The overall method of this particular study was the case study approach. For this method I have adopted the model of Robert Yin.[54] In the majority of social science textbooks this method is seen as simply an exploratory stage in some other type of research strategy. To distinguish his approach from that use, Yin defines a case study as 'an empirical enquiry that:

- investigates a contemporary phenomenon within its real-life context; when
- the boundaries between phenomenon and context are not clearly evident; and in which
- multiple sources of evidence are used.[55]

Case studies can adopt either quantitative or qualitative strategies and aim either to *explain* causal links in the data, or *describe* the real-life context in which the phenomenon occurs, or *explore* a relatively unclear situation. In this particular study I intended to *explore* the relatively unclear situation regarding the nature and function of charismatic glossolalia in the UK in the mid-1990s. Yin also advocates the role of theory building prior to the conduct of any data collection. Whilst some knowledge of the theories concerning the nature and function of glossolalia had been acquired, the emphasis was upon the subjects' theological praxis.

For Yin, there are four criteria listed for judging the quality of the case study research design.[56] The first is *construct validity*. In the past case study designs have been criticized for inadequately developing an operational set of measures and for 'subjectivity' employed in the collection of data. In response, Yin proposes (1) the use of multiple sources of evidence, encouraging divergent lines of enquiry; (2) establishing a chain of evidence, that makes 'explicit links between the questions asked, the data collected and the conclusions drawn';[57] and (3) a review of the draft report by the key informants. Second, the *internal validity* of the project is especially important for explanatory types of research. The problem of the accuracy of inference is anticipated and dealt with by tactics of pattern-matching, explanation-building and times-series analysis. Third, the *external validity* is noted, that is, the ability to generalize from the findings. Yin argues that case studies are not sampling units and should not be chosen for this reason. A case study is selected as a laboratory investigator selects an experiment topic. In that sense multiple case studies should be considered like multiple experiments (or multiple surveys). In these circumstances the method of generalization is 'analytic generalization', that is a previously developed theory is used as a template with which to compare the empirical results. If more than one case study supports a particular theory then replication may be claimed.[58] Fourth, *reliability* is the final test. The solution proposed by Yin is accurate documentation of the study and the development of a *case study database*. 'A good guideline for doing case studies is therefore to conduct the research so that an auditor could repeat the procedure and arrive at the same results.'[59] In this exploratory study multiple sources of evidence are used and links between questions, data and conclusions are made.

Participant Observation

The participant observation was carried out over a seven-month period in which I visited the Sunday worship on eight occasions. The first occasion was in November 1995 and the last was in May 1996. On arrival I made mental notes on the physical setting, conversations and identity of certain key people. These were written down in the situation when possible, usually during the sermon, when it was very acceptable to take notes. Consequently I took detailed notes of the sermons in particular and used the time to add any other comments. Upon my return home I immediately typed up my notes on to my computer and added anything that I remembered about the visit.[60] I noted the time that I was in the service and the sequence of events and conversations of the occasion. I also observed my general impression about the worship and feelings at the time. I tended to focus my attention specifically on the sermon, the use of the 'spiritual gifts' and conversations afterwards, because of the difficulty of sustaining concentration on every detail for such a prolonged visit.[61] I did not, however, assign pseudonyms to individuals at this stage but waited for the writing-up stage for this to be done. The pseudonym for the church that I have adopted is 'Aigburth Community Church'.[62]

Documents

The documents relating to the church include, first of all, the Sunday information sheet, called a 'newsletter'. This was not available every Sunday. I have five newsletters from which to draw information. Second, one of the church leaders gave me copies of the foundation documents of the church, which are entitled: (1) 'Aigburth Community Church: The Developing Vision', (2) 'Foundations, Cornerstones, Framework, Bricks and Mortar', (3) 'Aigburth Community Church: Recognizing New Leaders', and (4) 'Aigburth Community Church: Notes for the Leadership Meetings'. To this is added the Training Manual for the Alpha Course, since this was used during the time of the case study.[63] Information regarding the Alpha course was supplemented by *Alpha*

News, which is a free newspaper distributed via the *Church Times* and other avenues, to inform people about the course.[64] Finally, after the Alpha course was completed, the house groups continued in their times of study by using a book by Nicky Gumbel entitled *A Life Worth Living*.[65] This was also used to guide the sermon series during Lent and to connect with the house group studies at the same time.

Interviews

After visiting the church a number of times I was introduced to the congregation more formally in the newsletter.[66] In addition to this I was able to give a notice in the service in order to explain my project and invite people to speak to me after the service, if they were happy to be interviewed.[67] After this service I was given 11 names of people who would be willing to help. These people were volunteers and were not coerced by the leadership of the church. The list was to alter slightly in the process of arranging the interviews, so in total nine interviews were conducted, which included 13 people.

The interviews were semi-structured and after the initial background information was written down the interviews were tape-recorded and subsequently transcribed.[68] For an outline of the interview schedule, see Appendix 1. Although I followed the schedule in principle, I would follow up interesting lines of conversation and occasionally miss questions out in the process. This meant that on the whole I had a clear set of answers to the main questions I was asking and also a lot of other useful information that added to the basic description. It was from this type of information that new questions were to emerge. A feedback session with interviewees enabled the interview schedule to be revised (see the italicized questions in Appendix 1).

Data Analysis

Data analysis was conducted by means of content analysis of field notes and interview transcripts.[69] This analysis was conducted using the *Nota Bene Orbis* computer programme, which is a free-form text retrieval system.[70] Categories from the initial set of questions were defined and explored by means of content analysis. This kind of computer analysis was supplemented by a close reading of hard copies of field notes and interview transcripts. I found the use of colour coding to be especially useful.[71]

Case Description: Aigburth Community Church

The Aigburth Community Church (hereafter ACC) first met together in 1991 and came out of another independent charismatic church, which continues to exist less than a mile away from where the church meets. People freely admit that the birth was difficult and traumatic, but that it had the full support of the parent church fellowship. Some people might see it in terms of a split, others in terms of a church plant. The first three leaders of the church were Frank, Philip and Debra,[72] and they had been part of a seven-person leadership team in the previous church. When they first began to meet they did not have a church polity but decided that their attitude should be based on the story of the cave of Adullam (1 Samuel 22): that is, no questions would be asked and no pre-conditions laid down. If anyone needed a place of shelter, then they would be welcome as part of the church.

The start in 1991 was followed in the New Year by a weekend away at Llandudno in 1992, at which a name for the church was chosen. It was chosen to reflect the character of the church as a place of community and peace and a church aiming to reach out into the wider community. It was by now meeting in a primary school building. At this weekend away the scriptural foundations of its *raison d'être* were established. This was followed in 1993 by another time away at Blackpool and in 1994 at Elim Bible College, Nantwich, during which the vision for the church was described and its church polity defined. By the summer of 1994 the leaders were able to look back at the first three years of the church's life and talk in terms of the end of the beginning. At this juncture it was decided that all three leaders would 'resign their commission'. However, Philip and Debra were happy to continue in leadership, but Frank stepped down. He was replaced by Michael, and an elder, Thomas, was appointed as a general overseer. At the time of my visits Michael, Philip and Debra were all acting as leaders, with Thomas continuing in the eldership role.

In a document entitled 'Aigburth Community Church: The Developing Vision' the identity and self-understanding of the church is described. The church defines itself by saying:

We have never wanted to be a church which is authoritarian, ruled by edict, directed by the vision of the few. Our style is to have open consideration of the issues facing the church, to look for input from all members, and to walk through the process together.

This can be summarized by consideration of the following.

Foundations

During the foundation period of the church a number of scriptural passages guided the thinking of the members. These included Zechariah 4:2–9, 8:4; Haggai 2, especially 2:9; Zephaniah 3:14–20; Nehemiah 2:17; Joel 2:26; and Ezra 1 – 6. The principles taken from Ezra have been particularly important. They are: (1) worship first (Ezra 3:2–6); (2) get organized (Ezra 3:8,9); (3) gatekeep (Ezra 4:1–4); and (4) hear God (Ezra 5:1,2).

Cornerstones

The concept of building and the metaphor of stones were important to the church at this time. The scriptural basis came from 1 Peter 2:5, Ephesians 2:19,20 and 4:11–13. The members recognized their need for the Spirit of God to move them (Zechariah 4) and for them to depend upon God for their source of spiritual supply. They believed that God wanted to turn their barrenness into fruitfulness (Luke 1:5–19). Their feelings of unproductiveness had to change (Jeremiah 4:3). The belief that God had spoken to them and promised that, just as Zerubbabel completed the foundations of the temple, so God would complete his foundational work in the lives of the church members and build upon it. Based upon the text of Jeremiah 6:16 the church aimed to move forward by going back and re-establishing fundamentals. These include prayer and spiritual warfare, loving one another, and visible unity including ecumenical involvement.

Framework

The four foundational principles in Ezra were used in order to construct a framework.

1. Worship should be the first priority and a daily experience. This should be focused in Sunday worship 'with a real explosion of public worship, with the full expression of God's

gifting in the whole body'. Therefore prophets are encouraged to prophesy and spiritual gifts sought. The gifts of dance, poetry, visual art and 'all other forms of creative expression' are encouraged. An appreciation of silence in worship is also promoted together with the gift of meditation. Finally, the musicians are encouraged to work hard at their gifts and to expand the material with which the church has to worship. 'Most of all, we seek the continual blowing of the Spirit through the church.'

2. Organizing the work was the second principle in the framework. To this end five trustees were appointed: Adam, Jane, Mark, David and Philip. They established the Aigburth Community Trust from February 1993. A group of people responsible for the finances was established and chaired by Derek. Members of the group were Joan (Treasurer), Ian, Fleur, Adam, Andrew, Steven and Philip. The leaders stressed that they valued input from everyone and in particular those who had specific wisdom or expertise on certain matters. The leaders wanted 'to state a commitment to kingdom-building, not empire-building'. This meant beginning to work together with other churches in the area and missionaries in other countries.

3. Gatekeeping is also considered to be a framework principle. The church was expected to develop close, loving and supportive relationships within the church. Issues that appeared would be dealt with openly, with people encouraged by 'speaking the truth in love'. Disagreement with the leadership was permitted and discussion of differences encouraged. The fallibility of the leadership was stressed.

4. Finally, the vision is of a listening church. To this end members are encouraged to listen to God in personal prayer and meditation and through other people.

Bricks and Mortar

The basic pattern of church life was defined as including the following. (1) House groups would meet midweekly. (2) Sunday worship would include a teaching programme, usually from a book of the Bible,[73] with the last Sunday of each month being a family service. The Lord's Supper would be celebrated fortnightly and outside speakers invited to preach from time to time. (3) Youth work would be on the agenda with the intention to do work ecumenically and to build a church group. (4) Pastoral care would be regarded as an important concern and house group leaders as well as church leaders are to be used in this ministry. (5) Prayer is considered vitally important and a strategy would be under consideration from the beginning.

Other categories that are to be mentioned under this heading include Outreach, which focused on the need for stressing the principles of marriage and the provision of support. The issue of a paid worker for the church was also under review.

Leadership

The leadership structure that was suggested at the church weekend away in 1994 was a 'flat triangle' model of leadership, including leaders, elders and deacons. 'The intention is to see people serve in their most suitable role without too much sense of hierarchy. Leaders direct and govern, elders consult and advise, deacons manage and carry forward the work of the church.' The enlarged leadership including deacons did not, however, materialize and the model of leaders and elders was adopted, with the aim to create a wider 'task force' to help manage the work of the church. A full-time worker, Alexander, was appointed for a year from September 1994.

The vision of the church can be summarized in the following phrases:

- A worshipping church
- A learning church
- A serving church

These phrases encapsulate the ethos of the ACC.

Sunday Worship

A full analysis of Sunday worship is offered in chapter 5 so a brief summary is offered here. As mentioned above, the church meets in a primary school, in the assembly hall of the school. The school is situated on the border of an urban/suburban residential area of the city. The entrance to the room that is used is difficult to locate and on my first visit I felt somewhat uneasy about finding my way into the assembly hall. Even though there was a notice on the main gate informing people of a Christian worshipping community and the time of worship, the precise location of entry is unclear. An adjacent classroom is used for the children's Sunday school activities and a room for the crèche is adjacent. The assembly hall is quite small and contains the usual primary school decoration with paintings and children's work on display. The only difference for Sunday worship is the addition of a music band located in one corner around the piano, and the rows of chairs set out for worship and a lectern and microphone at the front. An information stall is usually set up at the back of the room where people enter and from where newsletters are obtained.

The congregation gather around 10.30 a.m. Although the service is scheduled to start at 10.30 a.m. it very rarely started on time. The congregation contained a mixed age range of people, but mostly people under the age of 50, with a good number of young families and some students, mostly from a neighbouring college of higher education. The numbers of the congregation average at about 60–70 people. The church has an atmosphere of informality about it with most people dressing casually but nevertheless smartly. It is clearly a church that appeals to the middle classes, with most of the members coming from the professional sectors. No offertory is taken during the service, but a box is located at the back for those who wish to donate money.

The main band contains a guitarist, bass player, pianist and drummer, with other musicians joining in from time to time. The chairs are set facing the wall where the overhead projector screen is situated. All the words to the songs appear on the screen. The service usually follows the pattern of an introduction followed by number of songs. At this juncture the children and Sunday school teachers leave the service to have their classes and the notices are given, usually with a good degree of Liverpudlian humour. Often this is followed by a quieter and more reflective time of worship with songs, readings and meditations. This is usually followed by the sermon, which takes between 25–35 minutes. The communion may come next in the sequence, or it may come before the sermon. After the sermon there is an opportunity to reflect upon it and, depending upon time, further songs may be sung with the opportunity for people to share anything that they feel to be important to them or the church. The service usually concludes with a song and a prayer.

After the service coffee is served in the adjacent room, where the children have had their Sunday school class. This is a good opportunity to meet people and chat. I found this, in some ways, the most helpful time of the Sunday activity as far as the research project was concerned. I found people to be genuinely interested in the research and willing to talk about themselves and their view of the church. My key contact, Barbara, was initially very helpful in introducing me to people in the church. However, once I got to know the leaders, especially Philip and Debra, I found that I did not need her mediation, but that the relationships I had formed with others were sufficient for the case study to proceed satisfactorily.

From the conversations I was able to gather some interesting pieces of information about the church.

Philip talked with me on my first visit about the influence that certain theologians had had upon him at a meeting he had attended.[74] At this meeting it had been suggested that the independent charismatic churches take advantage of the mainstream liturgies when wishing to celebrate communion. It was particularly interesting for me to be suddenly confronted with the commandments extracted from the 1662 Book of Common Prayer service of the Lord's Supper during my first visit to the church!

I also had a conversation with Philip about the area of prosperity theology. He told me some people who had sympathy with that theology had been part of the church, but had been given 'short shrift'. He had no time for that theological position.

On another occasion I had a conversation with Michael, one of the leaders. He talked about worship and liturgy and mentioned the influence of Dave Tomlinson.[75] He said that the church wishes to embrace a variety of styles of worship and aims to be a 'broad' church.[76]

This was followed by a conversation with Ian, who was a market researcher and interested in empirical research. He confirmed my socio-economic impression of the church: most of the church members were white-collar workers, of whom most would be graduates. For example, only a couple of families did not own a car.

Ecumenism

It was evident from the first visit to the church that ecumenism was considered important. An ecumenical covenant, including ACC, was signed in 1996. This shows a willingness to work with other churches in the area, and in the words of the covenant document, 'to express visible unity by not doing separately what we can do better together'.

Interviewees

The first interview was with a woman called Julie. Julie was the oldest member of the church, aged between 60–69, and a divorcee. She had been retired a number of years from working as a special needs teacher. She had also fostered children for almost 20 years. She described her church background as Church of England, although her mother had been a Baptist and her father a Methodist. She had been 'christened and confirmed' at the age of 16 and had trained as a Sunday school teacher. She said that she became a Christian by attending ACC. She joined the church in January 1994 and would say that she was born again on 29 March 1994. This was followed in May by an experience of healing, which was unspecified.

The second interview was with a woman called Jane. Jane was aged between 30–39, and married to Frank, one of the original church leaders. She was currently working in the civil service as a rent officer. Previously she had trained and qualified as a barrister. She had a Baptist church background, being baptized at the age of 15 or 16, when her parents had been converted and attended a Baptist church. She subsequently attended the parent church for 10 years before transferring to ACC.

The third interview was arranged to be with Steven and his wife Kate, but upon arrival at their house they had forgotten about the arrangement and had a dinner guest called Jeremy in attendance, who was also a member of the church. Since they had finished their meal, they all decided that they would like to be interviewed. Steven and Kate were aged between 40–49, while Jeremy was aged between 30–39, and single. Steven was a self-employed architect by profession, while Kate was a nursery school teacher. Jeremy worked in a factory as a bottle maker. All three had Church of England backgrounds, although Kate had classical Pentecostal experience as well, while Jeremy became a Christian 20 years ago through a Liverpool City Mission church. All three had been members of the parent church but had also been part of the group that formed ACC when it started. The interview was a difficult interview to transcribe, partly because of recording failure, but also because Jeremy's Liverpool accent was so strong and yet so softly and quickly spoken that he was very difficult to hear, let alone record!

The fourth interview was with Rebecca. She was aged between 50–59 and married. She described herself as a 'housewife' although she had done some secretarial work in the past. She came from a Baptist church background and became a Christian at the age of 16 or 17. She attended another New Church Fellowship in Liverpool for 16 years before joining ACC. She had joined the church from its the earliest days.

The fifth interview was with a married couple in the church called Robert and Ruth. They were both aged between 30–39. Robert described his occupation a 'Christian painter and decorator', while Ruth was a nurse working in the residential care sector. Both had Church of England backgrounds but had previously been involved in the parent church before involvement in ACC.

The sixth interview was with Philip, a leader, who was married to Debra, one of the other church leaders. He was aged between 40–49 and worked as a director of a charity. Philip had a classical Pentecostal background with the Assemblies of God denomination. He had been involved in the parent church for 15 years before leaving to be a founding member of ACC.

The seventh interview was with Adam, aged 30–39, one of the trustees of the church. He was married to Fleur. They were both musicians and members of the finance committee. Adam was a self-employed solicitor working with a firm of solicitors as a partner. He became a Christian at school through the Christian Union and had some contact with the Church of England and a Methodist/ United Reformed Church. He had also worshipped at a Baptist church and the parent church. He was a founding member of the ACC.

The eighth interview was with Emily, a recent graduate aged between 20–29. She was single and described her occupation as an artist, having obtained an art degree. She did some part-time teaching with an adult education course but was technically un-employed. She had a Church of England and Methodist background but had also been taken to a spiritualist church as a child. As a student in Liverpool she had visited a number of churches in the city and had finally settled at ACC.

The ninth interview was with Rachel and Basil, a married couple. Basil did not speak in tongues but nevertheless sat in on the interview and answered questions as well. They were both aged between 30–39. Rachel was employed as an occupational therapist within a psychiatric hospital while Basil worked at a secondary school teaching Latin. Rachel had become a Christian at the age of 22 and attended the parent church to ACC immediately. Basil had a Roman Catholic background and been involved in a New Church Fellowship in another part of the country prior to also being involved in the parent church to ACC.

A Survey

The questionnaire was piloted with 12 people and adjustments were made to the questionnaire according to the full comments of respondents (see Appendix 2 for a shortened version). The study aimed to survey core members (house group members) of independent charismatic churches and any mainline Free churches who would be classified as charismatic in the Merseyside area. In order to locate these churches I contacted the co-ordinator of an important network of churches working together in the area. A person from an evangelical and charismatic network of churches assisted in the initial approach. He was very sympathetic to my work and permitted me to write a notice of my research that was published in the network's monthly newsletter. His support was to be crucial in helping me to gain the trust of church leaders. He provided me with a list of 43 church contacts belonging to churches he knew to be within the Charismatic Movement. Out of the 43 names on the list eight people either refused to participate or proved unable to be contacted, even after persistent attempts. This left me with 35 church leaders who were willing to discuss the project face to face.

Over a period of about three weeks I travelled throughout Merseyside explaining the project to these people, showing them the agreed procedure and taking them through the questionnaire itself. Out of this number 32 church leaders agreed, on behalf of their churches, to participate in the survey. The church leaders administered the questionnaire for me to core house group members (usually via their church administrator and the church computer database). I requested that house group leaders ask their members to complete the questionnaire during the meeting. I carefully explained the need for the list to be an objective list of current members of existing house groups, the numbering system and the need for confidentiality. This was agreed in all but one church fellowship, where the nature of the fellowship was _ad hoc_ and there was intentionally no membership structure.[77] Questionnaires were either returned by mail or collected by me. The overall number of churches involved in this study, for statistical purposes, is 29, and the overall response rate for questionnaires delivered to the churches is 633 from 1227, a 51.6% return. This is regarded as a very good sample.

Once the data set had been prepared it was checked and cleaned. This involved doing an initial frequency check and changing coding errors. This was followed by a random 10% check of the question-naires. The Eysenck Personality Questionnaire section was also checked manually. This was followed by crosstabulation checks where the frequencies of two variables can be checked in relation to each other (see below). Therefore there is good reason to be confident in the accuracy of the data set.

Description of the Research Population

As Table 4.1 below indicates, there are 11 New Churches and 12 Pentecostal churches, including the Assemblies of God, Elim and an independent Pentecostal church. There are two Brethren churches and two Baptist churches as well as one United Reformed church and one Evangelical church. This means that the sample is predominantly either classical Pentecostal or New Church. All these churches carry the charismatic label.

In the overall sample, 37.9% were male and 61.0% female (1.1% missing). Their ages were spread mainly between the 30–54 age range. These included 10.6% between 30–34, 14.4% between 35–39, 10.7% between 40–44, 10.9% between 45–49, and 13.7% between 50–54. The sample contained 17.7% of single people, with 66.5% married and 7.1% divorced. Their qualifications ranged from CSEs (6.2%), GCSEs (6.0%), O levels (16.9%), A levels (8.7%), Diplomas in Higher Education (17.9%), Bachelor's Degrees (17.2%), Master's Degrees (2.4%) and Doctorates (0.6%). The education levels were reflected in 6.3% in Class I (professional), 22.1% in Class II (lower professional), 18.6% in Class IIIN (skilled non-manual), 9.0% in Class IIIM (skilled manual), 2.8% in Class IV (semi-skilled), 1.1% in Class V (unskilled), 3.8% unemployed, 28.0% housewife/retired and 3.3% students. Most of the sample had been Christians for between 5–9 years to 24 years, thus reflecting the age range of the group. Most respondents had also experienced Christianity in previous denominations before settling in their current church. The largest group had experienced mainline Protestant denominations (45.7%).

The 29 churches, comprising eight different denominations, and their responses can be shown in the following table.

Table 4.1: The churches

Church number	Number of questionnaires	%	Denomination
1	11	1.7	New Church (Pioneer)
2	5	0.8	Brethren
3	28	4.4	Elim
4	14	2.2	New Church (Vineyard)
5	9	1.4	Baptist
6	3	0.5	Assemblies of God
7	10	1.6	Elim
8	16	2.5	Assemblies of God
9	47	7.4	Baptist
10	46	7.3	New Church (King's)
11	33	5.2	New Church (Covenant)
12	9	1.4	Elim
13	16	2.5	Elim
14	30	4.7	Pentecostal (independent)
15	11	1.7	New Church

Church number	Number of questionnaires	%	Denomination
16	10	1.6	URC
17	19	3.0	New Church
18	30	4.7	New Church
19	10	1.6	New Church
20	20	3.2	Brethren
21	41	6.5	Assemblies of God
22	12	1.9	Assemblies of God
23	13	2.1	New Church (Ichthus)
24	28	4.4	Assemblies of God
25	8	1.3	Assemblies of God
26	29	4.6	Evangelical (independent)
27	17	2.7	Elim
28	71	11.2	New Church
29	37	5.8	New Church (Faith)[78]
Total	633	100.0	

Definition of some Statistical Terms and Concepts

In order to assist the reader who is unfamiliar with statistics I shall define and describe some of the terms and concepts commonly used in this kind of empirical research.[79] For the sake of brevity I shall simply confine myself to the actual terms and concepts used in statistical tests that are displayed in the results.[80] For a discussion of the complete range of terms and concepts standard quantitative texts will need to be consulted.[81]

The term population is normally used of a complete set of people, values or events which can be held together by means of a common definition, for example, charismatic Christians. A sample is a collection from this population that we may assume is an accurate reflection of the characteristics of the wider population, for example charismatic Christians within the geographical location of Merseyside. Probability or random samples are chosen by some form of chance mechanism, for example, random numbers.

Alternatively, convenience or opportunity samples can be used. The assumption that the subjects within the sample are representative of the whole population may be made. The survey described above would be regarded as a convenience sample because it was not randomly selected but used a network list as its basis. Most church congregation sampling would be classified in this way. The number of successfully completed questionnaires returned from the sample is regarded as the response rate.

The questionnaire survey method asks a series of questions from the respondents. These items are entered into the computer database as individual variables, for example, gender, age and occupation, although several variables can be combined to measure a commonality, for example the concept of charismatic socialization. In this case, these variables function as a scale. When five questions probe different aspects of the same concept it strengthens the nature of the result. Variables are usually classified as: (1) nominal (names, for example church denomination); (2) ordinal (classifications arranged in rank, the differences between which are not necessarily equal, they either ascend or descend in frequency, for example educational qualifications); and (3) interval (like ordinal but the differences are similar in distance). Likert scales (named after R. A. Likert) are regarded as functioning as interval variables. Likert questions tend to make a statement and then ask the respondents whether they agree strongly, agree, are not certain, disagree or disagree strongly. Since the distance between agree and agree strongly is regarded as the same, these items are treated as interval variables. For example, in the questionnaire used in this research, I asked the question: 'How much have the following helped you to understand speaking in tongues?' The option 'famous preachers' is followed by the choices: 'very little 1 2 3 4 5 6 7 very much'. The respondent is asked to indicate where on the scale the influence of 'famous preachers' would be placed. Other options such as 'friends' and 'books' were also listed and followed by the same choices.

The notions of validity and reliability are important ones for empirical research. Validity refers to the appropriateness of the instrument for the measurement of an attitude or belief. In this context, validity refers to the content of the questions. The meaning of the words used in the questions should be appropriate to the concept being measured. The construction of the question is also

related to the notion of validity. It is usually termed operationalization. This is a difficult aspect of quantitative research. Often
complex concepts and theories, including theological theories, for
example the doctrine of the Trinity, can prove difficult to measure
by means of simple questions that are easily understandable by the
target group. Reliability refers to the consistency of the measurement. For example, the instrument devised to measure a dimension
of personality must be able to measure the same dimension
repeatedly if it is to be a useful tool. The reliability of scales constructed to measure an attitude or trait can be checked for internal
consistency using the Cronbach reliability test. This check gives an
alpha coefficient, which is a number between 0 and 1. The nearer
the number is to 1, the greater the reliability of the measurement,
but this depends to some extent on the number of items in the
scale. A scale with a greater number of items, say 9, would be
expected to generate a larger alpha coefficient than a scale of 3
items. If there were very little difference between the scores, then
the shorter scale would tend to be regarded as the more reliable of
the two.

Statistical analysis is based upon the discovery of the central
tendency, or average score, for variables in a particular sample.
Say, for example, that the scores for a particular variable were 1, 8,
12, 19, 44, 44, 45 and 51. There are 8 numbers and they add up to
224. The mean is therefore 224 divided by 8 = 28. The mode is
the number which occurs most often, in this case 44, while the
median is the middle number in a spread, that is, the halfway point
between the fourth and fifth numbers, 31.5. Statistical analysis is
also interested in the dispersion of the numbers around the mean.
To do this we subtract every number from the mean, square the
differences (to get rid of the negative numbers) add the differences
together, then average them and take the square root of the average
(to undo the effect of squaring). This number is called the standard
deviation. For the numbers above the standard deviation is
approximately 19.[82] The term that is closely associated with standard
deviation is variance. The variance of a set of numbers is the standard
deviation squared.

The term correlation refers to the idea of association between
two variables. This is often demonstrated when two variables (x
and y) are plotted together on a graph. There is said to be a

relationship of association or correlation if the items can be seen to slope up or slope down in a straight line, that is they are in a linear (straight) relationship. If they cluster, then there is no obvious correlation. A single figure expresses this relationship of association between the two variables, which is called the correlation coefficient. The range is between −1 to +1. A figure of −1 would indicate a perfect negative correlation, so that as one variable increases the other decreases. A figure of +1 would indicate a perfect positive relationship, so that the highest score in one variable is related to the highest score in the other variable. If the distribution of the variable is normal (indicated by a bell-shaped curve when the frequency is plotted), the correlation is calculated by Pearson's coefficient that is designated by 'r' (lower case). The notion of significance is an important concept and refers to probability. The most common designation is that the finding would have come about by chance less frequently than 5 times in 100 (P = .05), although once in a 100 (P = .01) and 5 times in 1000 are also used (P = .005).

An independent sample t test is used to compare the mean scores of two different groups (e.g. men and women) in relation to a continuous variable (e.g. the frequency of prophecy). The probability value for the t statistic indicates whether there is a statistically significant difference in the mean scores of the two groups. The t statistic represents the relationship of the sample mean to the true mean of the population. As the standard deviation reduces and the sample size increases the closer the sample mean will be to the true mean. The larger the t value the greater is the difference in means between the groups. If the probability value for the t statistic is significant then one can assume that the groups tested come from distinct populations with different characteristics.

A crosstabulation is used to understand the relationship between two variables and is based upon a simple frequency and percentage count. Although there are difference measures of association, the most commonly used one is the Pearson's chi-square (X^2) test. This test measures the independence of the items in the table based upon the expected frequencies compared to the actual frequencies. If the difference between the expected and actual frequencies is so great that independence is unlikely then the X^2 will be large. The statistical significance of the score is measured in the usual probability manner (see above).

Often in statistical procedures the use of the null hypothesis is employed, denoted by H_o. When seeking to compare samples of scores from the same or different populations, the null hypothesis is based on the idea of no difference. That is, the assumption that there is nothing 'going on' between the samples. It is the hypothesis that researchers would like to reject in favour of an alternative hypothesis, that the samples are different and therefore interesting.[83] In the studies that follow I shall simply use the positive sense of the hypothesis, that there is a statistically significant relationship between the samples or variables. In relation to the null hypothesis there are commonly two types of errors recognized by statisticians. The first is called a type I error. This occurs when the null hypothesis is rejected but turns out to be true because there has been a sampling error, for example through small and thus unrepresentative sampling. Therefore a significant relationship is thought to exist, but this is indeed false. The second is called a type II error and is the opposite of type I. In this case the null hypothesis is retained, that is the belief that there is no relationship between the samples of variables, when in fact there is a significant relationship.[84] This is again most often caused by a sampling error.

7. Conclusion

This chapter provides the basic information for all the empirical studies in Part Two. The description of methods for all the studies is contained here. This means that I have omitted the methods section almost entirely from these following chapters. Therefore readers will need to read the case study or survey examples in this chapter in conjunction with reading the individual studies. Readers will also find it useful to move back to them from time to time in order to refresh their understanding of the background to these other studies. I have written in this way in order to minimize the duplication of material throughout the individual empirical studies.

[1] A. Bryman, *Quantity and Quality in Social Research* (London: Routledge, 1996²) pp. 61–70.

[2] Ibid. p. 61.

[3] Ibid. p. 47.

[4] Ibid. p. 48.

[5] D. Hall and I. Hall, *Practical Social Research: Project Work in the Community* (Basingstoke: Macmillan, 1996) pp. 156–7.

[6] C. Robson, *Real World Research* (Oxford: Blackwell, 2002²) pp. 283–9.

[7] See, for example, J. Kitzenger, 'The Methodology of Focus Groups: The Importance of Interaction between Research and Participants', *Sociology of Health and Illness* 16.1 (1994) pp. 103–21.

[8] Bryman, *Quantity and Quality in Social Research*, p. 49.

[9] Hall and Hall, *Practical Social Research*, p. 181.

[10] Ibid. pp. 183–7.

[11] J. W. Creswell, *Qualitative Inquiry and Research Design: Choosing among Five Traditions* (London: Sage, 1998) p. 65.

[12] Robson, *Real World Research*, pp. 460–72.

[13] My doctoral dissertation gives greater details concerning qualitative data analysis: see M. J. Cartledge, 'Tongues of the Spirit: An Empirical-Theological Study of Charismatic Glossolalia' (PhD dissertation, University of Wales, 1999).

[14] D. A. de Vaus, *Surveys in Social Research* (London: University College London Press, 1985, 1994²) p. 3.

[15] For an assessment of surveys, see Robson, *Real World Research*, pp. 230–2.

[16] Ibid. pp. 260–8 describes the various types in full; cf. Hall and Hall, *Practical Social Research*, pp. 106–17.

[17] For a good introduction to experimental research, see Robson, *Real World Research*, pp. 110–33. A quasi-experiment is where 'random assignment and comparison groups has not been used' (p. 133).

[18] Ibid. pp. 360–1.

[19] Ibid. pp. 251–4.

[20] M. J. Norusis, *Guide to Data Analysis* (Upper Saddle River NJ: Prentice Hall, SPSS 8.0, 1998). The most recent update of this package is version 11.1.

[21] Robson, *Real World Research*, pp. 19–22, including a critique (p. 22); N. Blaikie, *Approaches to Social Enquiry* (Cambridge: Polity Press, 1993, 1995²) pp. 13–17; G. Delanty, *Social Science: Beyond Constructivism and Realism* (Buckingham: Open University Press, 1997) pp. 11–14.

[22] Although it was largely inductive in its earliest days, since it was believed that only sense experience mediated knowledge. However,

Critical Rationalism associated with Karl Popper argued for a deductive approach based upon the testing of theory and the falsification of hypotheses: see M. Williams and T. May, *Introduction to the Philosophy of Social Research* (London: University College London Press, 1996) pp. 25–32.

[23] Bryman, *Quantity and Quality in Social Research*, pp. 14–15.

[24] J. E. Loder, 'The Place of Science in Practical Theology: The Human Factor', *International Journal of Practical Theology* 4.1 (2000) pp. 22–43 (p. 28) refers to Albert Einstein's 'leap of imagination' to discover the theory of relativity.

[25] Bryman, *Quantity and Quality in Social Research*, p. 20.

[26] Ibid. pp. 50–61.

[27] Williams and May, *Introduction to the Philosophy of Social Research*, pp. 49–52; Blaikie, *Approaches to Social Enquiry*, pp. 36–45.

[28] Robson, *Real World Research*, pp. 23–4.

[29] Ibid. p. 26.

[30] Delanty, *Social Science*, pp. 39–58.

[31] Williams and May, *Introduction to the Philosophy of Social Research*, pp. 75–6.

[32] Bryman, *Quantity and Quality in Social Research*, p. 52.

[33] Williams and May, *Introduction to the Philosophy of Social Research*, p. 75.

[34] See H. Garfinkel, *Studies in Ethnomethodology* (Cambridge: Polity Press, in association with Blackwell, Oxford, 1984, original publication 1967).

[35] Bryman, *Quantity and Quality in Social Research*, p. 54.

[36] Robson, *Real World Research*, p. 197.

[37] Bryman, *Quantity and Quality in Social Research*, p. 55.

[38] Williams and May, *Introduction to the Philosophy of Social Research*, pp. 48, 63–4.

[39] G. G. Baum, 'Remarks of a Theologian in Dialogue with Sociology' in M. H. Barnes (ed.), *Theology and the Social Sciences* (Maryknoll NY: Orbis, 2001) pp. 3–11 (p. 7).

[40] Cited by Bryman, *Quantity and Quality in Social Research*, p. 57.

[41] For a theological reading of Weber see T. Ekstrand, *Max Weber in Theological Perspective* (Leuven: Peeters, 2000) and in relation to *Verstehen* see pp. 65–8.

[42] Bryman, *Quantity and Quality in Social Research*, pp. 58–9.

[43] Robson, *Real World Research*, pp. 26–9.

[44] Ibid. pp. 29–42; cf. Delanty, *Social Science*, pp. 129–31. The use of the word 'critical' in an emancipatory sense is different from theological understandings of the phrase 'critical realism'. See, for example,

N. T. Wright, *The New Testament and the People of God* (London: SPCK, 1993²) pp. 32–7, 61–4, 88–92, where it is understood in the sense of provisional and partial, and therefore revisable.

45 Blaikie, *Approaches to Social Enquiry*, p. 126.

46 It is the standard question of the philosophically orientated commentator: see Williams and May, *Introduction to the Philosophy of Social Research*, p. 11; and Blaikie, *Approaches to Social Enquiry*, p. 203.

47 Bryman, *Quantity and Quality in Social Research*, p. 104.

48 See J. W. Creswell, *Research Design: Qualitative and Quantitative Approaches* (London: Sage, 1994), who offers a very useful account of the different traditions and how they can be combined.

49 J. A. van der Ven, *God Reinvented? A Theological Search in Texts and Tables* (Leiden: Brill, 1998) pp. 58–60 argues that qualitative and quantitative research methods be understood as complementary within the empirical theological paradigm. Also see J. S. Dreyer, 'The Researcher: Engaged Participant or Detached Observer? A Reflection on the Methodological Implications of the Dialectics of Belonging and Distanciation for Empirical Research in Practical Theology', *Journal of Empirical Theology* 11.2 (1998) pp. 5–22.

50 P. Luscombe, *Groundwork of Science and Religion* (Peterborough: Epworth Press, 2000) p. 97 states: 'critical realism claims that the ideas of verisimilitude and approximate truth, however difficult to formulate, are the correct way forward. Scientists can have confidence that their theories are, on the whole, coming closer to a description of the state of the real world'. Cf. A. E. McGrath, *The Foundations of Dialogue in Science and Religion* (Oxford: Blackwell, 1998) pp. 154–64.

51 For example D. Silverman, *Qualitative Methodology and Sociology: Describing the Social World* (Aldershot: Gower, 1985) pp. 157, 170.

52 Baum, 'Remarks of a Theologian', p. 9.

53 R. K. Yin, *Case Study Research: Design and Methods* (London: Sage, 1989) p. 80.

54 Ibid. See also R. K. Yin, *Applications of Case Study Research* (London: Sage, 1993).

55 Yin, *Case Study Research*, p. 23.

56 Bryman, *Quantity and Quality in Social Research*, *passim* also discusses the problems in qualitative research of interpretation, theory's relationship to data, and generalization of case study research.

57 Yin, *Case Study Research*, p. 84.

58 Ibid. p. 38.

59 Ibid. p. 45.

[60] T. May, *Social Research: Issues, Methods and Process* (Buckingham: Open University Press, 1993) pp. 111–23; D. Silverman, *Interpreting Qualitative Data: Methods for Analysing Talk, Text and Interaction* (London: Sage, 1993) p. 145.

[61] B. L. Berg, *Qualitative Research Methods for the Social Sciences* (Boston: Allyn & Bacon, 1989) p. 71.

[62] To my knowledge there does not exist a church of this name, it is a pseudonym. Any resemblance to a church of this title would be purely accidental.

[63] *Alpha Training Manual* (London: Holy Trinity Brompton, 1993).

[64] *Alpha News*, December 1995, March 1996, July 1996.

[65] N. Gumbel, *A Life Worth Living* (Eastbourne: Kingsway, 1994).

[66] Newsletter, 15 December 1995.

[67] 7 January 1996.

[68] Berg, *Qualitative Research Methods*, ch. 2; May, *Social Research*, ch. 6; Silverman, *Interpreting Qualitative Data*, ch. 5.

[69] I used the guidance of I. Dey, *Qualitative Data Analysis* (London: Routledge, 1993) and J. Riley, *Getting the Most from Your Data: A Handbook of Practical Ideas on how to Analyse Qualitative Data* (Bristol: Technical and Educational Services, 1990).

[70] Baltimore: The Technology Group, Inc. USA, 1993.

[71] One of the most widely used computer software is now QSR NUD*IST Vivo (Nvivo), QSR International Pty, Melbourne, Australia, 1999–2000. See L. Richards, *Using Nvivo in Qualitative Research* (Bundoora, Victoria, Australia: QSR International Pty Ltd, 2000).

[72] In addition to the church name being a pseudonym, all personal names mentioned in this account are also pseudonyms.

[73] During my Sunday visits the teaching series most in evidence was a series on Philippians to tie in with the use in house groups of the book *A Life Worth Living* by Nicky Gumbel, cited above.

[74] Visit dated 19 November 1995

[75] Dave Tomlinson is famous for his book *The Post-Evangelical* (London: Triangle, 1995).

[76] Visit dated 17 December 1995.

[77] In this case the questionnaire was administered to those who came to their weekly meeting on a specific occasion.

[78] 'Faith' here refers to the Faith Ministries associated with Kenneth Hagin and Kenneth Copeland.

[79] Bryman, *Quantity and Quality in Social Research*, pp. 21–40 offers a good discussion of the preoccupation of quantitative research with concepts and their measurement, causality, generalization, replication and individualism.

80 I am indebted to William Kay for a copy of his chapter 'Empirical and Statistical Considerations' in W. K. Kay and L. J. Francis (eds), *Religion in Education* Vol. 3 (Leominster: Gracewing, 2000) pp. 431–72.

81 For example, see H. Coolican, *Aspects of Psychology: Research Methods and Statistics* (London: Hodder & Stoughton, 1999); K. D. Hopkins, B. R. Hopkins and G. V. Glass, *Basic Statistics for the Behavioural Sciences* (London: Allyn & Bacon, 1996).

82 This is example is extracted from Kay, 'Empirical and Statistical Considerations', pp. 444–5.

83 Coolican, *Aspects of Psychology*, p. 99.

84 Ibid. p. 107; Hopkins, Hopkins and Glass, *Basic Statistics for the Behavioural Sciences*, p. 176.

PART TWO
EMPIRICAL STUDIES

5

Charismatic Worship as a Performance of Spirituality

1. Introduction

The aim of this chapter is to follow the description of the church in chapter 4 by considering the nature of its worship through the matrix of charismatic spirituality. The notion of spirituality, as outlined in chapter 2, contains particular features which function as lenses through which we view reality and upon which we base other beliefs and values. These lenses also reflect the structure of spirituality since all aspects of life are mediated through this matrix. The structure of charismatic spirituality mentioned previously is based upon the idea of a worldview, which contains the elements of narrative, symbols and praxis (that is, a way-of-being-in-the-world). I intend to use these lenses to consider the picture of worship that emerges from visits to the congregation over a period of seven months. The methodology of the chapter is basically participation observation, but using the spirituality categories as organizing principles around which the material is clustered, and through which the church and its worship performance is viewed. The picture is built up by a close reading of the fieldwork notes and documents associated with the study. In this way it is hoped that a fruitful description is offered that can lead to further understanding and suggestions for renewed theological praxis. As part of the reflection offered in the study I shall also engage with ethnographic studies of worship as well as Pentecostal and charismatic scholarship on the nature of worship as the description progresses.[1]

2. Context and Liturgical Structure

The Aigburth Community Church (ACC) meets on Sunday mornings in a primary school and it uses the assembly room and the adjacent classrooms for the children's activities. The chairs are arranged so that the focus of the worship space is one side of the room, which contains the overhead projector, and to one side of this focus is the band. The leader of the service leads from around the overhead projector and sometimes uses a lectern.[2] The adjacent rooms are also used for refreshments that are served after each service. The service starts at 10.30 a.m., but this is a flexible starting time, and the service can start up to ten minutes late. It usually finishes around 12.30 p.m. There is no evening service. The church contains people of wide age range, but the majority are in their 30s or 40s, and married with children. I was informed by a member of the church, a market researcher, that 50% of the church is comprised of graduates and most of those originate outside of Liverpool. The church, therefore, is predominately middle class, racially white and culturally British, and most people would wear casual if smart clothes, and, judging from the use of the school playground as a car park, drive to church. The people in the church are both friendly and welcoming. Indeed, I was aware of the atmosphere of informality that permeates almost every feature of church life. It has a 'laid-back' quality that I found to be both inviting and relaxed.

The services are led by a variety of people with both men and women taking turns to lead. The church has three leaders, who are elected for a three-year period. This period may be extended if the church wishes. It is inevitable that the three leaders take more of a leading role in worship services. However, participation is full and expected from all members of the church. During my time attending the services 60–70 people attended the worship.

The leaders of the worship have to be people who are capable of leading worship in a sensitive and appropriate manner, given the ethos of the church.[3] In the services that I attended I noticed the way in which each leader skilfully managed the liturgical structure of the service. Although there is no formal liturgical structure, no order of service and no clues for the occasional visitor as to what is about to happen next, the members of the church have a clear understanding of the possible sequence of events.[4]

They also know what would be an appropriate thing to expect and to do at the various stages of the liturgy. This framework facilitates the flow of worship and yet allows space for encountering the Holy Spirit through the service. In a simple outline, the service can be seen to comprise a number of key components in the following sequence.[5]

- (Hello: pre-service chat, catching up)[6]
- Welcome and introduction
- A number of songs (2–4)
- Space for quiet reflection or activity
- Children leave the service
- Bridge
- Reflective songs
- Sermon and Bible readings
- Response
- Closure
- (Goodbye: tea and coffee are served)

As can be seen by this liturgical structure the service is a bounded experience in both time and space.[7] Although there is flexibility in terms of both time (services start late) and space (it can be used differently if desired, though never is), gathering and departure and are both definite. The meeting of the church members is for the purposes of worship, fellowship and edification in the faith. The relaxed atmosphere is therefore eminently purposeful, a kind of focused and instrumental leisure pursuit. The boundaries of a beginning and an end are also stated clearly within the liturgical structure of the service itself, with both a definite welcome and closure. The welcome and introduction can include the notices (even though a newsletter is usually available), the teaching of new music, introduction of the service theme or an opening meditation.

The service is continued by means of a series of songs or choruses, which would fall within the main repertoire of the Charismatic Movement in the UK, but other music is included on other occasions, such as hymns and advent carols. The songs are usually continuous and played so as to run from one to another. The musicians are extremely competent and able to lead the congregation into praise and worship according the style and mood of the music as well as the theme of the service. The congregational participation is full with heartfelt singing and clapping when the musical style invites such participation.[8] However, I would not regard this singing as high-energy charismatic worship, rather it has a mild charismatic quality.

The space that follows this time of praise and worship contains opportunity for a variety of activities that reflect the charismatic spirituality of the church. The notices may be placed here, followed by a time of prayer ministry if someone is mentioned during the notices. For example, during one service it was mentioned that a member of the congregation was bereaved. He was invited to come forward to receive prayer ministry from the leaders. New music has been taught during this space, or silence kept. During one occasion a person prayed aloud while music was being played softly. This was followed by a few people singing quietly in glossolalia. On occasions this space provides the opportunity for some members to exercise the gift of prophecy, or to share testimonies of what God has done.[9] An example of testimony was the news of three people coming to faith through the Alpha course.[10]

At this point in the service the children leave to go to their groups. There is Sunday school provision for children, according to age range. The church clearly values the participation of children in the worship and yet recognizes the need for children to engage in faith activities that are appropriate to their age and abilities.

During the departure of the children to the Sunday school classes there is an obvious disruption to the atmosphere of worship. Therefore, the service contains what I can only call a 'bridge' section.[11] This section enables the parents to rejoin the service and at the same time enables the remaining adults to continue in their worship. The bridge section, therefore, typically allows people to disengage briefly before re-focusing. It can include notices, often punctuated with Liverpudlian humour, preparation and the taking of Holy Communion, or an introduction to an area of intercession.

After the bridge has been crossed, so to speak, there is a time for quieter and more reflective songs. These are gentle and allow the congregation opportunity to engage in more personally orientated worship as well as giving space for people to participate through the offering of Bible readings, prophecy, or singing in glossolalia.[12] This section of the liturgy usually closes with an atmosphere of stillness and is often managed with great discernment by the service leader.[13] It is a contemplative style that has a meditative and reflective quality.[14]

The sermon usually follows this section and includes the Bible readings for the service. The preachers are usually members of the church, often the leaders, but there are frequent guest preachers at the service. These include missionaries known to the church, local ministers and acquaintances (I preached after my research had finished, to be followed by a professor of theology!). The congregation therefore experiences a variety of styles of preaching ministry from visitors. I shall explore the style of one of its own preachers below.

At this point, time does become a factor. If the service has taken a long time, then quite often it can close with a short prayer, or simply a notice that tea and coffee are now served next door. If there is time or if the service has been planned to include a post-sermon response time then other activities may follow. There may be a further song, Holy Communion,[15] prayer ministry, children sharing what they have done in Sunday school, or a further reflective space that could include prophecy or intercessions. If the service has not been closed directly after the sermon, then it is closed after this response time with a concluding song or a prayer. Occasionally, missionaries have been invited out to the front to be prayed for, after which tea and coffee is announced thus signalling the end of the service.

The church is thus seen to embody a spirituality in God which is imminent in the everyday lives of his people. The school as an everyday building is used for the purpose of kingdom building. The modern tools of education, such as the overhead projector and contemporary musical instruments, are used to facilitate praise and worship of God. Yet at the heart of this spirituality is fellowship and a community of faith which meets to worship, learn and serve one another. It is this spirituality which can also be analysed in terms of the spirituality categories mentioned in chapter 2, so it is to this analysis we now turn.

3. Spirituality Performed

As stated above, the performance of charismatic spirituality within this church and by these people is mediated through the lenses of narrative, symbols and praxis. Narrative usually gives meaning and shape to a particular spirituality and coheres the use of symbols and various types of praxis within its contours, so I shall leave this lens until the end and use it in relation to the other two lenses.

Symbols

Symbols can be both artefacts, such as buildings, and events, such as marches and festivals. They enable a connection to be made between something that is concrete and particular and that which is greater, transcendent or ultimate, such as meaning, reality, value, community or institution.[16] There are major symbols and minor symbols, but it is not until a researcher begins to engage and investigate a particular group that its unique use of symbols can be discerned and described. From my engagement with the church I would like to suggest that there are four important symbols that give expression to the identity of the charismatic spirituality located in this church. Three of the symbols are main symbols and one is a minor symbol that nevertheless augments the others. The main symbols are the building, modern musical instruments and the overhead projector, while the minor symbols are bread and wine. These main symbols may be surprising but it is through the ordinary that spirituality invests a high degree of meaning and value, especially when embedded within cultural conventions, however recently formed.

For ACC the building is significant. The fact that it is geographically situated within a particular community, comprising mixed housing of Victorian terrace and early twentieth-century semi-detached houses, suggests a commitment to a particular locality. However, with this commitment is symbolized a place of transition and change. The church has not invested in a building of its own, which suggests that it is travelling light within this present world. It uses a school to demonstrate the very practical and down-to-earth nature of Christianity. The God of these people is very interested in the everyday, the routine and the 'nitty gritty' of life in a Liverpool suburb. The church is not interested in building an empire of its own – rather it is interested in kingdom building for

God. It also symbolizes the bounded space in which the worship ritual takes place.[17]

The musical symbols are not those of a traditional church: there is no organ. The building and the musical styles correspond in this respect. Instead we have the band with the usual instruments of modernity and postmodernity: guitar, bass, drums and keyboard/piano.[18] Occasionally other instruments supplement this basic set of musical symbols. Charismatic or Iona styles of music are played, which fit much more easily than traditional church music accompanied by an organ.

The overhead projector (OHP) is the quintessential charismatic symbol or indeed icon. There is no need for stained glass windows because the OHP can show various pictures and images that are temporary and transient. This key symbol is useful because it projects a crucial mediator of beliefs and values, that is, charismatic choruses and songs. The repertoire of songs can be changed regularly as certain songs go out of fashion and new songs are introduced. Of course, this symbol requires good eyesight. It can sometimes be difficult for older people with less good eyesight to see or understands what the symbol is signifying! However, in charismatic worship what the symbol conveys can be internalized, so, for example, popular songs can be learned off by heart. It facilitates heartfelt worship and the use of bodily expressions such as the raising of hands without the constraints of having to hold a hymnbook. It enables words and music to be joined in worship and praise that is so significant in charismatic spirituality.

Alongside these major symbols of this particular expression of spirituality comes a more traditional set of symbols: bread and wine. These symbols are regularly used in worship to express communion with God and to remember the saving death of Jesus Christ upon the cross of Calvary. These symbols are frequent but not used every week. They may be used at different liturgical junctures and they are certainly not the key symbols in the repertoire of symbols, but they have made an important return and represent a re-appropriation of traditional theological symbolism within the new context of postmodern charismatic spirituality.

In the sense that all the members of this church owned and used these symbols throughout their worship they can be said to contribute to the performance of their spirituality.

Praxis

Praxis refers to a way-of-being-in-the-world. It refers to the ways in which beliefs and values are enacted and embodied. In worship it refers to ways in which charismatic spirituality works out in the doing of worship. It is not just a question of what is on the menu, but what does it taste like? What energy does it produce, and how can it transform people as they encounter the Holy Spirit, who inspires them to worship? There are a number of key praxis items that are worthy of description.

There is the actual singing of songs as a way of expressing one's being through action. At the front of the church is a worship leader, a musician, whose task it is to lead the band and interpret the playing of the music to the congregation in order to elicit as full a participation in worship as possible. This means that songs must flow from one to the other and that the leader must manage the transitions well so that the emphasis upon continuity can be demonstrated. In this way the congregation gathers momentum in the search for God. The singing of songs at the beginning of worship belongs very much to the search phase in charismatic spirituality. God is praised for who he is, but in the search is the expectation that the God of relationship will meet them as they seek him with their hearts.

The worship affords space, mostly for quiet and personal reflection, but it is also used for corporate activity. There are carefully planned and managed times of stillness in which people are encouraged to seek God for themselves and to find him in the space. If the building speaks of the imminence of God in the everyday, then these key praxis moments of quiet, stillness and reflection open up opportunities for the second phase of charismatic spirituality, namely encounter with the Holy Spirit. From out of this space can come the exercising of spiritual gifts such as glossolalia or prophecy, the sharing of Scripture, intercessory prayer and prayer ministry, testimony and items of news for prayer.

Stephen E. Parker suggests that worship in a Pentecostal context is orderly despite the 'space' that is opened up for the leading of the Holy Spirit to encourage the congregation through testimony and the exercise of spiritual gifts. He argues that this orderliness is evident in the way in which music is used to guide the con-gregational response, and that some charismatic manifestations can bring closure, for example, an interpretation of a message in tongues. The pastor remains in charge of the service even during moves of the Spirit. He also identifies the notion of restraint operating through the leaders as they manage the charismatic manifestations.[19] When this is compared to ACC, perhaps a less highly charged environment, all of these tools for establishing and maintaining order are in evidence. Even though the church does not have a pastor or minister when the service is in process the service leader has the authority to guide the use of the 'space' created for encountering the Holy Spirit.

The activity of preaching and listening to sermons is also a form of praxis. Sermons usually contain the reading of Scripture by the preacher although on occasions this activity may be done by others. The sermons, while having a narrative quality, nevertheless place the Bible in the centre of the activity and people tend to follow the sermon by turning to the relevant passages and reading these as the sermon progresses. At times, depending on the preacher, the sermon will be participatory and invite the congregation to take part by either answering questions or engaging in some group activity. The sermons often contain exhortations to change and become more like Christ and better witnesses to his love for the sake of others in the world.

There is also the praxis of friendship and friendliness that contributes to the atmosphere of welcome and acceptance. This way-of-being-in-the-world acts as an envelope around the whole worship service. People chat in a relaxed way before the service rather than walking around in a hushed awe, for they know that kind of praxis will follow later. During the notices or sermon there is good humour as the Liverpool wit comes to the fore! After the service people mingle freely and chat during coffee or while they clear the band or service equipment away. Newcomers are made to feel especially welcome and they are genuinely encouraged to return. This reflects the importance of the charismatic community as a social community. It is this community which enters charismatic worship together, already bonded in friendship.[20]

Daniel E. Albrecht outlines the congregational roles that can also be viewed as summarizing these forms of praxis within the worship context. First, there is the role of the worshippers themselves. They actively engage in the ritual of worship and participate fully. It is not simply about the preacher's performance, but also the worshippers' performance, which is an offering to God and an embodiment of spirituality. Second, the role of the prophet is directed towards the congregation, by the offering of words of prophecy, words of knowledge, or appropriate verses of Scripture. This often occurs within the encounter 'space' of the liturgical process. Third, the role of minister is that of caregiver, as the leader directs the sharing and the caring within the congregation. This is especially evident in times of prayer ministry when a number gather around a brother or sister in Christ to pray for his or her needs.[21] Fourth, the role of listener/learner is also significant. It is expected that all members of the church are disciples and are in constant need to be taught and learn from one another and ultimately from God. Therefore, listening is not passive, it is listening with a purpose: in order to do God's will. Fifth, the role of doer/disciple is as one who is 'a doer of the word'. This means that action and activity in obedience to Christ are valued highly both within the worship service and in everyday Christian life.[22]

Although there are elements that are not strictly worship praxis, they impinge upon the nature of services from time to time. The concern for teaching of new converts meant that the church was using the follow-up material to the Alpha course not only during the mid-week Bible study groups but also for a sermon series on the book of Philippians. The openness to other church traditions was demonstrated in the joining of a local ecumenical covenant and the exchange of preachers and others in the leading of worship. The church has attempted to practise good communication, with both a notice board at the back of the assembly room as an information point, as well as a newsletter produced most Sundays. These elements, while not unique to the church, nevertheless reinforce a charismatic spirituality that is open to the needs others, relational and committed to evangelism.

Narrative

It could be argued that all Christians fundamentally have a narrative, indeed a metanarrative, of creation, sin and redemption. Clearly this metanarrative is demonstrated in the life of this church. But there are also other narratives that indicate where these people have come from and where they think they might be going.[23] This narrative suggests who they think they are within the household of faith and what their contribution might be to the family of the church universal. There are a number of key stories that emerged from the data.

The history of the church suggests that it emerged from out of a difficult phase in the lives of a number of people while they were members of another church. They decided to leave that church to form a new one. While there are certain sensitivities to that other church, and previous tensions are played down, it remains part of the narrative. The founders of this church wanted something different in worship from 'endless choruses'. They wanted to explore variety in worship with sensitivities to other symbols and different musical styles, exemplified in the frequent taking of Holy Communion and Iona music. However, as part of the narrative of origins is a clear narrative of the leadership style. They represent a reaction to and a rejection of autocratic and authoritarian leadership. They embrace an egalitarian and community orientated approach to leadership that celebrates maximum participation.[24] The community itself takes responsibility for its own life and work. That community appoints by consensus three leaders, who are not hierarchically ordered, to serve the community. For example, at the bottom of the newsletter, the leaders are referred to as church contacts. An elder functions in a supportive role for consultation and advice.

Again, partly in reaction to the competition between local independent charismatic churches, ACC does not wish to build an empire and, given the numbers at the time of my research, it is clearly on the small side for such a church. It sees itself as offering a distinct vision that is open, broad and inclusive of difference within the New Church movement. The interest in the work of Dave Tomlinson, and post-evangelicalism, serves to keep the church exploring its own identity.[25] The church entered into an ecumenical covenantal relationship with other churches in the area towards the end of my research time. This suggests that an aspect of its narrative is co-operation. It sees itself as not having the whole truth with regard to Christianity but that it is willing to journey and learn from other denominations in the locality. This also includes the church from whence it came, since they jointly offered an Alpha course, thus engaging in a common evangelistic strategy.[26]

The controlling narrative features mentioned above must also be seen alongside a commitment to biblical authority, which is expressed in sermons, Bible study and discipleship. However, the use of the Bible both in worship and in personal narratives is clothed within the culture of the church. The church wishes to be seen as open and friendly, welcoming to strangers and visitors. It seeks to provide space for those who are seeking something slightly different from the standard charismatic fare. However, it does have boundaries that are policed when required. For example, I heard the story of some people who were interested in joining the church, but who began to expound their beliefs in prosperity theology. They were treated with respect but were given 'short shrift' theologically. Theological truth is important for the church, and despite the narrative of breath and inclusiveness, there are limits to what can be endorsed. The church is a missionary church both in terms of its own evangelism and support of overseas missionary work, even if it lacks engagement with local social issues.

4. The Preacher: Embodying and Communicating a Spirituality

As a way of illustrating the performance of spirituality within this church congregation I shall briefly describe a sermon delivered by one of the leaders, whom I have named Debra. Debra is married to Philip (a musician) and they are both leaders in the church. They are founding members of the church and embody the spirituality of the church in their lives and roles. I witnessed Debra in the role of worship leader and was especially interested to see her lead the Holy Communion part of the service on one occasion. Her ministry is fully recognized and affirmed within the community. She is a teacher by profession and in her late 40s. (This reflection is based upon field notes only. Ideally one would also have a taped copy of the sermon by which to check notes and reflections.)

At the time Debra preached the church was following a sermon series based on the book of Philippians. It was programmed as part of the follow-up strategy after the Alpha course had just taken place. The church was studying Philippians both in house groups and on Sundays. These studies were based on the book by Nicky Gumbel entitled *A Life Worth Living.*[27]

Debra spoke on the passage from Philippians 1:12–30. She used notes via the OHP to remind the congregation that Paul was writing this letter from prison and that it was a 'thank you' letter to the church in Philippi. She cited Eugene Peterson's paraphrase by means of the OHP to introduce the text of her sermon.

I want to report to you, friends, that my imprisonment here has had the opposite of its intended effect. Instead of being squelched, the Message has actually prospered. All the soldiers here, and everyone else too, found out that I'm in jail because of this Messiah. That piqued their curiosity, and now they've learned about him. Not only that, but most of the Christians here have become far more sure of themselves in the faith than ever, speaking out fearlessly about God, about the Messiah.

It's true that some here preach Christ because with me out of the way, they think they'll step right into the spotlight. But others do it with the best heart in the world. One group is motivated by pure love, knowing that I am here defending the Message, wanting help. The others, now that I'm out of the picture, are merely greedy, hoping to get something out of it for themselves. Their motives are bad. They see me as their competition, and so the worse it goes for me, the better – they think – for them.

So how am I to respond? I've decided that I really don't care about their motives, whether mixed, bad, or indifferent. Every time one of them opens his mouth, Christ is proclaimed, so I just cheer them on!

And I'm going to keep that celebration going because I know that it's going to turn out. Through your faithful prayers and the generous response of the Spirit of Jesus Christ, everything he wants to do in and through me will be done. I can hardly wait to continue on my course. I don't expect to be embarrassed in the least. On the contrary, everything happening to me in this jail only serves to make Christ more accurately known, regardless of whether I live or die. They didn't shut me up; they gave me a pulpit! Alive, I'm Christ's messenger; dead, I'm his bounty. Life versus even more life! I can't lose.

As long as I'm alive in this body, there is good work for me to do. If I had to choose right now, I hardly know which I'd choose. Hard choice! The desire to break camp here and be with Christ is powerful.

Some days I can think of nothing better. But most days, because of
what you are going through, I am sure that it's better for me to stick
it out here. So I plan to be around awhile, companion to you as your
growth and joy in this life of trusting God continues. You can start
looking forward to a great reunion when I come visit you again.
We'll be praising Christ, enjoying each other.[28]

Debra followed this introduction by using the OHP to give headings
for the sermon. She had four headings.[29]

- Gospel opportunities (1:12–14)
- Gospel priorities (1:15–18)
- Gospel purpose for living (1:19–26)
- Gospel patterns for life (1:27–30)

First, under the title of 'Gospel opportunities', she reiterated
that Paul was a prisoner in Rome. He has been imprisoned in
Philippi but had escaped miraculously. However, this time there
appears to be no escape. This time God was doing things rather
differently. She applied this message to the congregation by saying
that sometimes we feel trapped by circumstances, but that we should
remember that God has not forgotten us. He has a purpose for our
lives. He says: 'That's where I want you to be right now.' Often
we feel lost to the opportunities and we can be blind to the small
things. We need to pray about that on a daily basis, to pray for new
opportunities. It is probable that even Paul did not know all the
opportunities even he had to witness. Sometimes the slogan: 'Your
God is too small!' is appropriate to us. God is greater than we
think.

Second, under the title of 'Gospel priorities', she asked the
question: 'Does it matter about our motives?' This was supplemented by the question: 'Is that what Paul is saying here?' Debra
suggests that God is bigger than any one of us and that people can
be saved even if the preacher's motives are wrong. This is because
his word is living, and God is bigger than the preacher. She
contextualizes Paul's comments here by saying that there are
obviously people out there who were trying to get him. His
comments stand behind this reality.

Third, under the heading 'Gospel purpose for living', Debra says that Paul recognizes that he is part of a team. He was supported by the prayers of others. The key verse here is verse 21: 'For to me, to live is Christ and to die is gain.' She says that we could add the question: 'Is it?' There could be a question mark here for all of us. She recalled her fear of Communism years ago as a young mother and says that we do not need to be frightened. God will give us the grace that we need. It is not a question of life and death but of life and more life. She asks herself: can I say verse 26, 'so that by me being with you again your joy in Christ will overflow on account of me'? She believes she is improving in her discipleship, even if she has a long way to go!

Fourth, under the title 'Gospel patterns for life', Debra says that we should nevertheless contend for the faith. She compares this idea to the television programme *Gladiators*. The referee starts the game by saying 'Gladiators, are you ready?' and then blows the whistle. At this point the competitors become fully committed to the game. Likewise, we are to fix our eyes on the prize with no turning back. She reflects that as a child we may have played the game called 'tag' in the playground. When an individual is touched or 'tagged' then that person is deemed to be 'on' or 'it' and needs to catch others. Christ has 'tagged' us and we are 'it', or perhaps we should say Christ is 'it'. In this area the churches are beginning to work together for the sake of the gospel. If you are 'in seed' for God, then the by-product is true happiness. At this point Debra closed the sermon and the service leader closed the service also.

What Debra displays through her preaching is a commitment to preaching based upon the text. It tends to be in the style of evangelical preaching and teaching rather than charismatic narrative-orientated sermons. This, no doubt, comes from a close reliance upon the interpretation of Nicky Gumbel. However, there are hints of the narrative, symbols and praxis throughout the sermon. For example, the comment that Paul was part of a team reflects the team-orientated narratives of the church ethos. The use of the OHP as a teaching tool not only reflects her teaching skills but the spirituality of the church more generally since it can be used for words or pictures. The Alpha course, and its use by the church, adopts a wider charismatic spirituality that is linked to the charismatic evangelicalism of Holy Trinity Brompton, London. A different sermon that was thematically based would perhaps indicate a slightly different use of the narratives, symbols and praxis. Nevertheless, I would suggest that the common spirituality components described here would emerge and re-emerge over time, thus performing and reinforcing the spirituality of the worship community that is ACC.

5. Conclusion

In conclusion, this chapter has aimed to show how qualitative data from a church case study is able to reveal a useful picture of a particular charismatic community in worship. It is, of course, a time-limited study and the church has, I know, moved on and developed further since this original study was completed. The study also reflects the formative period of ACC as an institution because it was conducted within the early years of its establishment. Nevertheless, it is hoped that this portrait of a church's performance of spirituality through worship offers a model of the kind of case study that is an important possibility for contemporary practical theology.

6. Methodological Reflection

This study is essentially a re-reading of qualitative data by means of a set of conceptual lenses. However, if the data were not available, I could not re-read it in any sense at all. Therefore the prior starting point is my original research enterprise of doctoral study. I chose this church as a way of engaging with a New Church in Liverpool for the purposes of exploring glossolalia. It was conceived as an instrumental case study rather than as an intrinsic case study or purely ethnographical study. Having said that, I used key ethnographical tools of participant observation and documentary analysis as well as semi-structured interviews. The material I have used for this chapter comes mainly from the Sunday service participant observation field notes. I first wrote a description of the church in the conceptual terms of the study before engaging with material from Pentecostal and charismatic scholarship and ethnographical studies of congregations and worship services.

What can be suggested for a renewed theological praxis of worship and spirituality? The church stands well within the orthodox tradition understood in the Protestant sense of the term. Where there might be a renewed understanding is in a reaffirmation of the doctrine of the Trinity. There is no guiding formal liturgy to renew minds in the knowledge of this doctrine. There is gratitude expressed in love for those within the community of faith and a concern for those outside that is expressed in terms of evangelism. However, I did not sense a great compassion for the poor and the outcast expressed through intercessory prayer within the context of worship. Also, the ministry praxis of the church would be greatly enhanced by the incorporation of times of ministry where people could be prayed for healing. This ministry could demonstrate a more holistic approach to salvation.

In terms of pneumatology, I would suggest that the presence of the Holy Spirit is discerned in the gathering of people together who are seeking God. They seek God through each other's lives and in the corporate act of worship. I believe that the Holy Spirit is indeed meeting these people as they create a 'space' within their services to meet with the God whom they worship. As a consequence of their encounter with God they are being conformed to the likeness of Christ and bearing the fruit of the Spirit. They are growing in discipleship through the ministry of the Spirit and the Word, and are engaged in the ministry of evangelism and missionary outreach for the sake of the kingdom of God rather than their church.

---

[1] See, for example, M. D. Stringer, *On the Perception of Worship: The Ethnography of Worship in Four Christian Congregations in Manchester* (Birmingham: University of Birmingham Press, 1999); S. E. Parker, *Led by the Spirit: Toward a Practical Theology of Pentecostal Discernment and Decision Making* (Sheffield: Sheffield Academic Press, JPTS 7, 1996); D. E. Albrecht, *Rites in the Spirit: A Ritual Approach to Pentecostal/ Charismatic Spirituality* (Sheffield: Sheffield Academic Press, JPTS 17, 1999).

[2] Albrecht, *Rites in the Spirit*, pp. 127–33 regards this use of geographical space as a ritual space, or micro-world, in which worshippers experience God. He differentiates between congregational space, leadership space (including platform, band and projector screen) and

altar space (the space between the leadership space and the first row of congregational chairs). The altar space is a meeting space where the congregation symbolically meets God. This happens occasionally at ACC because of the lack of geographical space. There these distinct ritual spaces are compressed and overlap.

3 For a discussion of the way in which worship services are managed, including charismatic worship, see F. Watts, R. Nye and S. Savage, *Psychology for Christian Ministry* (London: Routledge, 2002) pp. 20–39.

4 Stringer, *On the Perception of Worship*, pp. 138–67 discusses his ethnography of a similar independent Charismatic Christian Fellowship. He acknowledges order, but fails to identify sequence, only components (p. 144).

5 For a comparison of the worship liturgy of an International Holiness Pentecostal Church, see Parker, *Led by the Spirit*, pp. 72–3. Note also the description by D. N. Hudson, 'Worship: Singing a New Song in a Strange Land' in K. Warrington (ed.), *Pentecostal Perspectives* (Carlisle: Paternoster, 1998) pp. 177–203.

6 The importance of gathering is demonstrated in pre-service greetings and conversations, observed by Parker, *Led by the Spirit*, pp. 94, 154–5.

7 Albrecht, *Rites in the Spirit*, pp. 124–41, 152–70 discusses the defining ritual frameworks of time, space and identity in relation to three congregational studies. He observes that the three congregations have a similar tri-part liturgical structure of (1) the worship (songs), (2) pastoral message, and (3) the altar/response (p. 126). He suggests that between each foundational or processional rite is a transitional rite that functions to join these foundational rites (especially pp. 153–4, 160–62). The liturgical pattern under discussion here, while containing those elements, is structured differently. For example, there is not always opportunity for a response after the sermon.

8 Ibid. pp. 143, 147 regards music as functioning as an auditory icon within Pentecostal spirituality and also considers bodily movement to have an iconic quality.

9 The use of testimonies is less ritualized in this church than perhaps in most Pentecostal denominations: cf. Parker, *Led by the Spirit*, pp. 95–9.

10 Stringer, *On the Perception of Worship*, pp. 152–5 describes charismatic worship as montage, that is, within the orderliness of the service there is 'disorder' because of the constant interruptions due to the high level of congregational participation. This nevertheless has an internal coherent quality to it, for example focused around the concept

of conversion. Through the medium of experience, that is the experience of chaos, there comes an experience of renewed order and transformation (pp. 159, 162). It is this montage which offers 'space' to be filled by the Other, however defined (p. 214). It is at this point that charismatics wish to talk about an intimate encounter with the Holy Spirit, even if other conceptualizations, such a 'liminality' or 'moments in and out of time and in and out of secular social structure', are also offered. Albrecht, *Rites in the Spirit*, pp. 209–11.

11 Albrecht, *Rites in the Spirit*, pp. 160–2 refers to this kind of bridge as a transitional rite.

12 Stringer, *On the Perception of Worship*, p. 146 found the level of congregation participation somewhat strange, even when compared to classical Pentecostal denominations which he knew. In my experience levels of participation depend largely upon the leadership, values and culture of the church and therefore can vary immensely.

13 Cf. Parker, *Led by the Spirit*, p. 101.

14 Albrecht, *Rites in the Spirit*, pp. 158–9.

15 Stringer, *On the Perception of Worship*, p. 149. Stringer regarded this as the most formal feature of the independent charismatic church liturgy he described.

16 F. W. Dillistone, *The Power of Symbols* (London: SCM, 1986) p. 13.

17 Albrecht, *Rites in the Spirit*, pp. 127–8 suggests that buildings are significant in revealing the worship and spirituality attitudes of particular congregations.

18 In this regard even the traditional visual icons of Pentecostalism are missing. There is no Bible on display, no pulpit and no altar rail, although the musical technology does compare with contemporary Pentecostalism. Cf. ibid. pp. 144–6.

19 Parker, *Led by the Spirit*, pp. 114–15.

20 Albrecht, *Rites in the Spirit*, pp. 212–13.

21 Ibid. pp. 138–41 nuances the liturgical leadership roles more specifically in terms of facilitator/co-ordinator, authority and expert/specialist. The roles of facilitator and authority are assumed by the leaders of ACC, but they tend not to assume the role of expert.

22 Ibid. pp. 136–8.

23 For a discussion of the importance of story in worship ethnography, see Stringer, *On the Perception of Worship*, pp. 97–105, and the way in which it engages us empathetically. He defines 'narrative' as an ongoing process without specific beginning and end, while stories are time-bounded and relate to specific events. I use narrative and story synonymously but use metanarrative to refer to the grand Christian

worldview narrative. He further suggests that 'story' is an ideal way in which to communicate the essential nature of an experience, perhaps the only way to communicate experience. He suggests that the story is not a true account of the experience but an analogy that allows the listener to empathize with the experience and have some sense of it (p. 206). I believe that there are significant problems with Stringer's appreciation of 'truth' and his understanding of how language functions in this regard. He basically wishes to propose an experientialist ontology that can have 'significance' without having 'meaning' (p. 212). Clearly, the ghost of Schleiermacher haunts us still! For a Pentecostal discussion of ritual space in terms of both meaning and significance, see Albrecht, *Rites in the Spirit*, pp. 134–5.

[24] Albrecht, *Rites in the Spirit*, p. 136 uses White's phrase, 'full democratization of participation'.

[25] D. Tomlinson, *The Post-Evangelical* (London: Triangle, 1995).

[26] See the *Alpha Training Manual* and videos (London: Holy Trinity Brompton, 1993).

[27] N. Gumbel, *A Life Worth Living* (Eastbourne: Kingsway, 1994).

[28] E. H. Peterson, *The Message: The New Testament in Contemporary Language* (Colorado Springs CO: Navpress, 1993) pp. 487–8.

[29] These headings are extracted exactly from Gumbel, *A Life Worth Living*, pp. 27–37, and indeed a lot of the content of the sermon is based on Gumbel's analysis of the passage, but the illustrations Debra uses are different.

6

Glossolalia and Postmodernity[1]

1. Introduction

The Charismatic Movement is now more popularly connected with the so-called Toronto Blessing and its associated phenomena. In the earliest days the Charismatic Movement adopted the spirituality of Pentecostalism and the focus was upon the crisis spiritual experience known as baptism in the Spirit,[2] incidentally often associated with Toronto-type phenomena, but more especially with speaking in tongues, otherwise known as glossolalia.[3] It is probably fair to say that glossolalia is given a less prominent place in the British Charismatic Movement now than it was in the late 1960s and early 1970s, yet it has not disappeared.[4] On the contrary, there is a theory that suggests it might in fact *become* more at home in the twenty-first century than before.

This is the theory of Harvey Cox on the question of charismatics and the future of glossolalia in the context of postmodernity.[5] Cox essentially writes about classical Pentecostalism in the United States, but he also considers Pentecostalism in Latin America, Europe, Asia and Africa. Since there is still a close connection between Pentecostals and charismatics, although differences must also be noted, it seems a natural progression to consider Cox's theory in light of the Charismatic Movement in Britain today. Therefore the aim of this chapter is twofold. First, to describe very briefly Cox's interpretation of Pentecostals and glossolalia in relation to his understanding of postmodernity, and second, to explore his theory with material collected from the Aigburth Community Church.

2. The Fundamentalist/Experientialist Scenario

Harvey Cox, like many other academics, is interested in the apparent cultural shift from modernity to postmodernity. He begins the final chapter of his book, *Fire from Heaven*, with a quotation from the lyrics of Sting, the singer and songwriter, from his song 'If I Ever Lose my Faith in You'.[6] The lyrics of the song suggest a loss of faith in both scientific progress and institutional religion leading to a lack of direction. This view, Cox argues, epitomizes the opinion of many people in the late twentieth and early twenty-first century. Both scientific modernity and conventional religion have failed to provide spiritual meaning for the masses of society. He understands this current shift to be characterized by changes from the cerebral to the intuitive, from the analytical to the immediate, from the literal to the analogical, and a move beyond the subject–object divide (presumably to inter-subjectivity, but this is implied rather than stated). People wish to participate and not merely observe, whilst attracted to archaic and mystical modes of perception and inductive ways of thinking.

Into this new situation, and within Pentecostalism, two contenders battle to provide the spiritual meaning which so many want and yet cannot find: fundamentalism and experientialism. Both of these, according to Cox, claim authentic links to the past and aim to use what is valuable in the past in order to apply to the present and the future. Fundamentalists are understood to be the most visible and are zealous, unswerving, impassioned and intolerant, seeing themselves as sole authentic representatives of religious tradition, in this case, Christianity. A by-product of modernity, fundamentalism is characterized by literalism and absolute truth claims encapsulated in the doctrine of biblical verbal inerrancy. On the other hand, the experientialists are disparate, inchoate and focus on 'experience' rather than a single authoritative voice. They use the historic Christian tradition as a 'toolbox', accepting some but not all of the worldview for the job at hand. The cohesion for such a position is located in the person rather than a system or institution, thus putting immense responsibility upon the individual. In church organization terms, this means the network rather than the hierarchy is preferred, the authority of the clergy is abandoned for the company of seekers. This, in turn, provides the setting for mining the treasures of the Christian tradition. Cox uses the phrase by Danièle Hervieu-Léger, 'spiritual bricolage', to describe a radical and personal form of spirituality with each individual 'constantly compiling his or her own collage of symbols and practices in the light of what coheres with their own changing experiences in the tortuous passage through life in a world where the old, allegedly comprehensive charts no longer command confidence'.[7] This results in an essentially pragmatic and 'deregulated' spirituality.

Cox realizes that Pentecostals will need to define what they mean by 'experience' or else a cult of experience and feelings could emerge, resulting in a form of New Age absorption that defies verbal expression and leads to confusion. He suggests that the crux of the debate between belief system and personal experience may lie in ecstatic worship and glossolalia in particular. For Cox, glossolalia is the recovery of what he calls primal speech.[8] This, together with primal piety (that is, trance, vision, healing, dream, dance, etc.) and primal hope (a millennial vision), is part of a core human religiosity labelled 'primal spirituality'. Speaking in tongues, according to Cox, responds to a feature of this spiritual crisis, which he calls 'the ecstasy deficit'. Tongues-speech is an ecstatic experience 'in which the cognitive grids and perceptual barriers that normally prevent people from opening themselves to deeper insights and exultant feelings are temporarily suspended'.[9] This ecstatic state is not irrational but is rather a way of knowing that transcends everyday awareness, in which communication occurs at a deep level. The risk of such communication is made possible in the context of a secure environment provided by a familiar framework of biblical stories and metaphors, and eschatological hope.

Cox uses the phrase 'primal speech', taken from the psychologists Ann and Barry Ulanov, to refer to a capacity for preverbal expression of needs, urges and emotions, which are so characteristic of infants.

Babies gurgle with pleasure, scream with pain, and howl with fear. They also communicate in vigorous bodily movements and facial expression. After we develop the ability to speak in words, these psychologists suggest, primary speech still continues as a kind of undercurrent. For obvious reasons it is never fully expressible in words. Could it be that what we find in Pentecostal and other churches is the resurfacing of this surging, ever-present undercurrent, bursting to the surface because the religious setting provides a reassuring environment where we can safely become as little children, at least temporarily?[10]

According to Cox, Pentecostals have moved from interpreting tongues as the supernatural ability to speak foreign languages or the infallible sign of the baptism in the Spirit.[11] Now it is seen as a means of deliverance from the 'iron cage of grammar', and as provision for those who do not have the ability or strength to pray using their own words. That the practice of glossolalia persists despite the changes in interpretation is due to the conviction that the Spirit of God is available to anyone in an 'intense, immediate, indeed interior way'.[12] It also signals the fact that the available religious idiom is inadequate and it is a mystical-experiential protest against the existing religious language. It usually takes place among culturally displaced people and is often found among the politically and socially disinherited. As such it is a form of cultural subversion. It helps to create a new religious subculture, one in which personal experience is amplified and affirmed.[13] It is thus in the context of postmodernity that such a role is to be anticipated if not already in evidence.

The question, of course, is how accurate is this portrait of the current cultural shift and the Pentecostal scenario within it? To attempt to transfer this theory across the Atlantic and to situate it within the Charismatic Movement in Britain would appear to be an interesting proposal. The following case study did not originally intend to examine the scenario proposed by Cox and the reflections offered here are *a posteriori*. It is nevertheless assumed that the description offered below is of interest and importance. The general context of the church is considered first before the specific question of glossolalia.

3. The Church Context: Aigburth Community Church

The link with Dave Tomlinson has been mentioned, with one interviewee having been influenced by his book entitled *The Post-Evangelical*.[14] It was discovered that the three current leaders had attended a teaching weekend in 1991 organized by Dave Tomlinson at which his postmodern ideas regarding worship had been discussed. One of the leaders had become frustrated with the monotony of endless chorus singing and longed for something else. The introduction to meditation and the use of silence in corporate worship appealed to her. This was complemented by the use of the creative arts in worship that appealed to another leader, who was an art teacher by profession. The use of Eucharistic liturgies from other traditions was also adopted, as evidenced by the use of the 1662 Book of Common Prayer commandments at my first service! The idea that the church should be a 'broad church' was adopted, with the freedom to experiment in worship the motto. This was required to cater for the different tastes. While not uncritical of the weekend – some of it was regarded by Philip as 'rubbish' – the weekend itself functioned to provide a continuing source of inspiration for the life and work of the church.

There is one other feature that is important to highlight at this point. In addition to the worship aspect of the church, there is an attitude of acceptance already mentioned. This also comes, in large measure, from the influence of Dave Tomlinson, who encourages people to doubt and to be able remain within a church. ACC also sees itself as a place where people can doubt and still remain within the Christian fellowship. As Philip observed, Dave Tomlinson's book 'reflects where people are at'. Again Philip is not uncritical of Dave Tomlinson and feels, perhaps, that he has gone too far down the postmodern track and suggests that his acceptance has become a kind of collusion.

The cause of the split of ACC from its parent church reflects an attitude of non-authoritarian leadership. Quite clearly members of the church who did transfer felt that the leadership was at fault, with matters getting 'out of control'. The informants played down this aspect of authoritarian leadership but an outside contact, familiar with the situation at the time, assures me this was the main feature he recollects from the episode. In this regard, it is significant that the leadership model adopted by the church is a 'flat triangle', with the downplaying of hierarchy.

The church recently signed an ecumenical covenant agreement with mainstream churches. It must be one of a few in the New Church movement to have done so nationally. It belongs to the

Evangelical Alliance group as well as the ecumenical group of churches. Its uniqueness in this regard for an independent charismatic church is surely wider than the region. Such ecumenical commitment suggests that it does not see itself as the sole representative of true religion. The fact that it can happily belong to the Evangelical Alliance in addition suggests something of the polarity expressed by Cox. Indeed the following features reinforce the tension of fundamentalism and experientialism within the church.

As recorded in the foundation documents (chapter 4), the Scripture citations and their use is at times literalistic. Not all the preachers were literalistic but this approach is sufficiently in evidence to warrant a mention. It is also clear from the use of the book of Ezra, which is applied directly in order to provide scriptural authority and inspiration for a basic framework for the church.

During one sermon the elder, Thomas, clearly showed anti-intellectual tendencies, which is a usual characteristic of fundamentalism, if omitted in the description by Cox. He declared that logic was the enemy of faith, that knowledge could be dangerous, and that faith is unscientific. This was counteracted in a private conversation afterwards by Philip. He remarked that he was positively disposed to higher education, evidenced in his possession of two degrees. Despite this, the suspicion of intellectual pursuits to issues of faith was something worth noting.

It was reported that three people had been converted during the Alpha course. This indicated that evangelism was on the agenda and that the church, despite its pluralism, was concerned to bring people into the faith. The idea that there was a gospel to be proclaimed was clearly in evidence.

Finally, in this section, it is important to observe that the use of glossolalia in the church was almost entirely private. Singing in tongues occurred corporately two or perhaps three times in a yearly period. The only occasion of public speaking in tongues that was clearly audible occurred during the period of my research, although I was not present on that occasion. No interpretation was offered at the time and no explanation given subsequently. A couple of times it was evident that some people were quietly speaking in tongues to themselves, after songs especially. But this was hardly public and lasted only a few seconds at a time. The private use of glossolalia among those interviewed had declined significantly for only a few. However, the majority of interviewees continued to use glossolalia privately on a daily or weekly basis.

4. A Church Leader's Interview (Edited)[15]

In order to focus on the question of glossolalia and postmodernity in the space available, one church leader will be used to provide the focus. I shall essentially use the interview transcript as a starting point from which to enter into the wider picture within the church's worldview.

Philip is one of the church leaders. He is aged between 40–49, is married to one of the other church leaders, and they have four children (two are fostered). He works as a director of a charity. Philip has a classical Pentecostal background with the Assemblies of God denomination. He had been involved with the parent church for 15 years and had been one of its leaders before leaving to be a founding member of the ACC.[16]

After the greeting, the initial conversation was about personality profiles and testing. Philip understood a recent profile that he had taken to be encouraging since it affirmed his ability as a leader. He was the kind that led when the situation demanded it.

★   ★   ★

MARK   What do you understand by the phrase speaking in tongues?

PHILIP   I've always understood that tongues consisted either of unknown human tongues or of angel tongues. I've heard examples given by reputable first-party observers of the use of human tongues that were unknown to the speaker but were known to speakers in the room at the time. So that's what I would understand them to be.

MARK   How long have you been speaking in tongues yourself?

PHILIP   Since I was 17, so 30 years.

MARK   Can you tell me about your initial experience? I know it's a long time ago.

PHILIP Oh no, I remember it. Being in a Pentecostal church the blessing of baptism in the Spirit accompanied by tongues was promoted. In certain circumstances, special meetings and conferences and stuff, there was always the opportunity for people seeking the blessing to meet and be prayed for. And I received the gift of tongues in 1968 in Butlins in Bognor Regis of all places, probably in the Gaity Ballroom or something [*laughs*].

MARK And did that accompany your baptism in the Spirit?

PHILIP Yeah, I would say so at the time, in view of what I knew at the time. I had been prayed for on previous occasions and arguably might have received other kinds of tokens of the Spirit's presence, which in other circumstances I might have interpreted at that time as being baptism in the Spirit. But certainly in terms of speaking in tongues I would say that was the day I was baptized in the Spirit.

MARK Given your understanding of tongues, accompanying baptism in the Spirit, do you think that it's still the norm?

PHILIP I always felt that was the norm. I was brought up in quite a theologically aware sort of church. The pastor of the church was, I would say, quite a profound student of the Word. He was a big Pentecostal minister for donkey's years and stretched back into the 1920s in Liverpool. It was the only Pentecostal church and where, going back to that time, there was significant debate and opposition including up to 1000 people turning up for a debate. So he was a guy who had investigated and come up with all the logic, and the support and the understanding of it, and he was very clear at teaching it. The core material was about the incidences in the Acts of the Apostles where there are something like five occurrences or reports of people baptized in the Spirit. I think on three occasions tongues were specifically mentioned. And on the occasions where they weren't mentioned, it was described that the onlookers saw or heard that the Holy Spirit had come upon them, so there is an implication of some external evidence.

MARK And do you still hold to that belief?

PHILIP   I think so, broadly. I wouldn't want to say if you haven't spoken in tongues, you haven't been baptized in the Spirit. But I think I'd still broadly follow the same line.

MARK   How frequently do you speak in tongues?

PHILIP   Not very frequently [*laughs*], probably once or twice a week, a small amount, not a lot.

MARK   How does your current experience compare to your original experience?

PHILIP   It is fair to say it's declined . . . down the years.

MARK   Why do you think that is?

PHILIP   I think the most accurate thing to say would be it's almost habit. It's something that you kind of practise or you don't practise. I suppose there'd be times early on where it was fairly natural to speak in tongues when I was pottering around, and when I was sort of praising God generally on my motorbike or whatever. And it's just a habit that I've got out of, I think, more than anything else. It still just occurs now and again, just a few sentences, probably the most would be a couple of times a week, you know. It's years since I've spoken in tongues publicly in the church. In fact I've only done that once or twice.

MARK   Would you wish to describe it as a language, despite what you've called it?

PHILIP   In terms of my own tongue, I think it's an interesting one. Something can be a language but you can be inadequate at speaking that language. You can be, I suppose, using the analogy of the English language, you can speak as a baby and you can use repetitive words and onomatopoeic words and things like. And I think when I speak in tongues nowadays it tends to be that. And I'm aware of times in the past when for various reasons I've spoke more extensively, at a time either at a prayer meeting or something out loud or to myself. There's almost like been a conscious effort to expand the vocabulary and to kind of spread it around and learn a bit more and allow the Spirit, you know, to lead a bit more.

MARK   And did that happen?

PHILIP   Yeah, I'm fairly sure that happened. What's more normal I think would be, I suppose, you get down to praying, and you tend to use, in English, expressions like, you know, 'thank you Lord' and 'praise you Lord'. To me like, using a tongue is on the same limited range, limited vocabulary of phrases as part of the general setting as you're getting down to praying in more detail, if you know what I mean. So I suppose the short answer would be yes, I would regard it as a language, in the sense of words which exist, words which have some objective existence somewhere as opposed to just sounds.

MARK   But you don't know what the language is?

PHILIP   No.

MARK   But somewhere in the real world, that is in human existence, or do you mean a heavenly sense?

PHILIP   Or in a heavenly sense, yeah, that's where, you know, I'm not sure. And of course the problem with that is it can always be a little bit of a get out because if you can't actually identify the human language that it is, you can say well it's a heavenly language. There's probably a whole load of languages in heaven that we don't know about.

MARK   Can you speak in tongues when you want to, or not?

PHILIP   I can do but I'd be inhibited to do so just within a kind of experimental way.

MARK   But are you in control?

PHILIP   Yes, it's there all the time.

MARK   Who would you say you are speaking to when you speak in tongues, to whom are the words directed?

PHILIP   I would say towards God. I can think of occasions when I've been praying quite fervently, not very many of them, but there's been the odd one or two. And I have felt that I've really got a grip of praying in tongues and really, almost as the Scripture describes it, as the Spirit praying for us because we're unable to find the words and the fervency in our own language.

MARK   And it's always God-directed?

PHILIP   Yeah.

MARK   Is this ability to speak in tongues limited in any sense to a particular time or place?

PHILIP   No, not for me.

MARK   When and where do you speak in tongues most often?

PHILIP   In prayer in private, in the home or, you know, driving or wherever, but when I'm on my own, or just praying with my wife.

MARK   You mentioned that you'd given a public tongue in the past. Can you describe this occasion?

PHILIP   Right. As I said that, I realized that's not actually correct. I was getting mixed up – what I've done publicly is give an interpretation of tongues but I can't actually recall having stood and given a message in tongues. I've prayed out loud in public places using tongues when a lot of other people have been doing the same kind of thing.

MARK   And maybe sung in the Spirit?

PHILIP   Yeah, I've sung in tongues quite frequently, yeah. Thank you for reminding me of that. That's something else I do quite frequently. Certainly in leading worship there've been a number of occasions when we've let the worship flow and people have begun to respond and sing and in those situations I often sing in tongues. And because I'm up the front leading it's in that sense it's audible, although it's not sung out for the congregation to listen to it's just me singing. And then that often turns into singing words of English, whether it's a translation or whether it's just a way of moving on I don't know.

MARK   How do you understand the idea of the interpretation of tongues? Can you tell me what understanding you have of that gift?

PHILIP   Well, in terms of my understanding of it, I think the key word is interpretation rather than translation. I suppose, if pressed on it, I'd say things like tongues may sort of contain the burden of the message and may open a door of thought and the interpretation picks up that thought. And at that point I think the distinction between interpretation and maybe prophecy starts to get a little bit blurred. I would say interpretation is a prophetic response to a tongue which kicks off from the burden of the tongue that's been given.

MARK   To whom is it directed?

PHILIP I've known interpretation of tongues to be directed in two ways really, either to a congregation in terms of God speaking to people, or to be inspired praise and worship which is interpreted, 'Oh Lord you are mighty', and stuff like that.

MARK   When you speak in tongues, how do you feel? Are there any particular emotions that you feel or that you go through?

PHILIP It's a fairly natural expression for me, so words would be like, you know, peace and nearness to God, I suppose, and things like that. I wouldn't describe it as ecstatic utterances . . . I mean I'm using that word ecstatic deliberately because that's obviously the terminology that's used: 'ecstatic utterances'. And I think that carries with it the sense of out of control almost, you know, like a well absolutely flowing over. That was probably the case when I was first baptized in the Spirit, and there's probably been the odd occasion since, when without being out of control, there's certainly been a real welling up. But the more general experience has been of it being one form of expression, a fairly natural form of expression. In public contexts it is associated with a feeling of nearness to God and a feeling of the Spirit coming upon me. They're the contexts in which it happens, you know. Whether one causes the other or whether these are two sorts of things that happen when you get near to God I'm not sure.

MARK   What effect do you think it has upon others who hear you or anyone else speaking in tongues?

PHILIP I think that given the context in which it happens for me, and in ACC, it would generally be associated with sort of warm and intimate feelings of worship. And with a variety of singing and things going on like that which I guess would be impressive in the sense that they're having an impression on people, but generally a positive impression. I've been in situations where the tongues expressed have been more wild and ecstatic and actually a bit more frightening.

MARK   What do you think about the record of speaking in tongues in the Bible?

PHILIP   The occurrences of tongues tend to be associated with new moves forward of the gospel and the Spirit into different contexts, hence the various incidences in Acts of the Apostles. It tends to be quite visible in the life of the church in the early stages in the early epistles and things of that sort, notably Corinthians, where there's misuse of tongues. I'd hesitate to draw the conclusion from that it was something which was very much an initial burst for the Apostolic age which was not important to a church. I would tend to feel that it was probably something that fell into disuse within the church. But it's difficult to draw the evidence from the New Testament. You've either got to conclude, say if you're looking towards the Pastoral epistles which are that much later, you've either got to conclude by the fact that it's not mentioned that it tended to fall a little bit into disuse and not be an issue. Or else the use and the theology was understood and under control and therefore didn't become an issue for them actually talking about it.

MARK   You mentioned about the misuse in 1 Corinthians: are you thinking of any particular kind of individual texts?

PHILIP   Yeah, I'm thinking of Paul's expression where he's having a go at the Corinthians about the mismanagement of things but actually makes a statement that he speaks in tongues more than any of them. 'I thank God I speak in tongues more than you all.' I would draw from that that tongues was an everyday part of Paul's experience and again, extrapolating from that, that there's no real reason why it should be anything other than a normal part of the experience of anyone. But that would be a fairly significant statement.

MARK   What Christian books about speaking in tongues or spiritual gifts have you found helpful, or general books about spiritual gifts that contained the gift of tongues?

PHILIP   Most of the things I've accumulated or read on tongues are a long time ago now, because in many ways over the last 20 years it's become a bit of a non-issue. This is either because it's toned down and fallen a bit into disuse in vaguely charismatic churches; or more particularly because I suppose 20–25 years ago there was quite a lot of debate about the rightness or wrongness of the origin, the source of tongues. I get the feeling that in a sense the charismatic approach to things has more or less swept the board and there's not a lot of people now who would vociferously stand out against these things. But the general attitude would be either accepting of it or promoting of it or living with it. I think so, and it may be that I'm out of touch with what's going on, and what's being published but I've not seen it referred to . . . I've not, for myself, tended to go down the line of being an apologist for certain things because it hasn't been an issue. I've not moved in circles where people have been making me go back to my roots and start defending it.

MARK   Has there been any other teaching material, tapes or video or anything like that, that you've found helpful?

PHILIP   No, never used anything of that sort. Back in my day, young man, we never had such things [*laughs*]!

MARK   I'm interested in a comment that you make earlier that tongues were a big issue but now it's not an issue in the Charismatic Movement. It's no longer overtly concerned with these things, or doesn't appear to be. Why do think that is? Why do you think there's been this downplaying of tongues? If it's so vital, if it is initial evidence, which you believe in baptism of the Spirit, why has it been downplayed?

PHILIP   OK, just working back to what I was saying. I think what you've just said probably is fair, I think. What I was initially saying was that the issue about being charismatic, i.e. believing in the baptism in the Spirit and associated miraculous gifts and things like that, seems to me to be in most cases almost like an old battle. In that it's not an issue. I don't keep much track of what goes on in the Christian world round about and things like that. But certainly there's been a bit of a sense that over the last ten years that one of the main things that Evangelical Alliance has done has been because of the kind of people that have been positioned there and have gained the respect of different churches. They've been trying to pull together, creating quite a bit of unanimity among wings of the church which in the past would have been quite dissenting in various ways. And I think Spring Harvest has tended to belong to a broadly charismatic framework and I'm not aware that there are many people, many mainstream people, who are standing up and actually resisting this and saying 'This is a work of the Devil. Miracles don't happen anymore, and tongues is a sign of a disturbed demon-infested person'. It is probably true to the experience of our church that tongues as an everyday phenomenon is much lower down in terms of usage and concern than it was in the early days. And I suppose that mirrors my own experience. It's almost like a novelty thing about it. In the early days of being baptized in the Spirit and filled with the Spirit and having the gift of tongues there is a lot of use of it, but it tends to sink a bit more into the background with other concerns.

MARK   Are there any other factors do you think in general for its demise?

PHILIP   I suppose you could answer that by saying: what are some of the things that have risen to prominence in terms of public worship in the last 20 years? Going back to the church I used to belong to, a Pentecostal church. Public worship was a piano and hymns and a lot of open worship where people could pray, give messages in tongues and prophesy. But it was very much a participative almost a Brethren-type approach, where people were expected to take part and to share particularly in prayer and was very restrained in the sense of terms of public music. One thing obviously happened over the last 20 years is that worship music, as a phenomenon if you like, has really grown rapidly. And I think one of the less useful outcomes of that is the fact that there's an emphasis now on front-led celebratory-type meetings with a lot of music. A lot of singing and correspondingly less opportunity for participation from people who are there, partly because of the size of meetings and partly because of style. A premium is set on having a worship leader who can engage the congregation and take them along in the flow, you know, and away you go. And in one sense that doesn't necessarily inhibit the use of tongues, and in another sense it doesn't particularly provide a very fruitful ground in which tongues can be used as part of personal meditative worship within a worship context. So there may be a factor that wasn't there in an earlier time.

MARK   Is there anything else, just before we close, that you can think of? Am I asking the right questions? Are there questions that if you were doing this study you would want to ask, but I haven't asked?

PHILIP   No, I think that makes sense. I mean just for the record, I was saying earlier on about having had first-hand accounts of tongues which had been genuine languages. I just mention one, just for interest whether it's of any interest to you. This happened in the church that I belonged to before I attended the ACC. It was reported by the pastor, and there's no reason to doubt the veracity of it. There had been a guy who was in the church for a while who had been a missionary in China, and a tongue was given by a local person in Mandarin, and he was actually surprised that there was a Mandarin speaker in the church. And of course on investigation it was a tongue. And there's lots of other stories but that's the only one that I can say I knew the person who was there, who actually heard this happen and knew the person who was the Chinese speaker. That's the nearest thing I get to something that I would say I'm confident that's a true account.

MARK   Thank you very much indeed.[17]

5. Fundamentalist/Experientialist Analysis

In order to reflect upon the fundamentalist/experientialist scenario in light of the data, I begin with the fundamentalist tendencies first. The following characteristics can be observed.

Philip is still conscious of his Assemblies of God (AOG) background. On the issues of speaking in tongues he referred to experience and reading material from his youth, citing Pentecostal writers such as Harold Horton and William Burton (omitted from this edited transcript). This was evident in his belief in the AOG doctrine of a second post-conversion blessing, as part of conversion-initiation, called baptism in the Spirit. The initial evidence of such occurrence was the manifestation of tongues speech.[18] Philip believed that this doctrine was normative. In keeping with his classical Pentecostal background, he believed that tongues speech was literally either human or angelic.

The use of the Bible by Philip suggests that it is not just a book of signs to be used pragmatically but rather that it carries divine authority (although the language of 'biblical inerrancy' is not in evidence). As such the Scriptures provide norms for the Christian life, not just good ideas. So, just as on the day of Pentecost the apostles spoke in xenolalia, that is, genuine human foreign languages, so it is expected as a possibility today. Philip believes the account of a reputable first-party observer regarding the claim that tongues speech in a particular instance was xenolalia, in this case Mandarin. He recognizes the difficulty in verifying such a claim but was clear that he believes in this instance that the report was genuine. He also believes that St Paul's experience of being able to speak in tongues was normal and normative.

Philip shows some signs of intolerance. He is intolerant of wild and 'ecstatic' charismatic phenomena. He is unhappy with such manifestations and feels that greater controls should be in place to check such matters. This is accompanied by a resistance to 'prosperity theology'.[19] A couple of people had joined the church with such a theology but they had been given 'short shrift'.

In contrast, the experiential tendencies can be seen in the following features.

Philip claims to have had experiences of the Spirit other than baptism in the Spirit. He recognizes that only some have the public gift of tongues with most having the private gift. He is not an apologist for tongues and in fact noted the decline in his own use of the gift. In this matter he shows signs of being a pragmatist. Although he still uses tongues, he has moved on and his spiritual experience base has shifted away from tongues as the focus of his spirituality. He would say that the novelty has worn off over the 30 years he has spoken in tongues.

He is not concerned with the promotion of speaking in tongues as the evidence of baptism in the Spirit. For him this issue, so hotly contested in the late 1960s and early 1970s, is no longer perceived as important. It is a non-issue and consequently a non-authoritarian approach is adopted.

The use of the gift of tongues within the church is almost entirely located in private use. This mirrors Philip's own practice. Only occasionally does singing in tongues occur and this is often instigated by Philip as a worship leader. The almost entire use of tongues within the private sphere is a sharp move from the public dominated use of classical Pentecostalism. Indeed, following the classical Pentecostal distinction between sign and gift, Philip regards tongues as only one of the gifts in the spiritual repertoire of the Christian. This is similarly described by another interviewee who understood the spiritual gifts to be like tools in a toolbox. Each has its use as appropriate to the need of the task.

While Philip dislikes the use of the word 'ecstasy', as it conjures up images of people being out of control, he did admit to having the occasional dissociational state initially with glossolalia. However, the main public use of tongues at ACC is by means of 'singing in the Spirit'. That is when a number of people collectively join to harmonize in the musical use of glossolalia. In the church context, this contributes to an atmosphere of mysticism, 'associated with sort of warm and intimate feelings of worship'. This mystical element in worship is not just through the use of tongues, but by the use of other mechanisms such as silence and meditation.[20] The symbols used to communicate with God at a deep level have been expanded. This suggests more of a postmodern turn that even Cox envisions.

6. Conclusion

It is suggested that Philip, as a leader of the church, is a good focal person through whom to view the rest of the church. With this in mind some comments are made regarding the future of glossolalia in a postmodern charismatic church.

The person of Philip demonstrates the conflict predicted by Cox. He contains within himself the two poles of fundamentalism and experientialism. He has been influenced substantially by Dave Tomlinson, yet retains his fondness for the classical Pentecostalism of his youth. He stands on a definite theology and belief system with one foot, yet with the other he paddles in the fast flowing streams of postmodernity. He is clearly more at home in the stream but does not want to jump in because of the consequences of such an action (drowning comes to mind!). He has not abandoned the classical Pentecostal narrative of tongues; it just no longer has the same relevance to church life that it once did. Therefore, there appears to be a disjunction between what he believes and what he practises as a church leader. The church does not promote either the baptism in the Spirit or the gift of speaking in tongues. It simply accepts the validity of them for the individuals concerned.[21]

The consequence of this disjunction is the privatization of glossolalia almost entirely.[22] Since glossolalia has little if any public role, its symbolic significance is obtained from private use where it becomes a symbol of private devotion.[23] If the primary use of glossolalia in classical Pentecostal and neo–Pentecostal interpretation is public, as evidence of a phenomenon in the conversion–initiation process, then the secondary use is private through personal devotion. (Notwithstanding the fact that sometimes people only ever spoke in tongues at their baptism in the Spirit.) In postmodernity this has been reversed. Instead, the private sphere is primary, with the public sphere having a secondary role. In the place of a definitive sign of the sacred (initial evidence), one finds a collection of symbols and mechanisms for enabling people to worship God and make sense of reality. In this church artistic expression, meditation, silence and Eucharistic liturgies have been adopted for this purpose.

Philip does not like Cox's term 'ecstasy' and I have some sympathy with him. In the material gathered from the interviewees, it was clear that glossolalia does meet a need, within their belief system, in terms of communication with God. There is a conviction that the person is meeting with God at a deep and personal level. I would suggest that the term best suited to describing this need is not the word ecstasy, but rather intimacy.[24] In this present culture, the superficiality of much of human discourse and engagement hides the human longing for intimacy. In religious terms, this need for intimacy is being met through the use of glossolalia, as people believe they are communicating at a deep level with God. But in a postmodern church this symbol is only one symbol through which such encounters occur.[25] Other symbols could be those associated with the Toronto Blessing as well as ones drawn from other different religious traditions. What can be said from this case study is that if postmodernity is a cultural reality, and not just a product of academic discourse, then the needs of people will be expressed in various religious symbols. In a truly postmodern age the nature of the symbols will vary and glossolalia will become only one symbol among many used in religious practice. It will be used for a time, dropped for another symbol and possibly picked up at some future date.

The definition of glossolalia in terms of primal speech raises an important question in terms of how Philip understood the linguistic nature of his tongues-speech. On this matter he said:

> In terms of my own tongue, I think it's an interesting one. Something can be a language but you can be inadequate at speaking that language. You can be, I suppose, using the analogy of the English language, you can speak as a baby and you can use repetitive words and onomatopoetic words and things like that. And I think when I speak in tongues nowadays it tends to be that . . .
>
> I suppose you get down to praying and you tend to use, in English, expressions like, you know, 'thank you Lord', and 'praise you Lord'. To me like, using a tongue is on the same limited range, limited vocabulary of phrases as part of the general setting as you're getting down to praying in more detail, if you know what I mean. So I suppose the short answer would be yes. I would regard it as a language, in the sense of words which exist, words which have objective existence somewhere as opposed to just sounds.[26]

This suggests that the understanding of Cox might have some basis, but that the interpretation one gives to the linguistic nature of the tongues speech will depend, to a large extent, upon the conceptual framework out of which one is working. Thus for Philip, he acknowledges similar characteristics to Cox, but nevertheless interprets the speech in terms of objective language, which is consonant with his Pentecostal background.[27]

Finally, a note of caution is worthy of mention. The positions described by Cox of fundamentalism and experientialism are indeed polarities. They represent the ends of the spectrum, and in some measure the framework of Cox is simplistic. While I regard Cox's framework as interesting and a useful conceptual model, I have reservations about the use of both these terms. In particular, the problematic nature of defining 'fundamentalism' is exacerbated by the pejorative connotation it carries. It is here that the problem of Cox's model becomes most apparent. To acknowledge the plurality of fundamentalism is one thing, but to elucidate the nature of fundamentalism in relation to evangelicalism is quite another, for example in relation to the Evangelical Alliance.[28] It is important that such elucidation takes place if the portrait of Pentecostalism and the Charismatic Movement is to be credible. Therefore, a more nuanced understanding of Evangelicalism in relation to the concept of fundamentalism is needed.[29] Such a nuanced approach could considerably sharpen the conceptual model that Cox has given us.

7. Methodological Reflection

This study started by responding to the theoretical work of Harvey Cox. I consciously wanted to engage with his theoretical proposals because of the significance of his work and the importance of the issue of cultural shift from modernity to postmodernity. That is why I started with a theoretical stance. Having done this, I began to re-analyse the qualitative data from the case study material. I did this by means of content searches and analysis. This was followed by a further engagement with the theoretical literature in a broader sense although focused around the primary concerns of Cox. This enabled me to both affirm and yet qualify the theoretical perspective of Cox on this significant matter. It is hoped that such a reflection will move the discussion forward in relation to the issue that he raises.

The focus of this chapter represents it original design, which was theoretically orientated, therefore the conclusion focuses rightly on comments which renewed understanding of the theoretical construct being tested. However, one recommendation can be suggested for renewed theological praxis. In terms of glossolalic praxis, it could be suggested that the gift of speaking in tongues be understood within the search-encounter-transformation model. That is, a search for God associated with a sense of beauty and awe, an encounter with God associated with intimacy and power, and a transformation by God associated with edification in the faith for the purposes of the kingdom of God. Clear teaching on the sacrament of the Lord's Supper and the doctrine of the Trinity could enable a Trinitarian and sacramental understanding of glossolalia to develop.[30] This recommendation could inform both public and private use of the gift in worship and prayer.

---

[1] This chapter was originally published as 'The Future of Glossolalia: Fundamentalist or Experientialist?', *Religion* 28.3 (1998) pp. 233–44. It now contains an edited version of the interview transcript that was omitted from the earlier published version. I am grateful to 'Philip' for his ongoing permission to use this material.

[2] P. Hocken, *Streams of Renewal: The Origins and Early Development of the Charismatic Movement in Great Britain* (Carlisle: Paternoster, 1986) p. 171; A. R. Mather, 'The Theology of the Charismatic Movement in Britain from 1964 to the Present Day', University of Wales, Bangor, 1982, p. 2.

[3] Glossolalia can be defined as 'free vocalization', that is, a connected sequence of speech sounds that do not belong to a language that the speaker knows and which the speaker cannot identify. The casual observer might suppose that the language was an unknown language. V. S. Poythress, 'Linguistic and Sociological Analyses of Modern Tongues-Speaking', *Westminster Theological Journal* 42 (1979) pp. 367–88 (p. 369).

[4] The influence of John Wimber and the so-called 'Third-Wave' movement of the 1980s may have been influential in this regard. 'Here there is neither recognition of a subsequent experience of baptism in the Holy Spirit nor of tongues as evidence of the Spirit's infilling' – V. Synan, 'The Role of Tongues as Initial Evidence' in M. W. Wilson (ed.), *Spirit and Renewal: Essays in Honour of J. Rodman Williams* (Sheffield: Sheffield Academic Press, JPTS 5, 1994) p. 78. Cf. K. Springer (ed.), *Riding the Third Wave: What Comes after Renewal?* (Basingstoke: Marshall Pickering, 1987), which appears to omit any comment on baptism in the Spirit and glossolalia.

[5] H. Cox, *Fire from Heaven: The Rise of Pentecostal Spirituality and the Reshaping of Religion in the Twenty-first Century* (London: Cassell, 1996).

6 Ibid. p. 299.

7 Ibid. p. 305.

8 Ibid. ch. 4.

9 Ibid. p. 86.

10 Ibid. pp. 88–9.

11 Ibid. p. 87. This may be questioned in terms of Pentecostal doctrinal formularies. For example, M. Poloma cites the official Assemblies of God position to be: 'The baptism of believers in the Holy Ghost is witnessed by the initial physical sign of speaking with other tongues as the Spirit of God gives them utterance (Acts 2:4). The speaking in tongues in this instance is the same in essence as the gift of tongues (1 Cor. 12:4–10), but different in purpose and use (*Statement of Fundamental Truths*, 1969).' *Assemblies of God at the Crossroads: Charisma and Institutional Dilemmas* (Knoxville: University of Tennessee Press, 1989) p. 39.

12 Cox, *Fire from Heaven*, p. 87.

13 D. Davies, 'Social Groups, Liturgy and Glossolalia', *Churchman* 90 (1976) pp. 193–205 (especially pp. 202–3).

14 D. Tomlinson, *The Post-Evangelical* (London: Triangle, 1995).

15 The original unedited interview would have been too long for this chapter. I have attempted to take a recorded conversation and turn it into written text for public consumption, which is always going to be reductionist in some way. The interview is dated 13 February 1996.

16 It is, perhaps, important to observe that Philip has as much experience in the New Church movement (formerly House Church movement) as he had in classical Pentecostalism. The other interviewees have wider Charismatic Movement involvement through mainstream denominational charismatic renewal, the New Church movement, or parachurch meetings, for example the Good News Crusade Camp (associated with Don Double).

17 The original interview lasted 57 minutes.

18 F. D. Bruner, *A Theology of the Holy Spirit: The Pentecostal Experience and the New Testament Witness* (London: Hodder & Stoughton, 1970) pp. 76–87; Synan, 'The Role of Tongues', pp. 67–82. For a recent Pentecostal statement on the evidential nature of tongues see R. P. Menzies, *Empowered for Witness: The Spirit in Luke–Acts* (Sheffield: Sheffield Academic Press, JPTS 6, 1994) ch. 13.

19 R. Jackson, 'Prosperity Theology and the Faith Movement', *Themelios* 15 (1989) pp. 16–24; P. Cotterell, *Prosperity Theology* (Leicester: Religious and Theological Studies Fellowship, 1993); T. Smail, A. Walker and N. Wright, ' "Revelation Knowledge" and Knowledge

of Revelation: The Faith Movement and the Question of Heresy',
Journal of Pentecostal Theology 5 (1994) pp. 57–77.

[20] For comment on the 're-mystification' of worship by means of
glossolalia and prophecy, see M. B. McGuire, 'The Social Context of
Prophecy: "Word-Gifts" of the Spirit among Catholic Pentecostals',
Review of Religious Research 18 (1977) pp. 144–5.

[21] It has been suggested to me that Philip's position is similar to the
position adopted by some within the Christian Missionary Alliance in
the USA, that is, the 'seek not, forbid not' position formulated by
A. W. Tozer in the 1940s. Cf. Synan, 'The Role of Tongues', pp.
73–5. However, that position was formulated because glossolalia was
hotly disputed and a cause of disunity. Philip is quite clear that tongues
speech is a 'non-issue', which is a very different context for such a
position indeed.

[22] See A. Walker, *Telling the Story: Gospel, Mission and Culture* (London:
SPCK, 1996) pp. 167–70 for comments on the privatization of religion
in postmodernity.

[23] I am aware also of some of Paul's writings in the New Testament as
stressing the primacy of the private use of tongues, and I have discussed
this elsewhere. See M. J. Cartledge, 'The Nature and Function of
New Testament Glossolalia', *Evangelical Quarterly* 72.2 (2000) pp.
135–50. Initially, it perhaps suggests a parallel to the premodern, but
in this case one might expect there to be a more frequent use of
glossolalia publicly which, in this context, does not appear to happen.

[24] Although it must be noted that the use of the word 'ecstasy' in relation
to glossolalia and modernity is not new and predates discussion of
postmodernity. See O. R. Whitely, 'When You Speak in Tongues:
Some Reflections on the Contemporary Search for Ecstasy', *Encounter*
35 (1974) pp. 81–94. However, a more recent study states that:
'Believers view this new relationship with God, whether it be
manifested in tongues or public testimonies, as a personal gift from
God given to the individual to enable him/her to communicate on
an informal, intimate level with God. Therefore, God gives the believer
a special prayer language to express this relationship.' See D. L.
Sequeira, 'Gifts of Tongues and Healing: The Performance of the
Charismatic Renewal', *Text and Performance Quarterly* 14 (1994) p.
139.

[25] On the subject of symbolism see F. W. Dillistone, *The Power of Symbols*
(London: SCM, 1986). Glossolalia as a symbol signifies a divine-
human encounter which transcends the boundaries of one's native
language as it points to both God's transcendence (it is above and
beyond the speaker's known human language) and God's immanence

(yet by means of human utterance). For a sacramental understanding of glossolalia, see F. D. Macchia, 'Tongues as a Sign: Towards a Sacramental Understanding of Pentecostal Experience', *PNEUMA: The Journal of the Society for Pentecostal Studies* 15 (1993) pp. 61–76.

26 Interview extract dated 13 February 1996.

27 A point well made by D. Middlemiss, *Interpreting Charismatic Experience* (London: SCM, 1996) ch. 3.

28 Cox, *Fire from Heaven*, p. 302.

29 See I. H. Marshall, 'Are Evangelicals Fundamentalists?', *Vox Evangelica* 22 (1992) pp. 7–24; M. Percy, 'Fundamentalism: A Problem for Phenomenology?', *Journal of Contemporary Religion* 10 (1995) pp. 83–91; and M. Percy, *Words, Wonders and Power: Understanding Contemporary Christian Fundamentalism and Revivalism* (London: SPCK, 1996).

30 See M. J. Cartledge, *Charismatic Glossolalia: An Empirical-Theological Study* (Aldershot: Ashgate, 2002) pp. 187–205.

7

Charismatic Women
and Prophetic Activity[1]

1. Introduction

My research in the area of contemporary prophecy started back in 1986 and culminated in a dissertation and a number of publications.[2] Since then I have focused on the related subject of glossolalia.[3] As I return to this subject, inevitably my thinking has moved on, and I now find myself asking a slightly different set of questions. In an attempt to answer these questions, I was prompted to turn to my quantitative empirical database that I gathered through my doctoral studies. I reviewed this data in order to see what kinds of observations could be made and this naturally led me back to the literature and the issues that arise there.

In my earlier work, I argued that prophecy as a concept should not be limited to the specific gift of prophecy, but that a broad definition of prophecy should start with the revelatory experiences through which Christians believe God communicates. This means that other prophetic types of experiences would also be considered under the rubric of prophecy.[4] Therefore, the category terms of 'the word of wisdom', 'the word of knowledge', 'the discernment of spirits' and 'the interpretation of tongues' would also be included as prophetic activity.[5] Worship and prayer tend to provide the context in which a revelation is received by someone and this would need to be relayed in order to be prophetic activity in a proper sense.[6] The revelatory experience may contain 'words coming to mind', a 'sense' of the message, visions, dreams and pictures, physical sensations and impressions and the interpretation of tongues (glossolalia).[7] Therefore one would expect there to be a close association between all the gifts which could be classified as prophecy, although a message directed to the congregation in the context of worship would appear to be what most Pentecostal and charismatic churches understand by the term.

In this chapter I aim to concentrate upon the concept of prophetic activity. This means that the power of definition as to what is and what is not prophetic lies with the individual person concerned. The survey data used in this paper assumes that the persons responding know what these categories are and can locate their Christian activity in relation to them. But in order to focus the paper I shall review the position of a key commentator on Pentecostalism and the questions that he raises.

2. Pentecostal/Charismatic Women and Prophecy Activity

Once again, I turn to Harvey Cox and his celebrated book on the subject of Pentecostal spirituality. In a key chapter he explores how many Pentecostal women have taken leadership roles within the church.[8] He particularly focuses on Aimee Semple McPherson,[9] but mentions other notable women such as Lucy Farrow, Marie Burgess, Florence Crawford and Maria Woodworth-Etter. These women, according to Cox, felt able to assume a public ministry because of the Pentecostal interpretation of Acts 2:17: that 'your sons and *daughters* shall prophesy'.[10] They assumed that this included the calling to *preach* the gospel as well as heal the sick. Indeed, Cox argues that when Pentecostals entered into theological alliances with the (so-called) Fundamentalists they also had to take a literalistic reading of 1 Corinthians 14:34 into account, that is the Pauline injunction that women should be silent in the assembly.[11] Therefore there remains a tension for Pentecostals in what ministries they encourage women to enter.[12] Globally, however, Pentecostal women play a significant role in testifying, prophesying, healing, counselling and teaching within the church.[13]

From Cox's own investigation, he posits two questions, which he then attempts to answer. First, '*How* do women justify the leadership roles they play in a church which seems to be controlled by men at the top and in which "official" theology (at least where literalistic interpretation of the Bible obtains) seems to forbid them?' Second, '*Why* are women drawn to Pentecostalism in such disproportionate numbers in the first place, and why do they feel it is so urgent to carry the word to others?'[14]

He answers both of these questions with reference to the ministry of Aimee Semple McPherson (1890–1944). In terms of the first question, he observes that she never paid much attention to official theology but, being sure of her vocation and calling, she organized her own work, church life and denomination. When she died, the church she founded, namely the Church of the Foursquare Gospel, numbered 410 churches and 29,000 members. It now numbers 25,577 affiliated churches and 1,700,000 members in 74 countries.[15] He also answers the first question by considering the testimony of Betty Lou Carter. He recalls her testimony in which she claimed to have been healed and called to a preaching ministry because of a prophetic and visionary experience. His reflection on this episode is as follows:

> It is clearly demonstrated why Pentecostals, who take the authority of the Bible very seriously but also believe in direct revelation through visions, have opened a wider space for women than most other Christian denominations have. What the Bible says is one thing, but when God speaks to you directly, that supersedes everything else.[16]

Cox classifies this kind of experience according to the well-known call–refusal motif. The individual initially rejects the calling because of how the Bible is read today. However, God will not accept the refusal and the person finally accepts the call and becomes obedient.

The prophetic nature of Aimee Semple McPherson's ministry is captured in one of her biographies. In the account of her early ministry with her husband, Robert Semple, in the company of William Durham, she discovered that she had the gift of interpreting tongues. Edith L. Blumhofer recounts that:

> It was under Durham's tutelage that Aimee discovered she had the gift of interpretation of tongues, a gift she exercised with frequency and eloquence for many years. Pentecostals believed that messages in tongues uttered in public meetings should ordinarily be interpreted by someone divinely gifted to express in English the heavenly message

given in the unknown language . . . The gift bestowed on Aimee a considerable degree of cultural authority within the congregation and made full use of the oratorical skills and persuasive powers that had won her medals during her school years. Stylistically her interpretations resembled Old Testament prophecies; long before she was famous, they were considered so remarkable among the many interpretations Pentecostals heard that they were frequently taken down steno-graphically and published as having meaning far beyond the local setting in which they were uttered.[17]

This account suggests that it was because of her charismatic authority that she gained the respect and *cultural authority* of early Pentecostalism.

Cox answers the second question by analysing how Pentecostalism works in the context of San José, Costa Rica. In this setting, family problems, such as alcohol abuse and marital unfaithfulness, are tackled. Women who are desperate to bring some kind of order to family life are being converted and subsequently introduce their husbands to Pentecostalism. While Third World Pentecostal women might believe that their husbands should be the head of the home, they interpret this to mean that he should accept responsibility to earn money in order to support the household.[18] Cox summarizes his understanding when he says:

For decades Pentecostals were persecuted in many parts of Latin America. So, since they could not gain access to the public arena, they worked mainly through family networks. This happened just as the old family structure was being weakened by new forms of production and made co-operative family work less economically viable and often took the man out of the home for long periods of time. But, the importance still attached to traditional familial connections provided a ready-made network for recruitment. The Pentecostal conviction that everyone has the responsibility to spread the word did the rest. Wives brought husbands, children brought parents, in-laws and cousins and aunts testified to each other. For women, the Pentecostal message provided the best way they could see to effect a genuine change in their family relations, to get their men to forgo some of the macho posturing the popular culture encourages, and to reorder the priorities on how the limited family income was spent.[19]

Cox also observes that as women joined the church they also benefited from a wider supportive group that enabled them to receive
skills and education.

One could summarize Cox's answers by saying that: (1) the space
that Pentecostalism provides with its radical egalitarianism of the
Spirit enables more traditional evangelical hermeneutical approaches
to be set aside in favour of full participation, especially by women.[20]
In this sense Luke–Acts takes priority over the Pauline and Pastoral
Epistles; and (2) that the role of familial networks in the Third
World provides a conduit for recruitment to Pentecostalism and
enables change in the quality of family relations, which is often
initiated and sustained by women.

Bernice Martin in an insightful article – not least because of its
uncovering of paradigmatic blinkers of the sociological and feminist
academy – draws both these aspects together in her description of
Pentecostal gender relations as paradoxical. She states that:

> It is true that women are seldom allowed to become pastors and there
> are usually restrictions on their participation in the leadership of the
> ministry of the Word as well as strict regulations controlling dress and
> bodily adornment, but women are especially favoured with spiritual
> gifts in a movement which is, after all, expressly constituted around
> the gifts of the Spirit. Women supply most of the healers and prophets,
> they are particularly prone to be 'slain in the Spirit', they receive the
> gift of tongues and the gift of prayer. Their extensive religious discourse
> steadily feminizes the Pentecostal understanding of God.[21] Above all,
> women have used the Pentecostal religious discourse to rewrite the
> moral mandate on which sexual relations and family life rest. In societies
> characterized by a tradition of male dominance they have been enabled
> to institute family discipline, sanctioned and effectively policed by the
> church community, which puts the collective needs of the household
> unit above the freedom and pleasures of men and which has called an
> end to the long-tolerated double standard of sexual morality.[22]

This means that Pentecostal men have been 'domesticated' and
restrained, even if the *de jure* system of patriarchal authority in church
and home remain intact. This greater shift in gender equality can
be accommodated provided that women do not usurp men's
authority, especially in the public domain. Therefore, while gifts of
the Spirit enable a radical egalitarianism, it is carried inside a formal

patriarchal casing. It appears to suit both men and women that this gender paradox remains unresolved. [23]

Therefore this chapter shall explore the empirical-theological consequences of two questions that will be posed of the empirical data. First, what is the social context of women in the sample? Second, what is the charismatic context of women's ministry in relation to prophetic activity? These two questions represent the areas located by Cox's questions, although I have reversed the order, and material gathered from the data will be used in order to engage with them afresh. The significance for this new data in relation to Cox's argument will be subsequently explored.

3. Method

For a summary of the method see chapter 4. In addition to standard questions concerning gender, age, marital status, qualifications, occupation and church denomination, a further key question for our purposes was also asked. It was phrased as follows:

- Please tick one box in each row to indicate how often in the past six months you have done the following things:
    - given a public utterance in tongues
    - interpreted tongues
    - sung in tongues
    - given a positive testimony about the Toronto Blessing
    - prophesied
    - danced in the Spirit
    - given a 'word of wisdom/knowledge'
    - received a definite answer to a specific prayer request
    - felt led by God to perform a specific action
    - given a prophecy privately to another person
    - been 'slain in the Spirit'
    - heard God through a dream or vision
    - given a testimony about miracles
    - experienced the Toronto Blessing
    - experienced 'laughing in the Spirit'
    - prayed for the salvation of specific people

The answer options were: none, 1–6, 7–12, 13–18, 19+.

4. Results

The following tables present the results of data analysis. I have used crosstabulation with a chi-square test, t test and correlation using Pearson's measure. These tests seek to discover the measure of association between different variables.

Table 7.1: Crosstabulation: gender and marital status (% within gender)

	Single	Married	Widowed	Divorced	Divorced and remarried
Male	19.2	72.1	0.8	4.6	3.3
Female	17.1	64.0	8.0	8.8	2.1
$X^2 = 20.94$	P = .000				

Table 7.1 shows that gender is significantly associated with marital status. The majority of respondents are married (72.1% of men and 64.0% of women).

Table 7.2: Crosstabulation: gender and qualifications (% within gender)

	CSE	GCSE	O level	A level	Dip HE	Degree	Higher degree
Male	7.9	8.4	14.2	8.9	23.7	30.0	6.8
Female	8.3	7.6	27.3	13.1	23.5	18.0	2.1
$X^2 = 26.74$	P = .000						

Table 7.2 shows that gender is significantly related to educational qualifications. The question asked respondents to name their highest qualification attained. The results show that more men have higher qualifications than women. For women the most dominant educational categories are O level (27.3% of women) and Diploma in Higher Education (23.5% of women).

Table 7.3: *Crosstabulation: gender and occupation (% within gender)*

	I	II	IIIN	IIIM	IV/V	*Unemployed*	*Housewife/ retired*	*Student*
Male	13.3	26.7	12.1	13.3	7.6	6.7	12.9	4.6
Female	1.8	19.7	23.1	6.5	1.8	2.1	37.8	2.6
X^2 = 111.26	P = .000							

Key:

Class I = professional (e.g. doctors, lawyers, accountants and surveyors)
Class II = intermediate (e.g. sales managers, nurses, teachers and aircraft pilots)
Class IIIN = non-manual skilled (e.g. typists, shop assistants and clerical workers)
Class IIIM = manual skilled (e.g. cooks, butchers, electricians and hairdressers)
Class IV = partly skilled (e.g. bar staff, bus conductors, postworkers and caretakers)
Class V = unskilled (e.g. cleaners, porters, window cleaners and messengers)

Table 7.3 shows that men attain higher occupation status compared to women. The largest single occupational category for women is housewife/retired (37.8% of women). Gender was not significantly related to the variables of age and church denomination.

Table 7.4: *Comparison of mean scores for men and women for charismatic activity*

	Men			Women				
	N	Mean	SD	N	Mean	SD	t	P
Interpretation of tongues	216	1.31	0.58	345	1.21	0.51	2.11	.035
Prophesied	214	1.97	1.23	350	1.55	0.91	4.33	.000
Word of wisdom/ knowledge	220	2.02	1.09	345	1.74	0.89	3.31	.001
Prophesied privately	215	1.73	0.98	346	1.52	0.78	2.70	.007
Slain in the Spirit	218	1.40	0.70	3.48	1.60	0.91	−2.90	.004

Table 7.4 shows the mean scores for men and women for the items from the key question that are significantly related to gender. The probability value (P) of the t statistic indicates that there is a significant difference between men and women in respect of the interpretation of tongues, prophecy, the word of wisdom and knowledge and private prophecy. For these items men have a significantly higher mean score. This indicates that they participate in these activities more frequently than women. For instance, the higher mean shows clearly that men exercise the prophetic gifts more frequently than women. However, women have a significantly higher mean score for being slain in the Spirit, otherwise known as

Table 7.5: The correlation between charismatic activity and prophecy (Pearson's r)

	Prophesied	Prophesied privately
Public utterance in tongues	.253**	.164**
Interpretation of tongues	.399**	.274**
Sung in tongues	.385**	.223**
Testimony of the Toronto Blessing	.328**	.273**
Danced in the Spirit	.304**	.177**
Word of wisdom/knowledge	.615**	.521**
Answer to prayer	.337**	.375**
Led to act	.366**	.386**
Slain in the Spirit	.183**	.175**
Heard God through dream or vision	.316**	.348**
Testimony about miracles	.194**	.259**
Experienced the Toronto Blessing	.249**	.257**
Laughed in the Spirit	.157**	.161**
Prayed for the salvation of others	.128**	.158**
Prophesied	—	.591**
Prophesied privately	.591**	—
** = significant at the .01 level		
* = significant at the .05 level		

falling to the ground under the power of the Spirit. It is interesting to note that being slain in the Spirit is also considered to be a feature of the so-called Toronto Blessing.

Table 7.5 shows how various variables measuring charismatic activity are associated with prophecy. The most strongly associated items are: (1) word of wisdom/knowledge with prophesied; (2) prophesied with prophesied privately; (3) word of wisdom/ knowledge with prophesied privately; (4) interpretations of tongues with prophesied; and (5) led to act with prophesied privately. But since these activities strongly inter-correlate it means that they provide an indisputable context for the exercise of prophetic gifts.

5. Discussion

In terms of the first question, it is clear the majority of charismatic Christians contained within the sample are women (61.0%) who are married and whose qualifications are at the level of O levels or Higher Education Diploma in the British educational system. Their social class is skewed by the large housewife/retired category that includes 37.8% of females. The majority is located between the categories of Class II, lower professional (19.7%), and Class IIIN, skilled non-manual (23.1%). This large housewife/retired category suggests that perhaps many of these women are housewives rather than retired. A crosstabulation of gender and age reveals that 17.7% of women are aged 60 and over and would therefore classify them-selves as retired as well as housewives. Therefore 20.1% of women who are non-retirement age are classified as housewives. This affirms their role as housewives to be proportionally significant and second only to the Class IIIN (23.1%). This would fit in well with the rough balance between working and non-working Christian wives in Britain. It suggests that while the home is important for women they are also taking advantage of the working opportunities that are available to them.[24] This means that the social context of women in Britain is possibly more complex than in Costa Rica, with its differently constructed labour market. They are not perhaps as dependent upon their spouses for financial security. Therefore, the social factor that Cox claims as being significant in the attraction of women to Pentecostalism cannot be sustained by this data.

In terms of the second question, it is clear from Table 7.4 that men prefer prophecy much more, compared to women. The charismatic context of prophecy for men is the wider use of other word gifts, namely the gift of interpretation of tongues and the word of wisdom/knowledge. Men strongly prefer the gift of prophecy over these other gifts, although this also sustains some conceptual overlap. Table 7.5 gives the wider context of charismatic activity for the sample as a whole. While there is a number of activities that significantly correlate with prophecy, it is the word of wisdom/knowledge that leads the group. This again suggests the close relationship of these two items. The inter-correlation between prophesied, prophesied privately and the female preference for being slain in the Spirit suggests that women also find prophetic activity important, although the activity of falling down under the power of the Spirit is perhaps the mechanism through which they receive these other prophetic activities.[25] The link with the Toronto Blessing in the contemporary charismatic church is suggestive of a new context for cultural authority in today's church.

Clearly the charismatic men represented in this sample find themselves using the word gifts mentioned above much more than women. It suggests that such regular activity is valued by men, otherwise the mean scores would not be so significant. However, the reason for the attraction of men to charismatic activity is beyond the information of the database. Yet one could suggest that perhaps it is a direct consequence of male institutionalization. In this case male charismatic authority supports institutionalized authority of the churches. However, it is also clear that female charisma finds *some* expression. In other words, some cultural authority is possessed and expressed by women. Unfortunately, the survey does not ask any questions concerning male 'headship' or leadership roles, otherwise female cultural authority could be tested in relation to this concept directly.

Margaret Poloma, as noted earlier, has observed that the Toronto Airport Vineyard Church (TAV), now called the Toronto Airport Christian Fellowship (TACF), was seen to encourage women at one level, namely by encouraging women in prophetic ministry. However, it is interesting that at an institutional level only one of the pastoral leadership team was a woman.[26] Does this mean that the encouragement of women to enter into prophetic activity functions as a means of inclusion and exclusion? It includes women and affirms their prophetic activity and ministry but also appears to contain them within this realm. Does it, paradoxically, exclude them from an institutional ministry since they are not affirmed at this level? If this is the case, it suggests that charismatic authority also carries the potential for marginalization of women who own it because of its capacity to threaten the institutional order.[27] Women, of course, may prefer the freedom of cultural authority and charisma over and against the restriction of institutional order. Nevertheless, for those women who feel called both to a charismatic and an institutional ministry, there is a tension in a way that perhaps does not exist for men.

6. Conclusion

To conclude this chapter, I offer one suggestion as to how many women combine their cultural authority of prophetic activity with institutional authority within Pentecostal and charismatic churches. It is through the notion of 'joint ministry', that is, being married to a man in ministry. The man holds the 'official' position of authority and guards the institutional order, seen especially in the notion of 'headship'. In the churches in the survey, men are also the main carriers of the cultural authority of prophetic activity. However, wives, by means of marriage, have access to leadership roles that would be otherwise denied them. This is illustrated in the early ministry of Aimee Semple McPherson who, through her marriage to Robert Semple, was able to minister and gain a significant amount of cultural authority by means of prophetic activity. This was seen through her use of the interpretation of tongues, which was probably the most important authoritative means of prophecy for Pentecostals because of the association with speaking in tongues that usually preceded it. But it was also demonstrated through visions. While in London with her husband Robert she received a vision of what she called the 'Dispensation of the Holy Spirit', which was a Pentecostal view of church history from the day of Pentecost to the parousia.[28] Thus her marriage *in combination with* her charismatic gifting enabled her to access a certain amount of cultural authority within the context of the Pentecostalism of the time.[29] Therefore, the interpretation of tongues and visionary statements belong together in the early ministry of Aimee Semple McPherson.

When we turn to the contemporary charismatic church we find a similar phenomenon, although not with tongues, but with the Toronto Blessing. Poloma seeks to answer the question to women's ministry in relation to women pastors, but if our analysis is correct, it is with the wives of pastors that we shall locate the locus of charismatic authority among women. This is indeed the case at the TACF. John Arnott is the senior pastor of the church. But when one begins to review the ministry of the church through the medium of its video material we see the emergence of John's wife, Carol.[30] Carol Arnott features in particular through the testimony of her vision while experiencing the Toronto Blessing. During a time when she is lying on the floor under the power of the Spirit, or slain in the Spirit, she has a vision of Jesus and the church. It is an eschatological vision about the end of the age and encourages anticipation of the parousia. It has its basis in Scripture, but it is a call to the contemporary church, the bride, to get ready for the bridegroom. The context for this vision is 'carpet time', not the interpretation of tongues. Vineyard charismatics do not subscribe to speaking in tongues to the same extent as classical Pentecostals. Instead the dominant narrative of the 'power encounter' through a time of ministry provides the theological and sociological context. Thus it differs in this respect from early Pentecostalism at the beginning of the century.

The commonality between the two examples concerns charismatic women involved in the appropriation of cultural authority by means of both prophetic activity *and* marriage to a church leader.[31] Therefore is it not surprising that the marriage provides a consistent factor in establishing the ministry of charismatic women. Prophetic activity is a means of gaining authority alongside their husband's more institutional authority. When the husband dies, as in the sad case of Robert Semple for Aimee Semple McPherson, or is removed from the scene, naturally the woman enters a time of crisis. This crisis is unresolved until the ministry is re-established either by the same mechanism of marriage or by means of a recovery of the original charismatic authority witnessed initially with her husband but this time without him. Indeed, it is not uncommon for women to continue in a successful ministry without their husband because of the initial experience of charismatic authority and its reception by a local church. In this way the church continues to be blessed by the prophetic activity of charismatic women. Of course, the key question concerns the ministry of single charismatically endowed women. To confine them to certain ministries in restricted parts of the world is not a satisfactory solution, nor was it ever so. The church universal needs their gifts and their ministries. Therefore, one could also say 'let your [single] daughters prophesy'! Amen, brothers?!

7. Methodological Reflection

This chapter, as I have already said in the introduction, was written initially as a journal article. For that purpose I reviewed my earlier work before re-analysing my survey database. This raised some interesting questions. At this point I reviewed the most recent literature and decided to specifically test the ideas associated with Harvey Cox by means of an historical lens, namely through the life and work of Aimee Semple McPherson. I subsequently reflected upon the findings theologically and in relation to the contemporary situation (Carol Arnott). I became alerted to the work of Bernice Martin and others and have supplemented the original article with further material for the purpose of this chapter. What emerges is a theological reflection on gender relations and charismatic activity.

The issues of pneumatology are complex in this area with the hermeneutical concerns being highly significant. It seems that Pentecostals will continue to emphasize Luke–Acts over Pauline material. This is partly driven by a predisposition for narrative and theology done in terms of *via salutis* rather than the Reformed *ordo salutis*. The work of Janet Everts Powers raises the issue of cessationist evangelical hermeneutics in relation to the ministry of women.[32] The arguments she advances need to be taken seriously. From the above discussion, it could be suggested that we should be grateful for the women who have faithfully served God, despite resistance from men! We need to have compassion on those who suffer in this imperfect world of gender relations; to have courage to persist and remain hopeful for the transformation of all things when there will be righteousness, joy and peace. I would like to suggest that churches frequently review the role of men and women in relation to institutional and charismatic authority and power. The marginalization of single gifted women called to Christian ministry needs to be addressed in practical ways for the sake of the kingdom of God. The study has highlighted the paradoxes of the Pentecostal and charismatic traditions in this regard. What is the Spirit saying to the church? Perhaps the Spirit is prodding us to listen to each other afresh, to understand each other's hermeneutical paradigms, the diversity as well as the unity of the biblical witness, and to enable a greater sensitivity in the church's use of the biblical texts.

---

1 This chapter was originally published as 'Charismatic Women and Prophetic Activity', *The Spirit and Church* 3.1 (2001) pp. 97–111. I have revised it for this present publication.

2 'Prophecy in the Contemporary Church: A Theological Examination' (Master of Philosophy dissertation, Council for National Academic Awards, 1989); 'New Testament Prophecy and Charismatic Prophecy', *Themelios* 17.1 (1991) pp. 17–19; 'Charismatic Prophecy: A Definition and Description', *Journal of Pentecostal Theology* 5 (1994) pp. 115–26; 'Charismatic Prophecy', *Journal of Empirical Theology* 8.1 (1995) pp. 71–88.

3 'Tongues of the Spirit: An Empirical-Theological Study of Charismatic Glossolalia' (PhD dissertation, University of Wales, 1999). A revised and abridged version is published as *Charismatic Glossolalia: An Empirical-Theological Study* (Aldershot: Ashgate, 2002).

4 For a typology based on field research, see Cartledge, 'Charismatic Prophecy', pp. 79–82.

5 Cartledge, 'Charismatic Prophecy: A Definition and Description', pp. 81, 88–99.

6 M. Turner regards New Testament prophecy as essentially oracular speech that was based on a revelatory impulse. For a full discussion of New Testament and contemporary prophecy, see M. Turner, *The Holy Spirit and Spiritual Gifts: Then and Now* (Carlisle: Paternoster, 1996) pp. 185–220, 315–28.

7 Cartledge, 'Charismatic Prophecy: A Definition and Description', pp. 82–8.

8 H. Cox, *Fire from Heaven: The Rise of Pentecostal Spirituality and the Reshaping of Religion in the Twenty-first Century* (London: Cassell, 1996) ch. 7.

9 See E. L. Blumhofer, 'Reflections on the Source of Aimee Semple McPherson's Voice', *PNEUMA: The Journal of the Society of Pentecostal Studies* 17.1 (1995) pp. 21–4; and J. M. Everts, 'Brokenness as the Centre of a Woman's Ministry', *PNEUMA: The Journal of the Society of Pentecostal Studies* 17.2 (1995) pp. 237–43.

10 Also noted by W. K. Kay as the legitimating text behind equal use of the gifts of the Spirit by men and women during the Sunderland Conventions (1908–14). See W. K. Kay, 'A Woman's Place is on her Knees: The Pastor's View of the Role of Women in the Assemblies of God', *Journal of the European Pentecostal Association* 18 (1998) pp. 64–75 (p. 66).

11 Cox, *Fire from Heaven*, p. 125. See also the discussion by D. G. Roebuck and K. C. Mundy, 'Women, Culture, and Post-World War Two Pentecostalism' in T. L. Cross and E. B. Powery (eds), *The Spirit and the Mind: Essays in Informed Pentecostalism* (Lanham, MD: University Press of America, 2000) pp. 191–204, who suggest that the allegiance between Pentecostalism and Evangelicalism in the 1950s and 1960s also coincided with a stress on the role of women as 'homemakers'.

12 See D. M. Gill, 'The Contemporary State of Women in Ministry in the Assemblies of God', *PNEUMA: The Journal of the Society for Pentecostal Studies* 17.1 (1995) pp. 33–6; S. Benvenuti, 'Anointed, Gifted and Called: Pentecostal Women in Ministry', *PNEUMA: The Journal of the Society for Pentecostal Studies* 17.2 (1995) pp. 229–35; S. C. Stanley, 'Spirit Women: Alma and Aimee Reconciled?', *PURITY AND POWER: Revisioning Holiness and Pentecostal/Charismatic Movements for the Twenty-first Century* (27th Annual Meeting of the Society for Pentecostal Studies in special session with the Wesleyan Theological Society, 1998, vol. 2-Z) pp. 1–13.

13 M. Poloma notes how the former Vineyard church at Toronto shows signs of valuing the prophetic ministry of women. See 'Charisma, Institutionalization and Social Change', *PNEUMA: The Journal of the Society for Pentecostal Studies* 17.2 (1995) pp. 245–52.

14 Cox, *Fire from Heaven*, p. 125.

15 Ibid. p. 127.

16 Ibid. p. 131.

17 E. L. Blumhofer, *Aimee Semple McPherson: Everybody's Sister* (Grand Rapids MI: Eerdmans, 1993, 1998²) p. 81.

18 Also noted by D. Martin, *Pentecostalism: The World their Parish* (Oxford: Blackwell, 2002) pp. 75, 99, how women influence their husbands to better things by appealing to 'unequivocal religious norms', 'and may also reinforce their argument by inconvenient prophetic revelations' (p. 99).

19 Cox, *Fire from Heaven*, p. 136.

20 See J. E. Powers, '"Your Daughters Shall Prophesy": Pentecostal Hermeneutics and the Empowerment of Women' in M. W. Dempster, B. D. Klaus and D. Peterson (eds), *The Globalization of Pentecostalism: A Religion Made to Travel* (Carlisle: Regnum/Paternoster, 1999) pp. 313–37. See also J. E. Powers, 'Recovering a Woman's Head with Prophetic Authority: A Pentecostal Interpretation of 1 Corinthians 11.3–16', *Journal of Pentecostal Theology* 10.1 (2001) pp. 11–37.

21 Martin, *Pentecostalism*, pp. 103–4, drawing upon Sicilian Pentecostalism, explains this by saying that while the Pentecostal God is 'the God and Father of our Lord Jesus Christ', the imagery of worship is of long-suffering, broken-hearted pursuer of human hearts 'lover and mother in one' (p. 103). In Sicily, the Virgin Mary is displaced by Sophia, Divine Wisdom, the Holy Spirit, who feminizies both the 'Father of all' and Jesus. 'Clearly, these mutations provide spaces in which to negotiate new roles. It can do this, it would seem, precisely because the "Father" is not toppled; as ever, a revolutionary attack would generate the resistances which guarantee its own future rigidity, whereas a radical conservation allows space for changes which are masked for safety. As a result over time they become merely accepted' (p. 104).

22 B. Martin, 'The Pentecostal Gender Paradox: A Cautionary Tale for the Sociology of Religion' in R. K. Fenn (ed.), *The Blackwell Companion to Sociology of Religion* (Oxford: Blackwell, 2001) pp. 52–66 (p. 54).

23 Ibid. p. 55.

24 Thus suggesting a reversal of the 'homemaking' stereotype associated with post-World War Two Pentecostalism. See Roebuck and Mundy, 'Women, Culture and Post-World War Two Pentecostalism', pp. 203–4.

25 It is interesting to note that Martin, 'The Pentecostal Gender Paradox', p. 54 observes that women are prone to being 'slain in the Spirit'!

26 Poloma, 'Charisma, Institutionalization and Social Change', p. 250.

27 This containment is expressed by Kay, 'A Woman's Place is on her Knees', p. 72, when he suggests that the Pentecostal male ministers prefer to value women's ministry in terms of prayer because it is a substitute for action (and thereby interference!). It is men who *both* pray and act. Women are confined to the ministry of prayer and domestic duties.

28 Blumhofer, *Aimee Semple McPherson*, pp. 87–8.

29 An interesting comparison is the ministry of Mary Boddy, the wife of Alexander A. Boddy, the founding father of British Pentecostalism, who exercised the gifts of the Spirit, as well as teaching and writing ministries. See Kay, 'A Woman's Place is on her Knees', p. 66.

30 See J. Arnott, *God's Love: Bottom Line* (Toronto Airport Vineyard, 272 Attwell Drive, Toronto ON, Canada, 1995).

31 D. Martin, *Pentecostalism*, p. 99 notes how in Pentecostalism husband and wife teams minister as a family to families and thus break the norm of an all-male clergy.

32 Powers, 'Recovering a Woman's Head With Prophetic Authority', *passim*.

8

Interpreting Charismatic Experience and the Toronto Blessing[1]

1. Introduction

The Toronto Blessing has raised important questions regarding Christian experience generally and in particular experiences associated with the Charismatic Movement. The phenomena associated with the Toronto Blessing, such as people falling or rolling over, laughing or weeping uncontrollably, and jerking and making strange noises that appear to have an animal quality all raise the eyebrows of observers. The obvious questions that spring to mind include: what is actually happening here? How can these activities be explained? Indeed, a variety of explanations have been and continue to be offered. These include sociological, psychological, physiological and theological explanations.[2] The movement itself appeals to church history and biblical texts to justify these experiences.[3] David Middlemiss in his book *Interpreting Charismatic Experience* advocates a philosophical and theological approach to assessing such experience, and offers a reflection in the light of the theory of hypnosis.[4] This idea in relation to the Toronto Blessing appears to be the first serious attempt of its kind. Previously John P. Kildahl had argued for a hypnotic interpretation of glossolalia.[5] However, Middlemiss makes no reference to the work of Kildahl, or indeed to any other psychological reflection upon glossolalia. Therefore it seems opportune to consider the argument of Middlemiss in the light of the work of Kildahl and those who have assessed his theory. In addition, it will be useful to consider the relationship of hypnosis to altered states of consciousness, since an understanding of charismatic experience in terms of altered states of consciousness has been proposed by Patrick Dixon. The earlier debate between

Felicitas D. Goodman and William J. Samarin on glossolalia and altered states of consciousness will be noted and used to inform the discussion. However, I shall also test some of these ideas in relation to survey data in order to provide independent comment upon them.

2. Charismatic Experience and Hypnotic Techniques

Middlemiss compares some of the common features in charismatic gatherings with hypnotic techniques and observes points of comparison. For the sake of brevity I have re-categorized his 23 points into three key areas.

First, Middlemiss compares the *situation* or context in which hypnosis can be practised with charismatic worship or Vineyard-style workshops. He argues that in both situations there is often a crowd in which individuals are hypnotized. People are encouraged to share accounts or symptoms of their experience one with another, either formally or informally. The atmosphere is regarded as safe and secure; it is both gentle and relaxed. There is a confidence in the leader and an expectation that something important and exciting is about to happen, often encouraged by the leader.

Second, the main *technique* that Middlemiss attributes to hypnotists and charismatic church leaders is 'suggestion'. People are aware beforehand of the kind of phenomena that occur and they are encouraged to be passive. This passivity is ideal for hypnosis. During times of 'ministry', Middlemiss suggests that the instructions to the person receiving prayer are comparable to post-hypnotic suggestion (that is, in a way congruent with the person's desires). In all of this the critical mind is bypassed. People are encouraged to accept the supernatural interpretation and detach themselves from the 'Western rational paradigm'. Those who prove stubborn may be bombarded with suggestions until they abandon resistance and suspend their critical faculties.

Third, the *effects* of hypnosis and charismatic experience are similar. These include, for example, a sense of time distortion, physical changes such as feelings of heat and cold, feelings of warmth in limbs, changes in heart rate and respiration, fluttering of eyelids and the movement of limbs into strange positions as muscles relax.

Some muscles may gain strength because sometimes conscious restraint imposed on muscular activity is removed during hypnosis. There are often reports of healing under hypnosis and Middlemiss suggests that these healings are mainly of the psychosomatic variety, since most people hypnotized and involved in the Charismatic Movement are normal and healthy. Indeed he observes that it is mostly healthy people who are able to be hypnotized. Psychologically disturbed people generally do not respond well to times of 'ministry'.

Middlemiss claims that there are significant similarities between charismatic phenomena and the effects of hypnotic techniques. The leaders are not practising hypnotic techniques consciously but unconsciously. Therefore, the conclusion reached is that the Charismatic Movement has unintentionally tapped into the psychological techniques of hypnosis. This raises the question of whether hypnosis is acceptable as a Christian practice. If it is a means of bypassing the conscious mind to get access to the subconscious, one needs to ask: 'What has been placed in the mind when it was in this state?'[6] Middlesmiss contends that the experience itself is too ambiguous to be a reliable sign of the work of the Spirit.

Although Middlesmiss is familiar with some of the literature in the field of hypnosis, he admits that the literature is vast and that various theories offer different explanations. This is certainly true. However, one would expect, as in any academic discipline, that Middlemiss would at least give a working definition of the term 'hypnosis'. This he prefers not to do but instead leaves the term undefined. Such a lack of clarity can only build on the popular understanding of hypnosis as a sleeplike state of insensibility with loss of volition.[7] The picture of a hypnotist swinging a watch is nevertheless abandoned so as to include charismatic worship leaders who apparently use hypnotic induction techniques.[8] The popular understanding of hypnosis is built upon implicitly while at the same time certain modifications enable the parallel to charismatic worship to be tenable. But behind this strategy is a methodological commitment to a theoretical perspective. From Middlesmiss's description it is clear that he stands within the 'trance' school of thought. Surely such a proposal would have been more significant had it contained a clear theoretical framework from the start.[9]

Instead, what we have is an *ad hoc* use of theory which, on the surface, appears to have a number of connections with charismatic experience.[10]

This assumption concerning the nature of hypnosis is therefore supplemented by other assumptions within this comparison of hypnosis with charismatic experience. The assumptions include: connections between hypnosis and charismatic experience in terms of (1) the same atmosphere, (2) the same phenomena and (3) by deduction, the same cause. The key issue, therefore, is the alleged causal relationship between hypnotic techniques, operating under certain conditions, to produce certain effects. In order to explore this idea further, some previous studies will be reviewed.

3. Speaking in Tongues and Hypnosis

John P. Kildahl in his book *The Psychology of Speaking in Tongues* tested five hypotheses.[11] First, that glossolalics were more suggestible, submissive, dependent and therefore more able to follow a leader than non-glossolalics. Second, that glossolalics initiated tongues speech while thinking about and feeling close to some kind of leader who is strong and masterful. Third, that glossolalia was a form of regression in the service of the ego. Fourth, that the emotional benefits of speaking in tongues did not last long. Fifth, that glossolalia was a real human language. He claimed that his results showed that the first three hypotheses were corroborated while the fourth and fifth were not. For the purposes of this chapter, his first hypothesis concerns us. A similar hypothesis to Kildahl's second is considered in chapter 10 within the discussion of glossolalia and the theory of socialization.

For Kildahl, his research showed that complete trust in the leader was vital. Tongues emerged out of a dependency syndrome and relied upon an external authority. The leader exerted pressure and sometimes people stopped speaking in tongues because they had 'fallen out' with the leader. They were therefore deprived of acceptance, contentment and well-being. Indeed, so close was the relationship to the leader that the tongue-speaker often developed speech which resembled that of the leader. Thus, for Kildahl, hypnotizability requires trust in someone else and constitutes the *sine qua non* of glossolalic experience.[12] If one is unable to be hypnotized, then one is unable to speak in tongues. Glossolalia is not synonymous with hypnosis but it is similar to it and has the same roots in the relationship of the subject to the authority figure. Post-hypnotic suggestion affirms that life will be better and that speaking in tongues is a sign of God's approval, which leads to a sense of well-being.

This theoretical perspective finds support in the work of E. Mosimann, who equated all ecstatic experience with hypnotic states. These states lead in turn to two negative dimensions, namely: (1) the domination of the unconscious mind; and (2) the susceptibility to suggestion.[13] There is also support in the work of H. E. Gonsalvez, who in a study of Catholic charismatics argued that glossolalics evidenced a greater tendency to the hysteric-type personality characterized by hyperexcitability, low frustration tolerance, emotionalism, instability, suggestibility and dependency.[14] However, A. A. Lovekin and H. M. Malony observe that only concerning one or two variables such as submissiveness or suggestibility do glossolalics differ from non-glossolalics.[15]

In contrast, a good number of scholars have argued against this from their own research. J. E. Coulson and R. W. Johnson compared a group of classical Pentecostals with Methodists. They found that those who did not speak in tongues were more *external* in locus of control than those who did speak in tongues. In other words, the non-glossolalics were more dependent on authority figures and more suggestible than glossolalics.[16] This confirmed the results of earlier research.[17] N. P. Spanos and E. C. Hewitt also tested the association between high levels of hypnotic suggestion and suggestibility.[18] They found that glossolalics matched non-glossolalics, with no difference found between the two groups regarding hypnotic suggestibility. Therefore they claimed to discorroborate Kildahl's hypothesis from their data. L. J. Francis and W. K. Kay also tested the hypnotizability-suggestibility hypothesis on a group of Pentecostal ministry candidates.[19] They proposed that a negative correlation existed between glossolalia and neuroticism, as defined by the Eysenck personality scale. That is, the greater the association with glossolalia, the lesser the neuroticism score. In this scale a high neurotic tendency would be consistent with high suggestible tendencies. The results confirmed a statistically significant negative correlation thus discorroborating the hypnotizability-suggestibility hypothesis. Finally, G. Neanon and J. Hair confirmed in their study, also using the Eysenck personality scale, that charismatic Christians were neither more neurotic nor more imaginatively involved than either non-charismatic Christians or the general population at large.[20]

4. Charismatic Experience and Altered States of Consciousness

Patrick Dixon has considered the phenomena associated with the Toronto Blessing in his book *Signs of Revival*.[21] He accepts that:

> the style of worship in some Vineyard meetings could slightly predispose some to a very mild hypnotic effect. The music is often gentle, almost soporific. But then so is Gregorian chanting in an ancient Cathedral, or the chanting of a long metricated psalm.[22]

The settings in which charismatic phenomena have occurred are, however, sufficiently varied for that explanation to be questionable. As Dixon himself explains:

> I have seen identical manifestations develop in a near identical way in meetings large, small and tiny, hyped up or low key, silent or noisy, strongly led or with an absence of clear direction, after worship or with no music at all.[23]

Indeed any simple explanation, according to Dixon, is likely to be inadequate since what we are witnessing is complex, with a variety of factors involved.

On the question of 'suggestion', Dixon argues that all behaviour is infectious (for example, the number of people who cross their legs and arms in the room at the same time). The effect of being in a social group is therefore present in a charismatic gathering. Every church service has its own culture and each culture gives clear signals about proper and improper behaviour. The Toronto Blessing has in many places taken the existing markers away and some have been left wondering how to react. Often manifestations occur after someone has just spoken about their experience and given an explanation about what has happened to him or her. It is in this circumstance that Dixon admits that suggestion and pressure can operate.

> The degree to which that [suggestion and pressure] is significant as an explanation of some of what happens to some people will depend of course entirely upon the atmosphere, the way in which things are communicated, the words and attitudes of the ministry team as they pray for individuals, and a host of other variables.[24]

The picture is very mixed and levels of suggestion are therefore unpredictable. Suggestion may well be an ingredient in the mixture, but it exists in *every* church context.

As an alternative explanation, Dixon proposes that people experiencing the Toronto Blessing are experiencing a profound religious experience. It is an experience of an altered state of consciousness (ASC) within a group context and is often deeply cathartic. He defines an ASC as that state between our normal waking state and our unconscious sleeping state. It is the state of the daydream or the vision.[25] For example, consider Peter's trance (Acts 10), Isaiah's vision (Isaiah 6), or the visions of Daniel, Ezekiel and John (Revelation), while Paul gives an account of being 'caught up into a third heaven' (2 Corinthians 12). These biblical descriptions all appear to have the quality of an ASC. Dixon describes ASCs as including: alterations in thinking (for example, concentration, memory, judgment, perception of reality), an altered sense of time, loss of control (for example, feelings of helplessness, dizziness, weakness), changes in emotional expression (for example, frustration, fear, anxiety, sadness, euphoria), body image changes (for example, feelings of heaviness, weightlessness, numbness, tingling), perceptual changes (for example, visual imagery), changes of meaning or significance (for example, insight, illumination, truth), sense of the ineffable (for example, vivid memories which are difficult to communicate), feelings of rejuvenation (for example, hope, renaissance, rebirth), and hypersuggestibility (for example, 'People may uncritically accept the ideas and commands of others while in an ASC. This is something to be aware of . . . This is not a hypnotic state, and control is not passing to another human being').[26]

Dixon describes the triggers of ASCs physiologically as including: lack of food (compare Acts 10), sensory deprivation (for example, solitary confinement), sensory stimulation (for example, bombardment by sound and light), increased alertness or concentration, decreased alertness or relaxation of critical faculties and body chemistry alterations (for example, dehydration, sleep deprivation, drugs). However, he argues that within Christianity techniques are not stressed as the means by which we are to meet God. Rather, no effort of our own apart from repentance and the reception of forgiveness through Christ's sacrificial death can produce a close relationship with God.

I conclude this section by allowing Dixon to speak for himself.

All an altered state of consciousness does is to confront us with the reality that there is more to life than we ordinarily see, feel and touch. There is a spiritual dimension to existence. An ASC does not bring us into God's presence, but it can make us aware of a presence to be brought into. The nature of a spiritual experience during an ASC will depend on the beliefs of the person and those around him or her.

Many Christians would agree that all ASCs are likely to open doors, but the question is, open them to what? An ASC in the middle of a seance or during a voodoo ceremony could be highly dangerous. However, an ASC during an act of Christian worship could be a helpful and healing experience, which is life changing and long lasting in its beneficial effect on body, mind and spirit.

Some may find this whole discussion uncomfortable, denying that they have ever had an ASC. But who has not knelt at the communion rail and felt something outside themselves? Who has not sat in a place like King's College Cambridge and been transported to a sublime height with the soaring ethereal notes of the choir? Who has not for a moment imagined they have caught a glimpse of heavenly glory itself in a fading sunset, or been aware of the presence of God in the instant between sleep and wakefulness?

The charismatic and Pentecostal movements have been driven perhaps by a celebration of altered consciousness and the recognition that our normal conscious state is a very shallow place from which to cultivate an awareness of all God is. There has been a widespread discovery that the experiences of prophets like Isaiah and the apostle

Paul, while unique, are an indicator of what the prophet Joel promised when he said that old men would see visions and young men would dream dreams when the Holy Spirit was poured out.[27]

5. Speaking in Tongues and Altered States of Consciousness

Felicitas D. Goodman's book *Speaking in Tongues: A Cross-cultural Study of Glossolalia* contributed to the vigorous debate concerning glossolalia in the 1960s and 1970s.[28] This book continues to be of primary importance from a behavioural science perspective, since Goodman is both a linguist and an anthropologist. It is her debate with William J. Samarin, another linguist, that has contributed significantly to contemporary scholarship. It is only fitting therefore that I should take note of her work as part of that discussion with Samarin.[29]

Goodman argues that there is significant cross-cultural agreement between glossolalic utterance in each of the settings she has studied, which is a clearly defined linguistic pattern. It comprises: a threshold of onset, a brief rising gradient of intensity, a peak and often precipitous decay. Goodman suspects that an ASC is the key to the cause of glossolalic speech, so she formulates a hypothesis. She claims that: '*the glossolalist speaks the way he does because his speech behaviour is modified by the way the body acts in the particular mental state, often termed trance, into which he places himself*'. In other words, glossolalia is considered to be an 'artifact of hyperaroused mental state' (conceptualized in Chomskyan terms, that is, 'the surface structure of a nonlinguistic deep structure, that of the altered state of consciousness').[30]

Goodman's hypothesis is derived from her work with the team of Professor E. Bourguignon on the subject of cross-cultural study of dissociational states.[31] The focus of that study was dissociational states, *not* glossolalia. Nevertheless, some glossolalia was included for Goodman to have made the association. However, in the formulation of the hypothesis, it is vital that literature of the movement (that is, Pentecostalism) be consulted, not just the behavioural science studies. Had Goodman done this with some rigour, she would have appreciated that dissociation can sometimes accompany glossolalia, but that it is not to be attributed as the cause of it. Samarin puts it clearly when he says:

> Goodman's treatment is erroneous, speculative, contradictory, and incredible, because of her relentless hold on an idée fixe. Yet her empirical base was simple enough: the vocalizations of Pentecostals who appeared to be in a state of dissociation. It was because she believed her hypothesis (on the causal relation between vocalization and dissociation) that she has gone to such extremes to prove it. A more careful person, working within the best scientific tradition would have taken pains to *disprove* it. If she had failed at that, she would have had more reason to believe the hypothesis.[32]

It may be added that recent studies have tended to run contrary to Goodman's thesis. For example, N. P. Spanos and E. C. Hewitt argue that their results disagree with the trance hypothesis of Goodman.[33] Likewise G. Stanley, W. K. Bartlett and T. Moyle suggest that Goodman's hypothesis is misguided.[34] This evidence would seem to suggest that ASCs do not always accompany glossolalia, even if alleged cross-cultural data is marshalled to support the claim. So it is to the empirical data that we now turn in order to test these theoretical perspectives further.

6. Method

From the theoretical discussion, there are key questions that can be posed of the questionnaire survey data. These may also be stated by means of hypotheses, which can be tested in relation to the data. Before this, however, I need to explain an important personality measure that was used in the study because it is especially relevant to this discussion.

Eysenck Personality Questionnaire

H. J. Eysenck studied personality traits of a large number of people.[35] These traits were subsequently grouped into 'dimensions' of personality. These dimensions are related to human physiology, in particular: (1) responses to external stimuli by the brain (extraversion or introversion); (2) the autonomic nervous system (anxiety/

neuroticism or stability); and (3) male hormonal or brain activity (tough-mindedness or tender-mindedness).[36] The dimension of dissimulation was added at a subsequent stage as a check. This questionnaire uses these four dimensions to measure personality. (1) The *extraversion* scale measures sociability and impulsivity. The opposite of extraversion is introversion. A typical extrovert likes parties and has many friends, preferring social occasions to isolation.[37] (2) The *neuroticism* scale measures emotional liability and over-reactivity. The opposite of neuroticism is emotional stability. A high-scoring neurotic is anxious, depressed, sleeps badly and suffers from psychosomatic disorders.[38] (3) The *psychoticism* scale measures underlying personality traits which at one extreme define psychotic mental disorders. The opposite to psychoticism is normal personality. The high-scoring psychotic is cold, impersonal, lacks sympathy, is unhelpful and unemotional, and is paranoid that people are against him or her. The low scorers on the psychoticism scale are empathetic, altruistic, warm, peaceful and pleasant, although they may be less socially decisive people.[39] (4) The *lie* scale measures dissimulation, or lying, and consequently it is also a measure of honesty. It also measures a tendency to social conformity, as well as lack of self-insight, or immaturity.[40] Those who score low on the lie scale have a tendency to social conformity. For the purposes of this research, I shall interpret low lie scale scores as a tendency to social conformity. Recent research has suggested, contrary to earlier research, that charismatics in general are stable (scoring low on the neurotic scale) extraverts.[41]

Hypotheses

1. Experience of 'trance' affects self-control for tongues speakers.

2. Neuroticism, as a dimension of the Eysenck Personality Questionnaire (EPQ), is associated with low self-control among tongues speakers.

3. Neuroticism (EPQ) is associated with greater charismatic activity.

4. Neuroticism (EPQ) is associated with experience of the Toronto Blessing.

5. Lack of self-control among tongues speakers is associated with experience of the Toronto Blessing.

Three questions were asked of respondents regarding the nature of self-control and trance with respect to speaking in tongues. These were:

- Can you speak in tongues when you want to? Tick box answers give the options: yes, no, sometimes, don't know.
- Are you in control of yourself when you speak in tongues? Tick box answers give the options: yes, no, sometimes.
- Are you in a 'trance' when you speak in tongues? Tick box answers give the options: yes, no, sometimes.

In relation to experience of the Toronto Blessing, a question was asked as part of a selection:

- Please tick one box in each row to indicate how often in the past six months you have done the following things:
  – Experienced the Toronto Blessing
  The answer options were: none, 1–6, 7–12, 13–18, 19+

The neuroticism dimension was used from the EPQ measures. As mentioned above, high-scoring neurotics also tend to be prone to suggestibility. The reliability of this measure was given a Cronbach alpha coefficient of .8318 (12 items).

Charismatic experience was also tested by means of the Charismatic Experience Scale (CES). This scale of measurement included individual items relating to prophecy (two items), words of knowledge/wisdom, answer to prayer, leading to perform actions, and hearing God through a dream or vision. Therefore, it measures levels of charismatic experience and has a Cronbach alpha coefficient for reliability of .8212 (six items). Both these reliability coefficients are good scores that enable confidence in the results below.

7. Results

Table 8.1 shows that the vast majority of the respondents are able to speak in tongues when they want to, feel themselves to be in control of the process and refuse the language of 'trance' very

Table 8.1: Frequency counts

Speak when want to (%)		In control (%)		Trance (%)	
No	15.0	No	6.0	No	82.5
Sometimes	6.0	Sometimes	5.5	Sometimes	1.4
Yes	71.7	Yes	73.3	Yes	1.1
Don't know	2.8	Don't know	–	Don't know	–
Not applicable	4.4	Not applicable	15.2	Not applicable	15.0
Total 100.0		Total 100.0		Total 100.0	

strongly. The very small number of respondents who are categorized as 'don't know' or 'no' in relation to speaking when want to, being in control or trance represent the small minority who perhaps sense what some would call an ASC.

Table 8.2 Crosstabulation: 'speak when want to' by 'in control' (% total)

	In control		
	No	Sometimes	Yes
Speak when want to			
No	3.6	0.8	2.6
Don't know	1.1	0.4	0.6
Sometimes	0.9	0.9	4.9
Yes	1.5	4.3	78.4
$X^2 = 181.62$	P = .000		

Table 8.2 shows that most tongues speakers in the sample can both speak when they want to and believe that they are in control. This association, as demonstrated by the high X^2 value, is statistically significant.

Table 8.3 shows that neuroticism correlates negatively with the charismatic experience scale (CES), suggesting that the greater the charismatic activity the lower the neuroticism score. It also correlates negatively with 'speak when want to', suggesting that an answer 'yes' to this question is associated with low neuroticism scores.

Table 8.3: Correlations (Pearson's r)

	N	TB	CES	Speak when want to
In control	NS	NS	.107*	.553**
Speak when want to	−.213**	.092*	.206**	
CES	−.194*	.273**		
TB	NS			
★★ = significant at the .01 level.
★ = significant at the .05 level.

Neuroticism, however, is not correlated with experience of the Toronto Blessing in a statistically significant way. The inter-correlation between experience of the Toronto Blessing and the CES is positive and statistically significant, as is that between 'speak when want to' and the experience of the Toronto Blessing. There are also positive correlations between being 'in control' when speaking in tongues and the CES, as well as 'speak when want to'.

8. Discussion

The hypothesis (1) stating that experience of 'trance' affects the levels of self-control among tongues speakers is uncorroborated by this data. The results show that there is a high degree of self-control among tongues speakers. There is a small minority who do feel that their control is lost. These are statistically insignificant for the sample as a whole. But perhaps they reflect those respondents who are self-conscious of their mental state and experience what we might call an ASC.

The hypotheses (2–4) stating that neuroticism is associated with low self-control among tongues speakers, or greater charismatic activity, or experience of the Toronto Blessing are also uncorroborated by this data. The results show that neuroticism is significantly associated with 'speak when you want to' but that the direction of association is with respect to a low neuroticism score. Therefore, the weaker the neuroticism score, the greater the sense of being able to speak in tongues when one wants to. This is also reflected in the correlation between neuroticism and the CES. A negative correlation suggests that low–scoring neuroticism scores are related to greater charismatic activity. The significant positive intercorrelation between experience of the Toronto Blessing, 'speak when want to' and CES is to be expected.

Finally, the hypothesis (5), stating that lack of self-control among tongues speakers is associated with experience of the Toronto Blessing, is uncorroborated. These variables are not found to be associated in any statistically significant way. Indeed, there is a positive correlation between being in control when speaking in tongues and the CES that also tells against this hypothesis.

This means that the hypnosis theories, described in the literature above, continue to have little basis in empirical research. This research, by linking questions concerning control and the EPQ neuroticism dimension to speaking in tongues and charismatic experience more widely, has been able to suggest a new dimension to the debate. The theories which have been used in relation to speaking in tongues (Kildahl and Goodman), the Toronto Blessing and in relation to charismatic experience more generally continue to be uncorroborated empirically. In theological terms, of course, more still needs to be said concerning how ASCs are significant in relation to Christian spirituality.

9. Conclusion

I want to suggest, in line with the empirical data, that the language of control is not incompatible with the language and experiences of ASCs. There may indeed be a spectrum of intensity within the range of ASCs that somehow corresponds to greater or lesser control. It may be that if I were to ask questionnaire respondents to explain the answers they stated, I would discover that the issues of personal control are not abandoned in ASCs states, but reordered in some way that still enables ASC to be experienced. It is with this caveat from the above discussion that I offer some thoughts by way of concluding.

First, as Dixon freely admits, ASCs are indeed complex states. To focus upon only one way of considering such phenomena would appear, therefore, to be reductionist. ASCs are part of our common humanity and as such are conditioned by variables such as individual differences, social context, language and culture. That ASCs are part of many different cultures and religions should enable us to affirm the common humanity of such experiences, whatever the religious interpretation given to them.[42] However, to admit to that common basis is not to discount the specifically Christian interpretation of the Holy Spirit using such experiences for his purposes. Therefore, to acknowledge this much is to affirm that God is the sovereign Lord of all creation. Any theological approach which seeks to understand charismatic phenomena will ultimately need to incorporate insights gained from other disciplines, even if the discourse addressed is theology.[43]

Second, ASCs have been used by the Holy Spirit as a means by which revelation has been imparted. In Old Testament times, the prophets experienced some quite startling experiences. Consider, for example, the opening chapters of the book of Ezekiel, which by the standards of twentieth-century Western rationalism would be considered bizarre! It would be difficult not to interpret these type of experiences in ASC terms, unless one had a priori reasons for doing so. New Testament examples, as already mentioned, include Peter (Acts 10) and Paul (2 Corinthians 12). It is interesting that Peter entered a trance state and received a revelation about food while waiting for a meal! Yet there is no indication to suggest that this revelation was inauthentic because of this context. On the contrary, the revelation proved to be highly significant for the early church. There are those within the Toronto Christian Fellowship who have claimed certain visionary and prophetic revelation whilst having an ASC.[44] It would be unwise to dismiss the prophecy out of hand just because it was associated with an ASC. Criteria for the testing of prophecy must be applied consistently whatever the context of the proclamation.[45]

Third, ASCs are part of different Christian spiritual traditions, though rarely acknowledged. A comparison has been made in the past between silence, liturgy and glossolalia.[46] The same applies to other types of experience, which enable prayer and worship. The space of silence or the rhythm of liturgy both open up the opportunity to encounter God the Holy Spirit. The charismatic experiences of singing songs of praise or prayer ministry can sometimes result in ASC experiences. In these cases the outward form of the experience is more dramatic and spontaneous than other types. Therefore, whilst the experience of ASCs in the charismatic tradition is similar to other traditions, the mechanism appears to be very different. The outward forms of silence, liturgy and prayer ministry resulting in charismatic phenomena are dissimilar, yet the outcomes are often remarkably similar: a meaningful worship experience.

Fourth, ASCs may be categorized within the process of sanctification. If sanctification is regarded as the process by which the believer is conformed to the likeness of Christ by the work of the Spirit, then charismatic experiences could be integrated at this point. Subsequent to conversion-initiation, which includes the reception of the Spirit,[47] the Spirit enables the believer to grow in grace and holiness. Charismatic experiences are often described as experiences of Christian growth, healing and reconciliation. As such they have the potential, readily realized in many cases, to draw the believer closer to the Lord. This often results in greater joy in Christian service, a concern for the unevangelized, the poor and the disadvantaged.[48] Such activity has serious implications for the mission of the church.[49]

Fifth, I have suggested elsewhere that just as glossolalia is a symbol of divine-human encounter, so the phenomena associated with the Toronto Blessing may be too.[50] The nature of the symbols are different, but the sign value appears to be very similar. That is, glossolalia can function as a symbol of intimacy between the person and God. This aspect has also been attributed to the Toronto Blessing.[51] The mystery of the experience (it can never be fully captured in words) indicates something of the divine, while the very physical nature of a lot of the phenomena (laughing, crying, jumping, falling) point to the humanity involved in the encounter. Or put slightly differently, the mystery signifies the transcendence of God, the physical expressions signify the immanence of God in created humanity. This may be considered in light of the perceived shift in culture: from modernity to postmodernity. In modernity certain symbols were important as definitive signs, for example, glossolalia as the initial physical evidence of baptism in the Spirit.[52] In postmodernity a whole range of symbols are used with no priority given to any one. Therefore charismatic phenomena associated with the Toronto Blessing are varied with no single phenomenon given priority over any other. Indeed, just as some have argued for a sacramental quality to speaking in tongues,[53] so many of the phenomena associated with the Toronto Blessing may be interpreted in sacramental terms.[54] As the Spirit is active in the sacraments and 'by whose power alone hearts are penetrated and affections moved',[55] so the Spirit may perform a similar function through other occasions. In baptism and the Lord's Supper, the themes of death and resurrection are central (Romans 6:3–4; Luke 22:14–20), and it is these themes which also, from time to time, mark the interpretation of such phenomena by individuals concerned. The experience of falling to the floor (dying) and getting up again (rising) naturally evokes these biblical metaphors. I would therefore suggest that it is this apparent sacramental quality which enables many to find growth in their Christian lives.

10. Methodological Reflections

This chapter started life as a journal article. It was written at a time in my research when I was thinking through issues related to charismatic experience and glossolalia. As I read Middlemiss's book I was made aware of a philosophical tradition of theology that simply did not engage with social science research. It seemed to me that Middlemiss was promoting a position that had been advanced before, only he was not aware of it. I subsequently developed some aspects of my reflection in the Hilborn collection of papers to which I was invited to contribute.[56] However, it was not until I had the opportunity to prepare the text of this book that I actually had chance to test the survey data properly and see what could be found.

Since this chapter is highly theoretical in its orientation, its empirical-theological significance lies in the testing of theologically related hypotheses on survey data. It seeks to reconceptualize an issue that has previously been conceived as problematic. This study does not remove that problematic issue entirely but re-theologizes it in a way that enables both charismatics and non-charismatics to appreciate the wider theological and anthropological context. It also illustrates the ways in which practical theology can utilize social psychology to explore issues in Christian spirituality. In terms of a renewed theological praxis, it could be suggested that an incorporation of an understanding of ASCs within charismatic theology could provide a means by which to appreciate the natural side of phenomena. When these ASCs are placed within an explicit understanding of the social psychology of worship a pastorally responsible strategy is made possible. The affections of love and joy are most often associated with the encounter phase of charismatic phenomena, but not always. Very often the moments of encounter can be painful and great care is needed to offer love and compassion to those who weep before the Lord. We must suspend judgment until we can hear and then understand the story of the person concerned. In the meantime we bless what we discern to the be the work of the Spirit and look forward to seeing the fruit of changed lives. Therefore we treat the people being ministered with dignity and respect, not least because they are being renewed in the image of God in Christ.

---

[1] This chapter was originally published as 'Interpreting Charismatic Experience: Hypnosis, Altered States of Consciousness and the Holy Spirit?', *Journal of Pentecostal Theology* 13 (1998) pp. 117–32.

[2] There is a significant amount of literature on the Toronto Blessing: see my references in 'Interpreting Charismatic Experience', p.117. The most recent collection of material is found in D. Hilborn (ed.), *'Toronto' in Perspective: Papers on the New Charismatic Wave of the Mid-1990s* (Carlisle: Evangelical Alliance/Paternoster, 2001).

[3] It has to be said that the biblical approaches used to support the blessing are far from satisfactory. See S. E. Porter, ' Shaking the Biblical Foundations? The Biblical Basis for the Toronto Blessing' in S. E. Porter and P. J. Richter (eds), *The Toronto Blessing – or is it?* (London: Darton, Longman & Todd, 1995) pp. 38–65.

[4] D. Middlemiss, *Interpreting Charismatic Experience* (London: SCM, 1996) pp. 241–52, Appendix: Enthusiastic Phenomena and Hypnotic Techniques.

[5] J. P. Kildahl, *The Psychology of Speaking in Tongues* (London: Hodder & Stoughton, 1972).

[6] Middlemiss, *Interpreting Charismatic Experience*, p. 252.

[7] G. F. Wagstaff, *Hypnosis, Compliance and Belief* (Brighton: Harvester Press, 1981) p. 211.

8 The use of relaxation techniques is a case in point. Here Middlemiss's lack of clarity allows him to use hypnosis as a common category to classify both sets of hypnotic and charismatic phenomena. Certainly feelings of relaxation are present in both settings. However, unrelaxed subjects can also be hypnotized, and not all relaxation is hypnosis: for example, watching television or reading a novel. See ibid. p. 212.

9 Indeed, a role theorist would argue that hypnosis is simply the action of a person taking on the role of the hypnotic subject. The modern hypnotic subject plays the 'game' according to rules laid down by the hypnotist, cultural notions of 'hypnosis' and individual attitudes and perceptions. Role theory was developed by T. R. Sarbin, building upon the work of R. White. It has been developed by T. X. Barber and the cognitive behavioural school. See N. P. Spanos and J. F. Chaves, *Hypnosis: The Cognitive-Behavioural Perspective* (New York: Prometheus, 1989) and Wagstaff, *Hypnosis, Compliance and Belief*, p. 220. Such a theoretical perspective would tend to exclude the charismatic setting as a place where hypnotic activity could take place, since it is dependent upon the recognition by both leader/presenter and congregation/audience that hypnosis is already taking place or is about to take place. For an overview of the main theoretical perspectives, see T. R. Sarbin and W. C. Coe, *Hypnosis: A Social Psychological Analysis of Influence Communication* (New York: Holt, Rinehart & Winston, 1972) ch. 5.

10 On the matter of an *ad hoc* hypothesis 'plucked out of the air' Middlemiss says: 'Such a hypothesis has the epistemic status of a guess, and while it may be a correct guess, one could never know whether it is correct until it has been tested in some way' – *Interpreting Charismatic Experience*, p. 205. Middlemiss, whilst acknowledging it as a pitfall to avoid, nevertheless fails to do so himself!

11 Kildahl, *The Psychology of Speaking in Tongues*, pp. 38–9.

12 Ibid. pp. 54–5.

13 See A. A. Lovekin and H. M. Malony, *Glossolalia – Behavioural Science Perspectives on Speaking in Tongues* (Oxford: Oxford University Press, 1985) p. 83.

14 H. E. Gonsalvez, 'The Theology and Psychology of Glossolalia' (PhD dissertation, Northwestern University, Evanston IL, 1979) pp. 104–11.

15 Lovekin and Malony, *Glossolalia*, pp. 74, 77.

16 J. E. Coulson and R. W. Johnson, 'Glossolalia and Internal-External Locus of Control', *Journal of Psychology and Theology* 5 (1977) pp. 312–17.

17 Lovekin and Malony, *Glossolalia*, pp. 72, 84, 85.

[18] N. P. Spanos and E. C. Hewitt, 'Glossolalia: A Test of the "Trance" and Psychopathology Hypotheses', *Journal of Abnormal Psychology* 88.4 (1979) pp. 427–34.

[19] L. J. Francis and W. K. Kay, 'The Personality Characteristics of Pentecostal Ministry Candidates', *Personality and Individual Differences* 18.5 (1995) pp. 581–94.

[20] G. Neanon and J. Hair, 'Imaginative Involvement, Neuroticism and Charismatic Behaviour', *British Journal of Experimental and Clinical Hypnosis* 7.3 (1990) pp. 190–2. See also H. B. Gibson, 'Imaginative Involvement, Neuroticism and Charismatic Behaviour: A Note on the Use of the EPI Scales', *Contemporary Hypnosis* 8.2 (1991) pp. 109–11.

[21] P. Dixon, *Signs of Revival* (Eastbourne: Kingsway, 1994).

[22] Ibid. p. 247.

[23] Ibid.

[24] Ibid. p. 251.

[25] For a consideration of this type of experience in terms of hypnagogic states and imagery, see D. Tappeiner, 'A Psychological Paradigm for the Interpretation of the Charismatic Phenomenon of Prophecy', *Journal of Psychology and Theology* 5 (1977) pp. 23–9; cf. M. J. Cartledge, 'Charismatic Prophecy', *Journal of Empirical Theology* 8.1 (1995) pp. 74–6, 87. For my personal reflection on the Toronto Blessing in ASC terms, see 'A Spur to Holistic Discipleship' in Hilborn (ed.), *'Toronto' in Perspective*, pp. 64–71.

[26] Dixon, *Signs of Revival*, p. 265.

[27] Ibid. pp. 277–8.

[28] F. D. Goodman, *Speaking in Tongues: A Cross-cultural Study of Glossolalia* (Chicago: University of Chicago Press, 1972).

[29] W. J. Samarin, *Tongues of Men and Angels* (New York: Macmillan, 1972).

[30] Goodman, *Speaking in Tongues*, p. 8 (italics original).

[31] Ibid. p. 3 cites E. Bourguignon, *A Cross-cultural Study of Dissociational States* (Columbus: Ohio State University Research Foundation, 1968). Goodman uses the term 'dissociation' and phrase 'dissociational states', together with the term 'trance', as synonyms for an altered state of consciousness, also called 'hyperarousal' or 'hyperaroused state'. By this she means a 'divorcement from ordinary reality'. Ibid. pp. 59–60.

[32] W. J. Samarin, 'Speaking in Tongues: A Cross-cultural Study of Glossolalia by Felicitas D. Goodman, Chicago: University Press of Chicago, 1972' *Language* 50.1 (1974) p. 209. It is useful to observe here that Samarin falls into the Popperian school of thought. See

W. K. Kay and L. J. Francis, *Drift from the Churches: Attitude toward Christianity during Childhood and Adolescence* (Cardiff: University of Wales Press, 1996) pp. 163–5; also J. A. van der Ven, *Practical Theology: An Empirical Approach* (Kampen: Kok Pharos, 1993) pp. 115–18.

[33] Spanos and Hewitt, 'Glossolalia', pp. 432–4.

[34] G. Stanley, W. K. Bartlett, and T. Moyle, 'Some Characteristics of Charismatic Experience: Glossolalia in Australia' *Journal for the Scientifc Study of Religion* 17.3 (1978) pp. 269–77.

[35] H. J. Eysenck and M. W. Eysenck, *Personality and Individual Differences. A Natural Science Approach* (New York: Plenum Press, 1985).

[36] W. K. Kay, *Personality and Renewal* (Cambridge: Grove, Renewal 3, 2001).

[37] L. J. Francis and T. H. Thomas, 'Are Charismatic Ministers Less Stable? A Study among Male Anglican Clergy', *Religious Review of Research* 39.1 (1997) pp. 61–9 (p. 61).

[38] Ibid. p. 61.

[39] Ibid. p. 62.

[40] Kay and Francis, *Drift from the Churches*, pp. 78–9.

[41] Neanon and Hair, 'Imaginative Involvement, Neuroticism and Charismatic Behaviour', pp. 190–2; Francis and Kay, 'The Personality Characteristics of Pentecostal Ministry Candidates', pp. 581–94; L. J. Francis and S. H. Jones, 'Personality and Charismatic Experience among Adult Christians', *Pastoral Psychology* 45.6 (1997) pp. 421–8; Francis and Thomas, 'Are Charismatic Ministers Less Stable?', pp. 61–9; S. H. Louden and L. J. Francis, 'Are Catholic Priests in England and Wales Attracted to the Charismatic Movement Emotionally Less Stable?', *British Journal of Theological Education* 11.2 (2001) pp. 65–76. I am grateful to Leslie Francis for a copy of these items.

[42] M. Mitton, *The Heart of Toronto* (Cambridge: Grove, Spirituality 55, 1995) recognizes that in the church there is 'a deep mistrust of our humanness' (pp. 8–9). By this he is referring to the negative attitude towards any open display of emotions. Once again the dualism between matter and spirit is lurking in the background!

[43] See chapter 2.

[44] See the prophecy by C. Arnott in the video *God's Love – Bottom Line* (Toronto: Toronto Airport Vineyard, 1995).

[45] See M. J. Cartledge, 'Charismatic Prophecy: A Definition and Description', *Journal of Pentecostal Theology* 5 (1994) pp. 114–20.

[46] R. A. Baer Jr., 'Quaker Silence, Catholic Liturgy and Pentecostal Glossolalia: Some Functional Similarities' in W. E. Mills (ed.), *Speaking in Tongues: A Guide to Research on Glossolalia* (Grand Rapids MI: Eerdmans, 1986) pp. 313–27.

47 See M. Turner, *Power from on High: The Spirit in Israel's Restoration and Witness in Luke–Acts* (Sheffield: Sheffield Academic Press, JPTS 9, 1996); M. Turner, *The Holy Spirit and Spiritual Gifts: Then and Now* (Carlisle: Paternoster Press, 1996).

48 See M. Poloma, *The Toronto Report: A Preliminary Sociological Assessment of the Toronto Blessing* (Bradford-on-Avon: Terra Nova, 1996).

49 It is interesting to observe at this point that one of the most significant churches in the UK to be influenced by the Third Wave and the Toronto Blessing, Holy Trinity Church, Brompton, has also launched the most influential evangelistic tool in Britain, the Alpha Course. See *Alpha Training Manual* (London: Holy Trinity Brompton, 1993).

50 See chapter 6.

51 Mitton, *The Heart of Toronto*, pp. 23–4.

52 See V. Synan, 'The Role of Tongues as Initial Evidence' in M. W. Wilson (ed.), *Spirit and Renewal: Essays in Honour of J. Rodman Williams* (Sheffield: Sheffield Academic Press, JPTS 5, 1994) pp. 67–82.

53 F. D. Macchia, 'Tongues as a Sign: Towards a Sacramental Understanding of Pentecostal Experience', *PNEUMA: The Journal of the Society for Pentecostal Studies* 15.1 (1993) pp. 61–76.

54 For example, a sacrament may be defined as 'an outward and visible sign of an inward and spiritual grace' – W. H. Griffith Thomas, *The Catholic Faith* (London: Church Book Room Press, 1904, revised 1920, 1929, 1952) p. 103.

55 J. Calvin, *Institutes of the Christian Religion*, J. T. McNeill (ed.), F. L. Battles (tr.) (Philadelphia: Westminster Press, 1960) book 4, ch. 14, § 9, p. 1284.

56 See Cartledge, 'A Spur to Holistic Discipleship', pp. 64–74 (p. 69).

9

Faith and Healing

1. Introduction

The Pentecostal and charismatic movements have often been associated with the ministry of healing in the church. The influence of the Charismatic Movement in the Church of England has been so significant that the ministry of healing by all sectors of the church is now widespread, in a way that would have been unthinkable only a few years ago.[1] Of course, such a ministry is not without its detractors, and there are examples of bad theological praxis as well as good. Although the healing ministry of the church has continued down the centuries,[2] it is perhaps in this age of therapy that it has become more popular. This may account for the wider interest in healing across the theological and church spectrum. This significant feature of Pentecostal and charismatic theological praxis was, however, given a boost by healing associated with the Toronto Blessing in the 1990s, and prior to that the influence of the ministry of John Wimber.[3]

In the literature of the Pentecostal and charismatic movements one can find all kinds of discussions of the relationship between faith and healing. Most of these discussions relate to the ministry of Jesus in the gospels and whether his ministry is paradigmatic for the church today.[4] So it is worth reconsidering what features the gospels provide for Pentecostal and charismatic discussion.[5] Clearly, not all healing in the New Testament is linked explicitly to expressions of faith.[6] But there are four aspects that I believe have a direct bearing on the subject.

First, within the narrative of the gospels, healing is sometimes directly associated with the faith of a person. Thus Jesus can say to the woman suffering from bleeding who touched his cloak, 'Daughter, your faith has healed you' (Mark 5:34 and parallels). He can say to two blind men, 'According to your faith will it be done to you' (Matthew 9:29), and to Bartimaeus, 'Go, your faith has healed you' (Mark 10:52 and parallels). To the person healed of leprosy who returns to thank Jesus, he says, 'Rise and go, your faith has made you well' (Luke 17:19).

Second, healing is sometimes explicitly associated with the faith of others. For example, in the story of the healing of the paralytic, we read that when Jesus saw their faith (that is, the faith of the man's companions), he said to the paralytic 'Your sins are forgiven', after which he rises and walks (Mark 2:5). To the centurion seeking help for his servant, Jesus exclaims, 'I tell you, I have not found such great faith even in Israel' (Luke 7:9). Jesus' response to the faith of the Syrophoenician woman ('even the dogs under the table eat the children's crumbs' [Mark 7:28]) is to grant the healing of her daughter from demonic possession (Mark 7:29).

Third, there is an association made by Jesus between lack of faith and the limitation of healing. In Mark 6:1–6 we read of Jesus teaching in the synagogue of his hometown. This caused amazement from friends and family and dishonour to the person of Jesus (v. 4). Although Jesus did lay his hands on a few people and heal them, Mark records that he could do no miracles here (v. 5). The reaction of Jesus is that he is amazed, but for him it is with respect to their lack of faith (v. 6). This lack of faith is also demonstrated by the disciples in relation to healing. They are unable to heal a boy with an evil spirit (Mark 9:14–29 and parallels), and Jesus is exasperated, stating, 'O unbelieving generation . . . how shall I put up with you?' (Mark 9:19). In the Matthean discussion of the disciples' failure, Jesus explains that they failed because of their lack of faith (Matthew 17:20). Jesus says that if they have faith as small as a mustard seed then they can command the mountain to move and it will do so, since nothing is impossible for them (Matthew 17:20).

Fourth, there is a link between faith and healing with deliverance from demonic influence. This has been already noted with respect to the episode of a boy with an evil spirit (Mark 9:14–29 and parallels) and the Syrophoenician woman's daughter (Mark 7:24–30 and parallels). There is also an interesting juxtaposition in another gospel passage. In Matthew 9:27–34 we have the story of Jesus healing two blind men (vv. 27–31), followed immediately by the healing of a dumb man who was also demon possessed (v. 32). After the demon had been 'driven out', the man spoke (v. 33). Thus faith and healing are also associated with belief in demonic forces at work and associated with some illnesses.[7]

To consider how these ideas are used within Pentecostal and charismatic theological praxis, it is useful to explore some of the theological models that are proposed by writers and preachers in the field.

2. Pentecostal and Charismatic Theologies of Faith and Healing

Henry H. Knight III, in one of the most illuminating articles on the subject of the theology of healing within the Pentecostal and charismatic traditions, has elucidated a number of different perspectives.[8] The article juxtaposes the concepts of God's faithfulness with God's freedom. The difficult question as to why a person is not healed is answered with respect to these two concepts. If God is always faithful, then the question becomes whether the person has met the sufficient condition(s)? Or if God is always free, has he chosen not to heal that particular person? Knight also considers the role of faith in the scenario. Is faith to be understood as trusting scriptural promises or trusting the person of Jesus Christ? And whose faith is necessary for such healing? Very often, from a pastoral perspective, the faith question is focused in terms of the actual person seeking healing. Does he or she have sufficient faith?

The Faith Movement teaching, associated with the names of Kenneth Hagin Sr, Kenneth and Gloria Copeland, Fred Price, Charles Capps, Robert Tilton and Savelle and Kenneth Hagin Jr., has given a very specific answer to this question. Faith Movement teachers argue that Christians are entitled to the blessings of Abraham through the cross of Christ. These blessings are received through faith and are the blessings of salvation, physical health and material prosperity.[9] The reception of such blessings is by means of the 'faith formula', otherwise known as positive confession.[10] To exercise positive confession one simply claims the healing based upon the promise of Scripture and then acts upon that confession in faith apart from what sensory evidence to the contrary there may be.[11] Although it is believed that anyone can tap into the universal spiritual laws that make positive confession possible, Christians have divine authority to claim the promises in Jesus' name. Such faith has power to change one's circumstances and create a new reality for oneself. This means that one need only pray once. Indeed, to pray twice is to doubt God. There is no need for petition, simply to make a positive confession. Knight III explains this position in terms of an emphasis upon God's faithfulness at the expense of God's freedom. Healing is automatic if based upon faith confession. Faith in this theology is about trusting in God's promises in Scripture, rather than trusting in God himself.[12] A faithful God has no choice but to act, this is how he has intended it to be.[13]

Agnes Sanford also stresses God's faithfulness to heal but in a very different way from the Faith Movement. She believes that the believer's words are not causal, but rather they help to channel God's healing. Positive faith is necessary but not in the way in which it is expressed in the Faith Movement. Prayer, for Sanford, should be persistent, because it is only through persistence that we become more open to the flow of God's healing power through us. These ideas are endorsed by Morton T. Kelsey, who believes that God is always available to heal the person having positive faith. Such a person is therefore open to the healing light within him or her.[14]

Kathryn Kuhlman and Charles Farah are cited by Knight III as writers who stress the sovereign freedom of God. Kuhlman is persuaded that believers are to trust in God rather than the formula of positive confession. Faith is necessary but it does not guarantee healing since a person can believe with his or her mind but not heart. It is heart-based belief that is true faith and it is a gift of God. Such faith is an event rather than being a possession. Healing therefore happens when the person receives faith for that particular healing.[15] For Farah, healing is due to God's sovereign love and decision. It is a mystery as to why some people are healed and not others. It is generally God's will to heal, but not necessarily in some specific situations.[16]

Knight III also describes writers who have aimed to integrate both aspects of God's faithfulness and freedom. Francis MacNutt believes that healing is part of the gospel and stems from God's compassion. Faith should be placed in God, not in our faith. While some people are given the gift of faith that allows them to pray in confidence, the virtue of faith is available to all believers, and is the basis of petitionary prayer. God works in a climate of love, not power, therefore prayer should be persistent. James K. Wagner believes that faith in the healing Christ must be present for healing to occur, but this may not necessarily be from the patient. John Wimber and Ken Blue, representing a Vineyard perspective, maintain that it is God's desire to heal because of his compassion and love. However, God is free and his actions are mysterious.[17] Therefore all ministry is partial and our obedience is never perfect. Faith confession is rejected; nevertheless the link between faith and healing is understood as being significant.[18] Faith is defined as a childlike trust in the loving character and purpose of God.[19]

Keith Warrington has noted the obvious connection between healing and exorcism within British Pentecostalism.[20] Most Pentecostals would accept the existence of a personal devil and influential demons,[21] although much theology in this area is generated by means of popular preaching and writing. He summarizes the main tenets of current belief as:

1. The devil and his demons are antagonistic foes of the church.
2. They have been eternally overcome by Christ.
3. They still affect individuals malevolently.
4. They can be resisted and overcome by and through Christ.[22]

Although many Pentecostals would understand that Satan is the cause of all suffering, the majority would separate sickness from demonic elements. In some cases, it would nevertheless be believed that demonic influences have caused sickness. The dualistic tendencies of the New Testament are often taken to extremes by Pentecostals and charismatics who simply talk in terms of either God's kingdom of light or Satan's kingdom of darkness.[23] It is in this cosmological context that much discussion of healing and demonology occurs.

3. Key Questions

In order to test one of the most pastorally difficult questions associated with faith and healing, namely whether the faith of the person seeking healing is believed to be great enough to secure healing, the data from the questionnaire will revolve around the question:

- Do you believe healing will always occur if a person's faith is great enough?

  (Answer options: yes, no, don't know.)

The questionnaire, unfortunately, does not contain supplementary questions, such as in whom or what is such faith placed (person or promises), but it nevertheless gives an indication of the kind of influence such teaching has had in the churches surveyed.

In order to obtain a picture of the types of people who associate themselves with such a position, answers to this question are compared to background variables, Christian experience variables, and a question that uncovers attitudes towards demonology. This is because there is a link between belief in healing and belief in a demon worldview. Also, because this whole area raises questions of epistemology, for example, the Faith Movement teaching denies the reliability of sensory data for the spiritual life, a question which highlights preferred ways of knowing is also related to the faith and healing question. These questions can be summarized thus:

- The background variables of gender, age, marital status, qualifications and occupation.
- Christian experience: Christian age and church denomination.
- Do you believe that Christians are in daily conflict with demons? (Answer options: yes, no, don't know.)
- Which way of knowing do you *prefer* to trust?

Either	*Or*
(a) intellect	(b) intuition
(a) personal senses	(b) logic
(a) picture language	(b) literal expression
(a) detached observation	(b) individual participation
(a) mysticism	(b) reason

From the theoretical discussion and these questions, a number of hypotheses can be constructed to guide the investigation.

Hypotheses
1. Background variables are associated with the belief that healing will always occur if a person's faith is great enough.
2. Christian age is associated with the belief that healing will always occur if a person's faith is great enough.
3. Church denominations are associated with the belief that healing will always occur if a person's faith is great enough.
4. Demon worldview is associated with the belief that healing will always occur if a person's faith is great enough.
5. Attitudes towards epistemology are associated with the belief that healing will always occur if a person's faith is great enough.

4. Results

In order to be able compare the categories in which answers fall in a simple but powerful way, I have chosen to present data mostly by means of crosstabulations. A frequency count for the main variable under consideration gives a general context from which to interpret the subsequent crosstabulations.

Table 9.1: *Frequency of belief in healing always occurring if a person's faith is great enough*

Answers (%)	
No	58.8
Don't know	10.4
Yes	24.6
Not applicable	6.2
Total	100.0

Table 9.1 shows that the majority of respondents do not believe that healing will always occur if a person's faith is great enough. However, there is a sizeable proportion of just under a quarter

believing in the proposition. A small proportion (10%) is undecided on the matter. This is consonant with the spread between men and women with very little difference between the genders.

The background variables that are insignificant in relation to the key proposition include gender, age and marital status. However, educational qualification is associated with the belief that healing will always occur if one's faith is great enough. The correlation score is −.206 (significant at the .01 level, Pearson's r). The negative score indicates that the lesser the education qualification the greater the probability that the proposition is believed. A similar relationship is established with occupation, another indicator of socio-economic status.

Table 9.2: *Crosstabulation: Occupation by belief in healing always occurring if a person's faith is great enough (% within occupation)*

	Faith and healing		
Occupation	No	Don't know	Yes
Class I	75.0	15.0	10.0
Class II	78.2	11.3	10.5
Class IIIN	61.9	12.4	25.7
Class IIIM	44.0	16.0	40.0
Class IV/V	60.7	2.8	36.5
Unemployed	57.1	9.5	33.3
Housewife/retired	60.0	9.1	30.9
Student	40.0	15.0	45.0
$X^2 = 47.39$	P = .001		

Table 9.2 shows the crosstabulation of occupation with the proposition that healing will always occur if a person's faith is great enough. The majority of respondents do not subscribe to the proposition. This data also show that the higher the social class the less likely the respondent is to subscribe to the proposition. This is especially seen with respect to Class I and Class II. The relationship of these two items is statistically significant.

Christian age is associated with the proposition with a correlation score of −.134 (significant at the .01 level, Person's r). The negative score indicates that the lesser the Christian age the greater the probability that one might believe in the proposition. Church denominations, however, are not significantly associated with the proposition.

The belief that Christians are in daily conflict with demons is also associated with the proposition. The correlation score is .111 (significant at the .01 level, Pearson's r) and the positive score indicates that the greater the belief in one of these propositions the greater the belief in the other.

The influence the epistemology variables have on the proposition is seen in tables 9.3 and 9.4.

Table 9.3: Crosstabulation: Way of knowing (1) by belief in healing always occurring if a person's faith is great enough (% within way of knowing)

	Faith and healing		
Way of knowing	*No*	*Don't know*	*Yes*
Intellect	76.6	10.0	13.4
Intuition	58.8	11.6	29.6
$X^2 = 19.35$	P = .000		

Table 9.3 shows the crosstabulation of preference for way of knowing in terms of either intellect or intuition with the proposition that healing will always occur if a person's faith is great enough. Although the majority of respondents do not subscribe to the proposition, there is a proportionally higher number of respondents who do subscribe to the proposition from those who prefer to trust the intuition way of knowing compared to intellect. The relationship of these two items is statistically significant.

Table 9.4 shows the crosstabulation of preference for way of knowing in terms of either personal senses or logic with the proposition that healing will always occur if a person's faith is great enough. Although the majority of respondents do not subscribe to the proposition, there is a proportionally higher number of respondents who do subscribe to the proposition from those who

Table 9.4: Crosstabulation: Way of knowing (2) by belief in healing always occurring if a person's faith is great enough (% within way of knowing)

Way of knowing	Faith and healing		
	No	Don't know	Yes
Personal senses	62.5	8.6	28.9
Logic	72.0	13.4	14.6
X² = 13.35	P = .001		

prefer to trust the personal senses way of knowing compared to logic. The relationship of these two items is statistically significant.

The other variables used to assess the influence of epistemology in relation to this proposition are not statistically significant.

5. Discussion

Hypothesis 1 proposes that the background variables are associated with the belief that healing will always occur if a person's faith is great enough. The background variables of gender, age and marital status are not statistically significant and therefore do not corroborate this hypothesis. However, the background variables of qualifications and occupation are statistically significant. The data show that the greater the educational qualifications and higher the social status, the less likely the respondent is to believe in the proposition. Conversely, it could be suggested that this belief appeals more to the less-educated and lower social classes. These two variables are related, since education is one of the key pathways to social mobility. In the context of Britain, where there is free medical care, and only a small minority of the population choose and can afford to pay for private health care, the accent should fall upon educational attainment. It could also be suggested that different levels of theological sophistication are reflected in this data. The lower the educational level, the greater the predisposition to adhere to such a belief. Therefore, while this hypothesis is uncorroborated with respect to gender, age and marital status, it is corroborated with respect to educational qualifications and occupation.

Hypothesis 2 proposes that Christian age is associated with the belief that healing will always occur if a person's faith is great enough. The data show that the older the person is in Christian age terms, then the less likely he or she is to believe in the proposition. This relationship is statistically significant. This suggests that belief in the proposition is associated with Christian immaturity, assuming the older the Christian the greater the level of maturity in the faith. This observation may be related to faith development theories, suggesting that as faith grows, so it can accommodate greater complexity and paradox.[24] This means that such a belief has the greatest appeal to younger and more immature Christians. Therefore the hypothesis is corroborated.

Hypothesis 3 proposes that Christian denominations are associated with the belief that healing will always occur if a person's faith is great enough. The relationship of these two items is statistically insignificant and therefore these British denominations cannot be said to align themselves with, for example, the Faith Movement teaching.[25] This means that the socialization of this particular belief must cut right across the denominations, with no statistically significant distinction to be found between classical Pentecostal denominations and New Churches or churches associated with mainstream charismatic renewal. Therefore the hypothesis is uncorroborated.

Hypothesis 4 proposes the belief that Christians are in daily conflict with demons (demon worldview) is associated with the belief that healing will always occur if a person's faith is great enough. The correlation shows that the relationship between these two items is statistically significant. This means that the earlier association observed within the narrative of the gospels is also demonstrated here. It is also consonant with the predisposition of Pentecostals and charismatics to understand healing within the context of spiritual warfare.[26] While not all healing can be situated within a demonic context, there are a sufficient number of respondents who believe that the two are closely related. Therefore this hypothesis is corroborated.

Hypothesis 5 proposes that attitudes towards epistemology are associated with the belief that healing will always occur if a person's faith is great enough. The item contrasting 'intellect' with 'intuition' as ways of knowing is related to the proposition in a statistically significant way. The majority do not subscribe to the proposition; however, a good proportion of respondents who prefer 'intuition' do agree with the idea. The item contrasting 'personal senses' with 'logic' as ways of knowing is also related to the proposition in a statistically significant way. Again, the majority do not subscribe to the proposition; nevertheless a good proportion from those respondents preferring 'personal senses' do associate with the idea. Therefore both 'intuition' and 'personal senses' ways of knowing are significantly related to this belief. However, while 'intuition' can fit with Faith Movement teaching since it coheres with intuitive 'revelation knowledge', 'personal senses', on the other hand, certainly poses a problem for the teaching that stresses the reliance upon promise rather than sight. Perhaps these pairs need to be understood rather in terms of anti-intellectualism? Therefore, both options, 'intuition' and 'personal senses', are posed as opposites to 'intellect' and 'logic'. Indeed, one can suggest that faith that trusts in the promises of God does so even against intellectual respectability and the demands of 'logic'! The hypothesis is corroborated in relation to these items.

6. Conclusion

It is important to observe that the majority of Pentecostal and charismatic Christians involved in this survey do not subscribe to the belief that healing will always occur if a person's faith is great enough (58.8%). However, just under a quarter of the respondents (24.6%) do subscribe to the belief. The people who maintain this belief tend to: (1) have lower educational qualifications and lower social status; (2) be younger and more immature Christians; (3) believe in daily conflict of Christians with demons; and (4) tend to be anti-intellectual, preferring intuition and personal senses as ways of knowing over intellect and logic.

7. Methodological Reflection

This chapter began with an exploration of survey data around the variables of faith and healing. Once I had established that there was some interesting data, I reviewed the literature. This was followed by the formulation of specific hypotheses that were tested and reflected on theologically. The outcome was a renewed understanding of the types of people who hold to a strong faith healing position. It therefore provides information to enable church leaders better to understand the social context of this theology and its relation to the wider Charismatic Movement. The recommendation for renewed theological praxis is in relation to education.

The portrait of this group of Christians within the churches surveyed is important for a charismatic practical theology. This survey enables us to not only identify certain beliefs but also to begin to understand the social context within which such beliefs are held and sustained. By identifying contexts for believing we can address, in a positive way, how beliefs might be changed. The factors highlighted above also suggest routes for action. The key recommendation for renewed theological praxis can be suggested in terms of education. Church leaders should be encouraged to engage with the best of Pentecostal and charismatic scholarship in order to develop a nuanced understanding of the relationship between faith, healing and demonology both in the Bible and today. The key theological doctrine relates to faith in a personal God, not some force that can be tapped into and manipulated. Healing should always be conceived in the context of the kingdom of God, which is inaugurated but not yet consummated, thus retaining a balance between what has been and is being realized and what is not. The healing ministry should always be offered in love and compassion both for the healed and the unhealed. A renewed understanding can then be taught from the pulpit and caught within Pentecostal and charismatic church communities. This may also mean engaging in dialogue with Faith Movement teachers and others for the sake of the gospel and the people of God.

---

[1] See the report for the House of Bishops of the General Synod of the Church of England, *A Time to Heal: A Contribution Towards the Ministry of Healing* (London: Church House, 2000).

[2] See R. A. N. Kydd, *Healing through the Centuries: Models for Understanding Healing* (Peabody MA: Hendrickson, 1998).

3   See J. Wimber, *Power Healing* (London: Hodder & Stoughton, 1986).
4   K. Warrington, 'Major Aspects of Healing within British Pente-
    costalism', *Journal of the European Pentecostal Theological Association* 19
    (1999) pp. 34–55, who regards the ministry of Jesus as unique
    phenomenologically (p. 45).
5   To my knowledge, the most comprehensive discussion of healing
    and deliverance in the New Testament is by J. C. Thomas, *The Devil,
    Disease and Deliverance: Origins of Illness in New Testament Thought*
    (Sheffield: Sheffield Academic Press, JPTS 13, 1998).
6   W. J. Hollenweger, *Pentecostalism: Origins and Developments Worldwide*
    (Peabody MA: Hendrickson, 1997) p. 244. Kydd, *Healing through the
    Centuries*, p. 13 notes how John's gospel in particular does not record
    faith as a condition of healing.
7   Matthew 12:22 describes how Jesus healed a demon-possessed man
    who was both blind and mute. Jesus healed him with there being no
    indication of faith.
8   H. H. Knight III, 'God's Faithfulness and God's Freedom: A
    Comparison of Contemporary Theologies of Healing', *Journal of
    Pentecostal Theology* 2 (1993) pp. 65–89.
9   Ibid. p. 66.
10 See the description in W. K. Kay, *Pentecostals in Britain* (Carlisle:
    Paternoster, 2000) pp. 91–2.
11 T. Smail, A. Walker and N. Wright, '"Revelation Knowledge" and
    Knowledge of Revelation: The Faith Movement and the Question
    of Heresy', *Journal of Pentecostal Theology* 5 (1994) pp. 57–77 (p. 65)
    suggest that negative confession is a device to explain the fact of not
    being healed in the form of (bogus) syllogism of Aristotelian logic.
    Premise one: Those who confess that they are healed will be healed.
    Premise two: Those who do not confess their healing will stay sick.
    Premise three: Therefore all those who are not healed have made
    negative confession.
12 As M. Turner, *The Holy Spirit and Spiritual Gifts: Then and Now* (Carlisle:
    Paternoster, 1996) p. 343 says, with reference to the Faith Movement:
    'Its view of "faith" makes the latter an absolute power independent of
    relation to God (unbelievers can apply the same spiritual laws), rather
    than a way of expressing a filial relationship of dependence.'
13 Knight III, 'God's Faithfulness and God's Freedom', p. 69. See also
    the citation of Fred Price by Smail, Walker and Wright, '"Revelation
    Knowledge" and Knowledge of Revelation', p. 63.
14 Knight III, 'God's Faithfulness and God's Freedom', pp. 71–4.
15 For a discussion of Kuhlman's model see Kydd, *Healing through the
    Centuries*, pp. 181–97.

16 Knight III, 'God's Faithfulness and God's Freedom', p. 74–7.

17 In a critical engagement with the writing of Wimber, N. Wright, 'The Theology and Methodology of "Signs and Wonders"' in T. Smail, A. Walker and N. Wright, *Charismatic Renewal: The Search for a Theology* (London: SPCK, 1993) pp. 71–85 (pp. 79–82) discusses divine sovereignty and Wimber's radical Arminianism in relation to human faith.

18 Turner, *The Holy Spirit and Spiritual Gifts*, p. 343 highlights the tension in Wimber's thinking between the main reason for failure in healing as 'lack of faith' and his assertion that he never blames the sick person for their lack of faith if healing does not occur.

19 Knight III, 'God's Faithfulness and God's Freedom', pp. 78–86. For a discussion of Wimber's model see Kydd, *Healing through the Centuries*, pp. 46–59.

20 K. Warrington, 'Healing and Exorcism: The Path to Wholeness' in K. Warrington (ed.), *Pentecostal Perspectives* (Carlisle: Paternoster, 1998) pp. 146–76.

21 This kind of personal ontology is contested. See A. Walker, 'The Devil you Think you Know: Demonology and the Charismatic Movement' in Smail, Walker and Wright, *Charismatic Renewal*, pp. 86–105 (pp. 101–2).

22 Warrington, 'Healing and Exorcism', p. 173.

23 For a discussion of this subject see A. Walker, 'The Devil you Think you Know', pp. 88–9. He regards this dualism as feeding a 'paranoid' universe in which the world is dissected into either 'them' or 'us'. The antidote to such dualism is to reassert the tripartite arenas of the divine, the natural and the demonic. This dualism is also discussed in relation to the theology of Wimber by another contributor to the same volume (Smail, Walker and Wright, *Charismatic Renewal*): N. Wright, 'The Theology and Methodology of "Signs and Wonders"', pp. 71–85 (pp. 73–5), who also regrets the demise of 'the natural' in Pentecostal and charismatic theology.

24 For a discussion of developmental theories in relation to Christian faith, see F. Watts, R. Nye and S. Savage, *Psychology for Christian Ministry* (London: Routledge, 2002) pp. 100–18.

25 Note the discussion of this item by Kay, *Pentecostals in Britain*, pp. 101–3. His survey of 930 Pentecostal ministers produced data that suggest that more than half the ministers in the Apostolic Church (55.1%) and Church of God (60.8%) believe the proposition. The Assemblies of God (19.7%) and Elim (13.5%) ministers are less likely to put all the responsibility for healing on the faith of sick person. He contends that Faith Movement teaching is more likely to be held by

older ministers and those who have not received full-time theological education (p. 102).

26 W. K. Kay, 'A Demonised Worldview: Dangers, Benefits and Explanations', *Journal of Empirical Theology* 11.1 (1998) pp. 17–29 presents data suggesting that the Eysenck personality dimension (EPQ) of psychoticism is a significant causal factor in explaining a demon worldview (p. 25).

10

Glossolalia and Socialization[1]

1. Introduction

The Pentecostal and charismatic movements are now very influential globally. Yet it is only recently that studies have been undertaken which combine different approaches to them, such as sociology and theology together. In this chapter material is presented from the case study of Aigburth Community Church (ACC) and this is subsequently supported and developed by the survey data. The focus of the study is the phenomenon of speaking in tongues, otherwise known as glossolalia. For charismatics, the gift of tongues is understood to be a language of worship and prayer, and as such a means of communication to God. Classical Pentecostals understood it to be the definitive sign of an overwhelming experience of the Holy Spirit, called baptism in the Spirit. Initially those involved in traditional denominations also understood it in this way. However, with the influence of the Third Wave movement, focused around the ministry of John Wimber and the Vineyard denomination, this specific emphasis has waned. The New Church movement, formerly called the House Church movement, combines a variety of Pentecostal and charismatic strands together, but it also seeks to develop its own unique approach.[2] The church in this study, as described in earlier chapters, is to be located within this New Church movement.

For research purposes, I use the working definition of charismatic glossolalia proposed by V. S. Poythress. That is, glossolalia is a form of free vocalization:

Free vocalization (glossolalia) occurs when (1) a human being produces a connected sequence of speech sounds, (2) he cannot identify the sound-sequence as belonging to any natural language that he already knows how to speak, (3) he cannot identify and give the meaning of words or morphemes (minimal lexical units), (4) in the case of utterances of more than a few syllables, he typically cannot repeat the same sound-sequence on demand, (5) a naive listener might suppose that it was an unknown language.[3]

Poythress uses the term *T-speech* (tongues) to refer to Christian free vocalization within the context of worship and prayer.

This chapter seeks to review the case study and survey material concerning the theological praxis of glossolalia by means of those setting variables which suggest that glossolalia is acquired by means of socialization. By socialization is meant the process by which a person is integrated into a culture or subculture. In socialization the person learns the meanings of the subculture, identifies with them and is shaped by them. As Peter Berger says, 'He draws them into himself and makes them *his* meanings. He becomes not only one who possesses these meanings, but one who represents and expresses them.'[4] The most important discussion of this idea is by William J. Samarin.[5] He combines his insights as both a linguist and anthropologist, that is, in sociolinguistic terms, to argue that glossolalia is more properly understood as a learned experience. The social context at the very least provides certain clues which enable the individual to take a 'jump into the dark' and speak in tongues.[6]

Samarin's sources include responses to a questionnaire and a transcription of a tape recording of a Full Gospel Business Men's Fellowship meeting, where people were invited to receive the baptism in the Spirit. There were 84 questionnaire responses from different groups in Canada, Germany, England, Holland and the USA. They were mostly from middle-class Protestant members of the Charismatic Movement rather than established Pentecostal groups. Samarin investigated the acquisition of glossolalia by means of questions concerning: the desire to speak in tongues, friends and family who spoke in tongues, encouragement or exhortation, instruction or guidance about what might occur, difficulties encountered, first experience and expectations and the improvement of one's ability to speak in tongues as time passed.

Samarin argues that, strictly speaking, glossolalia cannot be learned in the sense that one would learn a normal human language. This is because each tongue speech is produced more or less *de novo*. However, in another sense glossolalia is learned because it is associated with becoming a member of a social group. The main requirement for someone to speak in tongues is a desire to do so as part of a search for a new or better religious experience. Often the instruction given to those seeking baptism in the Spirit is minimal concerning tongues. It may contain some instruction to submit oneself to God and to relax. This can be supplemented in a number of ways. For instance, a person may be advised: (1) to speak whatever comes to mind; or (2) to 'make sounds' of any kind, with allusions often made to childlike speech; or (3) to imitate the utterances of others as they speak in tongues; or (4) to repeat a brief meaningless utterance (which has already come to mind) in the hope that fluent productive glossolalia will follow; or (5) to repeat a meaningful word or phrase, for example 'El Shaddai' or 'Praise Jesus', as a means of speaking in tongues. Such instruction is often accompanied by an expectant atmosphere, constructed by the use of silence, hushed voices, the rhetoric of the preacher and fostered by the 'laying on of hands'.[7] However, Samarin qualifies these comments by saying that the social setting in which the acquisition of glossolalia occurs appears to be so varied as to make it irrelevant.[8] But the question is whether there is some underlying social influence which transcends local variations?

According to Samarin, the language learning instruction is to be summarized by saying that the respondents to his questionnaire were given no clear model as to how to speak in tongues, and that many of them had not heard glossolalia for long enough to conceive their own model of it. They did not know the phonological elements required to produce glossolalia or how to group these elements together in speech. All that they understood was that whatever they said would be 'real words from a real language unknown to themselves'.[9] In addition, Samarin argues that there will always be people for whom this minimal instruction does not apply. These people find themselves speaking in tongues without intending to do so, privately, and without any knowledge of the Pentecostal and charismatic traditions. However, such people are expected to be rare in number.

For Samarin, the instruction that is given in meetings is of little linguistic importance. Someone who has been exposed to glossolalia, however, can retain enough information so that he or she is able to use the same sound, intonation and paralinguistic devices. He suggests that it is more likely that glossolalic patterns be passed on within the circle of those who already speak in tongues. Therefore, glossolalic control improves, and people learn to use it in different ways.[10]

In summary, Samarin argues that the desire for deeper spiritual experience when linked to the setting variables located in the various contexts predisposes individuals to speak in tongues. The implicit assumptions within the Charismatic Movement create contexts in which the seeker is able to take a 'jump into the dark' and begin speaking in tongues.

2. Qualitative Method

As discussed in chapter 5, participant observation was carried out over a period of seven months in which I visited Sunday worship on eight occasions.[11] Documents relating to the church life were analysed, and included Sunday newsletters, foundation documents, which were written at the church's inception, the Alpha course material used by the church,[12] and the book by Nicky Gumbel.[13] Semi-structured interviews were conducted on nine occasions with a total of thirteen people taking part. The interviews were tape recorded and subsequently transcribed.[14] Some of the interview questions targeted the relevant areas of: church background and Christian experience, initial and current experience of glossolalia, frequency of use, contexts and sources of understanding or interpretation. Data analysis was conducted with the assistance of a free-form text retrieval system.[15]

3. Qualitative Data

All of those interviewed had wished to receive spiritual gifting from God when they initially found themselves speaking in tongues. There were five who specifically emphasized the fact that they had been seeking the gift (Steven, Rebecca, Ruth, Emily and Rachel), although the circumstances varied. For Steven in particular, the biblical injunction of 1 Corinthians 14:1, that one should 'eagerly desire spiritual gifts', was inspirational. However, *all* were influenced by some of the biblical teaching on the matter of spiritual gifts and glossolalia as it is mediated through the contemporary Charismatic Movement.

Most interviewees were able to confirm that they had been encouraged to speak in tongues by someone they knew or had met. There were five who linked it to their experience of baptism in the Spirit (Steven, Kate, Robert, Philip and Adam). One associated an initial experience of glossolalia with her water baptism (Rachel). Another person received the gift while seeking it privately at home (Rebecca). There were three others who received explicit instructions while seeking to speak in tongues.

First, Jane told the story of how she was prayed over by a Baptist minister friend and his wife. She was told to say whatever came to mind at a later time, when she was expected to pray at home. In other words, she was to verbalize what sounds came into mind. This she was able to do and remembers consciously deciding to say the 'words' she had in her mind.

Second, Ruth had also been prayed for in order to receive the gift. The advice she received, after having had a failed attempt two years previously, was to be 'practical'. She should not expect tongues to suddenly flow, she had to speak aloud any syllables which came to mind. This she was able to do. Subsequently, some time later, she attended a charismatic camp seminar on the subject of praying for a 'new' tongue. This she received and discovered it to be better than the 'old' one, to which she never returned.

Third, Emily had been seeking the gift for some time, but to no avail. She had been helping at a children's camp where the children had been speaking in tongues. She was frustrated by her own inability and sought counsel. She was advised that there was nothing that anyone else could do, that she had to do it herself. She was disappointed at the time but later 'decided' to do it. She said one 'word' and kept repeating that 'word' over and over again. She felt that it was like a baby language one had to repeat and practise. Subsequently more 'words' were added until she became fluent.

All the informants, except Julie, had experienced other forms of charismatic Christianity before coming to the ACC. In most cases it appears that the wider charismatic scene has more influence than their present church. Here tongues are rarely used in public. Therefore the socialization of people into the acceptance of glossolalia occurs largely from previous church experience or wider charismatic contact.

Finally, most of the interviewees felt that they had developed their glossolalia through some form of practice. More 'words' came as existing 'words' were used. Thus the speech became more fluent as longer time periods were spent using it. More purpose was developed and different uses discovered (for example, worship, intercession and spiritual warfare). Only two people felt that their glossolalia had declined in recent times. Philip felt that his use of tongues had declined through lack of practice, thus the habit had changed, while Adam believed speaking in tongues was now drier and less exciting than it had been previously. He preferred the use of silence when praying, but noticed that during a time of crisis he returned to using tongues. Finally, Basil had declared himself a non-tongues speaker. He had at one point received one 'word' in his mind but felt unable to proceed. He dismissed his inability to speak in tongues as due to being a linguist and a Latin teacher! He has nevertheless felt edified by the tongues speech of others.

4. Reflections on Qualitative Data

It is inevitable that the person's desire to speak in tongues is informed by the charismatic tradition he or she has encountered. The gift of tongues is legitimized by reference to the Bible, which informs the basic perceptions of reality through which the phenomenon is socialized. The variety of social contexts in which people learn and practise glossolalia indicates, as Samarin suggests, that the social setting is highly varied and perhaps not as stereotyped as might be thought in terms of the acquisition of glossolalia. In the ACC the public use of tongues is infrequent and largely limited to singing in tongues. This means that informants utilize the setting variables of the wider Charismatic Movement to support and reinforce their belief and practice. This is confirmed by the fact that only one informant (Julie) encountered tongues initially at ACC, where it was associated for her with becoming a Christian and joining a social group. Socialization occurred here, but more significantly at the Good News Crusade Camp and other occasions where the social expectation to practise glossolalia was considerably higher. It is also clear that those whose practice of glossolalia had decreased were people who had less contact, and therefore less continued socialization, with the wider Charismatic Movement than others interviewed (Philip and Adam).[16]

Although the social contexts vary immensely there appears to be a socialization process in operation. It may be expressed in weaker terms at one end of the spectrum, for example, being 'encouraged' to speak in tongues; or by simply picking up the clues from the social context. Alternatively, it can be expressed in more explicit terms at the other end of the spectrum, where the instructions given to seekers are clearly expressed. Both extremes are located within the data from the case study. The development of tongues speech recorded in the data also coheres with what Samarin describes. People develop their ability to speak in tongues not in isolation but within a Christian community, that is, within continued socialization. Therefore it is not surprising that individuals will consciously or unconsciously adopt certain language styles and perceptions which reflect their particular group, and in some cases other groups as well. However, this socialization interpretation simply draws out the largely implicit (but sometimes explicit) influences at work throughout the Charismatic Movement. Further research is required to elucidate the nature of the glossolalic experience for the minority who do not fit into this category, that is, those people who suddenly find themselves speaking in tongues without having any charismatic socialization whatsoever.

5. Quantitative Method

The questionnaire used for the survey contained a number of items that can be used to test the theory of socialization in relation to glossolalia. The following questions are relevant to our discussion.

- Do you speak in tongues?

  The answer options were: (1) nearly every day, (2) at least once a week, (3) at least once a month, (4) occasionally, (5) used to, but not now, (6) never.

- Have you been baptized in the Holy Spirit?

  The answer options were: (1) yes, (2) no, (3) don't know.

- If yes, did you speak in tongues at the same time?

  The answer options were: (1) yes, (2) no.

- Do you associate speaking in tongues with joining the Charismatic Movement?

  The answer options were: (1) yes, (2) no, (3) don't know.

- Does your speaking in tongues sound similar to the speaking in tongues of the person who first led you into this experience?'

  The answer options were, on a Likert scale: 1 = extremely little, 7 = extremely much.

- What is the purpose of speaking in tongues?

  The answer options were: (1) prayer, (2) prophecy, (3) worship, (4) spiritual battle. The answers were measured according to the Likert scale: 1 = extremely little, 7 = extremely much.

- How much have the following helped you to understand speaking in tongues?

  The categories were: (1) famous preachers (P), (2) church leaders (L), (3) friends (F), (4) conferences (C), (5) books (B), (6) magazines (M), (7) audio tapes (AT), (8) video tapes (VT), (9) personal Bible study (PBS). The answers were measured according to the Likert scale: 1 = extremely little, 7 = extremely much. This item is a significant measure of charismatic socialization because when tested together as a nine-item scale of measurement it achieved a Cronbach alpha reliability score of .8130. However, for our purposes, which benefit from seeing how the individual items work, I shall focus on its components.

Hypotheses

The following hypotheses were formulated in order to guide the research process.

1. Speaking in tongues is part of the socialization process of joining the Pentecostal and/or Charismatic Movement.
2. A person's tongues speech is influenced by the tongues speech of the person who prayed for them to be led into the experience.
3. Socialization factors influence the frequency of speaking in tongues.
4. Socialization factors influence the purpose of speaking in tongues.

6. Results

Table 10.1: Frequency Count

(1) Speaking in tongues (%)	
Never	15.5
Used to, but not now	0.6
Occasionally	14.8
At least once a month	4.7
At least once a week	18.5
Nearly every day	44.7
Not applicable	1.1
Total	100.0
(2) Baptized in the Spirit (%)	
No	3.9
Don't know	4.7
Yes	90.2
Not applicable	0.8
Total	100.0

(3) Speak in tongues at baptism in the Spirit (%)	
No	58.5
Yes	32.9
Not applicable	8.7
Total	100.0
(4) Associated with joining the Charismatic Movement (%)	
No	62.2
Don't know	9.0
Yes	24.3
Not applicable	4.4
Total	100.0
(5) Speech sounds like the person's speech who led me (%)	
Extremely little	49.6
Very little	5.7
Little	3.5
Neutral	2.7
Much	1.3
Very much	0.8
Extremely much	1.1
Not applicable	35.4
Total	100.0

Table 10.1 shows that the majority of respondents speak in tongues regularly and that they have been baptized in the Spirit (90.2%). The majority did not, however, speak in tongues at their baptism in the Spirit (58.5%), nor do they associate speaking in tongues with joining the Charismatic Movement (62.2%). Nor do they regard their tongues speech as sounding like the speech of the person who led them into that experience. The majority of those answering this question (49.6%) thought that the influence was extremely little.

Table 10.2: Correlation (Pearson's r) socialization factors and the frequency of tongues speech

	P	L	F	C	B	M	AT	VT	PBS
Frequency	.146**	.091*	NS	.132**	.134**	.100*	.107*	.128**	.256**

** = significant at the .01 level

* = significant at the .05 level

Table 10.2 shows that the frequency of speaking in tongues is influenced by the socialization factors, with the exception of friends. The most influential factor is personal Bible study.

Table 10.3: Correlation (Pearson's r) socialization factors and purpose of tongues speech

Purpose of tongues	P	L	F	C	B	M	AT	VT	PBS
Prayer	.243**	.242**	.205**	.198**	.274**	.140**	.222**	.139**	.395**
Prophecy	.243**	.234**	.124*	.221**	.136**	.153**	.228**	.259**	.211**
Worship	.227**	.209**	.133**	.196**	.220**	.122*	.182**	.178**	.340**
Spiritual battle	.204**	.156**	.116*	.196**	.177**	.144**	.193**	.188**	.268**

** = significant at the .01 level

* = significant at the .05 level

Table 10.3 shows that all the socialization factors are significantly correlated to the items of the purpose of speaking in tongues for prayer, prophecy, worship and spiritual battle. The most significant correlations are for the factor of personal Bible study in relation to the activities of prayer, worship and spiritual battle.

7. Discussion

Hypothesis 1 is uncorroborated by this data. Although the majority of respondents have experienced baptism in the Spirit they do not regard it as either associated with speaking in tongues or with joining the Charismatic Movement. This data suggest that approximately a quarter (24.3%) of respondents make such an association. Therefore, the element of socialization which understands speaking in tongues as a boundary marker that people experience in order to belong to a Pentecostal or charismatic group has only limited support.

Hypothesis 2 is uncorroborated by the data, according to which most of those answering the question regarded their tongues speech to be dissimilar to person who prayed for them to receive the gift. The fact that only 64.6% of the respondents answered the question may indicate a certain ambivalence towards the question.

Hypothesis 3 is corroborated with respect to all but one of the socialization factors and the frequency of speaking in tongues generally. The most important influences are personal Bible study, famous preachers, books, conferences and video tapes.

Hypothesis 4 is entirely corroborated. The socialization factors are associated with the purpose of speaking in tongues for prayer, prophecy, worship and spiritual battle. The most significant influence is personal Bible study, especially for prayer, worship and spiritual battle. Prophecy is, however, most influenced by video tapes. Again, the impact of personal Bible study must be noted.

8. Conclusion

In summary, these data suggest that Samarin overestimates the role that friends and family play with regard to learning to speak in tongues. There may well be encouragement and guidance as to what might occur but this does not correspond with direct imitation in most cases. For some there is a link to the experience of baptism in the Spirit, but this is now a minority experience within the British Pentecostal and charismatic movements. Certainly the socialization factors tested suggest a broad influence of the Charismatic Movement; the most significant influences are personal Bible study and church leadership. This suggests that while literature and media are significant, they play a secondary role compared to church leaders and charismatic and evangelical spirituality, which is rooted in personal Bible study. The significance of personal Bible study should not, however, surprise Pentecostal and charismatic

Christians, whose worldview is informed and shaped by the text of Scripture.

This study seeks to combine both theology and social science in a mutually enlightening manner. However, theology cannot be entirely reduced to social science without serious loss of identity. Rather, the practical theological approach affirms the idea that within the *charismata* grace works in and through human nature, including socialization processes. As Max Turner argues:

> even a 'learned behaviour' or a form of utterance initially psychologically induced might (in God's grace, and when directed to him in a doxology of love) *become* a 'supernatural' divine gift (even if not a 'miraculous' one), in the same fashion as a person's natural teaching gifts may become on occasion the spiritual gift of powerful preaching that 'brings all heaven down' to listeners.[17]

Therefore theology and social science may both illuminate the contemporary phenomenon of glossolalia in complementary terms. This social science perspective also highlights the limitations of the socialization theory: it can only explain or interpret glossolalia partially (the hypotheses were corroborated only partially).[18] Nevertheless, it identifies the importance of the wider sociological base in relation to which *most*, if not all, acquire and sustain glossolalia. It is in this sense that the perspective of Samarin can be understood to shed light on the social settings in which the prospective tongue speaker takes a 'jump into the dark'. It is theology in dialogue with empirical research (hence empirical theology) which begins to illuminate that darkness, or mystery, and helps practitioners and critics alike understand something of the *significance* of charismatic glossolalic praxis.

9. Methodological Reflection

This study considers the nature of an important sociological theory of socialization by first of all engaging with scholarly literature on the subject. Inductively gathered qualitative data is re-interrogated by means of this theoretical approach. The resulting material is reflected upon in the light of the original theoretical approach.

Some of the questions relevant to this theory are re-examined in the survey questionnaire database before being reflected upon in light of the original theoretical perspective. Recommendations to theological praxis are suggested in the light of this research so that a greater understanding of Pentecostals and charismatics in Britain is gained.

In this example, while the study is guided by theory, qualitative data precedes and prepares the way for quantitative data. However, it is possible for this position to be reversed, in which case qualitative data would offer in-depth descriptions and subtle nuances to the picture offered by the quantitative data. As this study shows, a serious engagement with the actual theological praxis of Pentecostals and charismatics by means of qualitative and quantitative empirical data can equip researchers and church leaders with different types of knowledge upon which to base strategies for renewed theological praxis at local, national and international levels. The study highlights the important socializing role of personal Bible study and the influence of church leadership. Therefore practical strategies could be put in place to enhance and supervise the effectiveness of both roles in relation to socialization in general and the acquisitions and use of glossolalia in particular. Spiritual gifts are given to the church as the community of God to be used within a context of gratitude and love for the sake of the kingdom. The key use of glossolalia is in terms of worship and prayer; and opportunities should be modelled for the sensitive and appropriate use of this gift in church services and small group settings. A recognition of the fact that the Holy Spirit uses socialization processes but is not constrained by them can assist us to understand how grace intertwines with nature.

---

[1] The qualitative basis for this chapter was published previously as 'The Socialization of Glossolalia' in L. J. Francis (ed.), *Sociology, Theology and the Curriculum* (London: Cassell, 1999) pp. 125–34.

[2] A. Walker, *Restoring the Kingdom: The Radical Christianity of the House Church Movement* (London: Hodder & Stoughton, 1985); N. Scotland, *Charismatics and the Next Millennium – Do they have a Future?* (London: Hodder & Stoughton, 1994).

3 V. S. Poythress, 'Linguistic and Sociological Analyses of Modern Tongues-Speaking: Their Contribution and Limitations', *Westminster Theological Journal* 42 (1980) pp. 367–88 (p. 369).

4 P. Berger, *The Social Reality of Religion* (Harmondsworth: Penguin, 1973) p. 25.

5 W. J. Samarin, 'Glossolalia as Learned Behaviour', *Canadian Journal of Theology* 15 (1969) pp. 60–4; W. J. Samarin, 'Language in Resocialization', *Practical Anthropology* 17 (1970) pp. 269–79; W. J. Samarin, *Tongues of Men and of Angels* (New York: Macmillan, 1972); W. J. Samarin, 'Glossolalia as Regressive Speech', *Language and Speech* 16 (1973) pp. 77–89; W. J. Samarin, 'Making Sense of Glossolalic Nonsense', *Social Research* 46.1 (1979) pp. 88–105. See also the discussions by A. A. Lovekin and H. N. Malony, *Glossolalia: Behavioural Science Perspectives on Speaking in Tongues* (Oxford: Oxford University Press, 1985) and M. M. Poloma, *The Assemblies of God at the Crossroads: Charisma and Institutional Dilemmas* (Knoxville: University Press of Tennessee Press, 1989).

6 Samarin, *Tongues of Men and of Angels*, p. 55.

7 Ibid. pp. 50–8.

8 Ibid. p. 61.

9 Samarin, 'Glossolalia as Learned Behaviour', p. 62.

10 Samarin, 'Glossolalia as Regressive Speech', p. 87.

11 T. May, *Social Research: Issues, Methods and Process* (Buckingham: Open University Press, 1993); D. Silverman, *Interpreting Qualitative Data – Methods for Analysing Talk, Text and Interaction* (London: Sage, 1993).

12 *Alpha Training Manual* (London: Holy Trinity Brompton, 1993).

13 N. Gumbel, *A Life Worth Living* (Eastbourne: Kingsway, 1994).

14 B. L. Berg, *Qualitative Research Methods for the Social Sciences* (Boston: Allyn & Bacon, 1989) ch. 2; May, *Social Research*, ch. 6; Silverman, *Interpreting Qualitative Data*, ch. 5.

15 *Nota Bene Orbis* (Baltimore: The Technology Group Inc., 1993); I. Dey, *Qualitative Data Analysis* (London: Routledge, 1993).

16 Berger, *The Social Reality of Religion*, p. 26.

17 M. Turner, *The Holy Spirit and Spiritual Gifts: Then and Now* (Carlisle: Paternoster, 1996) p. 310.

18 V. H. Hine, 'Pentecostal Glossolalia: Toward a Functional Interpretation', *Journal of the Scientific Study of Religion* 8.2 (1969) pp. 211–26 (p. 221).

Appendix 1:
Speaking in Tongues: Interview Schedule

In light of feedback from the first set of interviews, Appendix 1 was modified. Changes to questions or new questions are in italic.

DATE: ....

TIME STARTED: ....

PLACE: ....

NAME: ....

ADDRESS: ....

TELEPHONE: ....

SEX: ....

AGE GROUP: −19/20–29/30–39/40–49/50–59/60–69/70–79/80+

MARITAL STATUS: ....

FAMILY: ....

OCCUPATION: ....

CHURCH BACKGROUND: ....

PRESENT CHURCH AFFILIATION: ....

1. What do you understand by the phrase 'speaking in tongues'?

2. *When did you first hear someone speaking in tongues?*

3. *When did you start speaking in tongues in relation to first hearing it?*

4. How long have you been speaking in tongues?

5. Can you tell me about your initial experience?

6. *Was there a key person or people who helped you speak in tongues?*

7. How frequently do you speak in tongues?

8. How does your current experience compare to your initial experiences?

9. *Can you trace any development in your speech?*

10. Would you wish to describe it as a language in any sense?

11. Can you speak in tongues when you want to or not?

12. Who would you say you are speaking to when you speak in tongues?

13. *What is the intended aim of speaking in tongues?*

14. Is the ability to speak in tongues limited to a particular time or a place?

15. *Would you say that anyone can speak in tongues?*

16. Where and when do you speak in tongues most often?

17. Have you spoken in church meetings, whether small groups or larger congregations?

18. Did anyone give an interpretation?

19. How do you understand the idea of the interpretation of tongues?

20. How do you feel when you are speaking in tongues?

21. *Are there any particular thoughts which go through your mind at the time of speaking, or perhaps just before or after?*

22. *Are there any specific physical accompaniments which you associate with speaking in tongues*

23. *What effect do you think it has upon you the speaker?*

24. What effect do you think it has upon others who hear you?

25. *Do you associate tongues as being a sign of anything?*

26. *Do you use any particular sections of the Bible to help you understand what you are doing?*

27. What Christian books about speaking in tongues have you found helpful?

28. Is there any other Christian teaching material which you have found helpful?

29. Are you able to give me a sample of speaking in tongues which I can record? (2–3 minutes if possible)

30. Is there anything which you would like to add to what you have already told me?

Time Finished: ....

Appendix 2:

Charismatic Church
and Speaking in Tongues Survey

This survey is being given to a large number of
Charismatic Christians in the Liverpool area.
Please help by completing the questionnaire
and returning it as soon as possible.

Contact:
The Revd Mark Cartledge

Your replies will be completely confidential and anonymous.
The number at the top of this questionnaire is there only to
help us identify those who do *not* send a questionnaire back.

Thank you for your help.

MARK CARTLEDGE
PhD Student, Trinity College, Carmarthen

PREFACE

If you wish to expand on any of the questions in this survey please use the space provided on the back page.

Please help with this survey if you consider yourself to be a Charismatic Christian. Your replies are important to build up a full picture of the views of Charismatic Christians.

If you need any further information about this survey please contact the Revd Mark Cartledge at the address given on the cover.

© 1997 Mark J. Cartledge, William K. Kay and Leslie J. Francis

[Certain parts of this questionnaire have been omitted for the purpose of this appendix.]

PART 1. INSTRUCTIONS: This part of the questionnaire asks for some information about yourself and your church. Please tick the appropriate boxes.

1. What is your sex?

male	1
female	2

2. What is your age?

under 25	1
25–29	2
30–34	3
35–39	4
40–44	5
45–49	6
50–54	7
55–59	8
60–64	9
65–69	10
70–74	11
75 or over	12

3. What is your marital status?

single	1
married	2
widowed	3
divorced	4
divorced and remarried	5

4. What qualifications do you have?
   Please tick the highest you possess.

CSE	1
GCSE	2
O level	3
A level	4
Dip HE	5
Degree	6
Master's	7
Doctorate	8
other	9
please specify	

5. What is your occupation?
   Please be as precise as possible.

6. How long have you been a
   Christian?

under 5 yrs	0	
5–9 yrs	1	
10–14 yrs	2	
15–19 yrs	3	
20–24 yrs	4	
25–29 yrs	5	
30–34 yrs	6	
35–39 yrs	7	
40–44 yrs	8	
over 45 yrs	9	

7. What church denomination do
   you attend currently?

Assemblies of God	1	
Baptist	2	
Church of England	3	
Elim	4	
F.I.E.C.	5	
House/New Church	6	
Methodist	7	
Quaker	8	
Roman Catholic	9	
United Reformed	10	
other	11	
please specify		

8. Which other denominations have
   you attended in the past?
   You may tick more than one box.

Assemblies of God	1	
Baptist	2	
Church of England	3	
Elim	4	

8. Which other denominations have you attended in the past?
(*continued*)

F.I.E.C.	5
House/New Church	6
Methodist	7
Quaker	8
Roman Catholic	9
United Reformed	10
other	11
please specify	

9. Are you an ordained person?

yes	2
no	1

10. Do you speak in tongues?

nearly every day	6
at least once a week	5
at least once a month	4
occasionally	3
used to but not now	2
never	1

11. Have you been baptized by the Holy Spirit?

yes	3
no	1
don't know	2

12. If yes, did you speak in tongues at the same time?

yes	2
no	1

13. How long have you been speaking in tongues?

under 5 yrs	0
5–9 yrs	1
10–14 yrs	2
15–19 yrs	3
20–24 yrs	4
25–29 yrs	5
30–34 yrs	6
35–39 yrs	7
40–44 yrs	8
over 45 yrs	9

14. Would you describe your 'tongue' as an earthly language?

yes	3
no	1
don't know	2

15. If yes, can you identify it?
Please specify.

16. Do you attend Charismatic Days/Conferences/Camps?

yes	3
no	1
used to but don't now	2

17. Do you read Charismatic literature?

yes	3
no	1
used to but don't now	2

18. Do you listen/watch Charismatic audio/video tapes?

yes	3
no	1
used to but don't now	2

19. Do you associate speaking in tongues with joining the Charismatic Movement?

yes	3
no	1
don't know	2

20. Can you speak in tongues when you want to?

yes	4
no	1
sometimes	3
don't know	2

21. Is speaking in tongues a means of persuasion?

yes	3
no	1
don't know	2

22. If yes, who is being persuaded?
You may tick more than one box.

God	4	
others	3	
myself	2	
other	1	
specify		

23. Are you in control of yourself
when you speak in tongues?

yes	3	
no	1	
sometimes	2	

24. Are you in a 'trance' when you
speak in tongues?

yes	3	
no	1	
sometimes	2	

25. Please tick one box in each row to indicate how often in the past six months
you have done the following things.

	none	1–6	7–12	13–18	19+
given a public utterance in tongues					
interpreted tongues					
sung in tongues					
given positive testimony about the Toronto Blessing					
prophesied					
danced in the Spirit					
given a 'word of wisdom/knowledge'					
received a definite answer to a specific prayer request					
felt led by God to perform a specific action					
given a prophecy privately to another person					
been 'slain in the Spirit'					
heard God through a dream or vision					
given a testimony about miracles					
experienced the Toronto Blessing					
experienced 'laughing in the Spirit'					
prayed for the salvation of specific people					

PART 2. INSTRUCTIONS: Please circle the appropriate number and answer for all the items.

1. How frequently do you address the following when speaking in tongues?

God	very little	1 2 3 4 5 6 7	very much
Jesus	very little	1 2 3 4 5 6 7	very much
myself	very little	1 2 3 4 5 6 7	very much
Satan	very little	1 2 3 4 5 6 7	very much
other, specify	very little	1 2 3 4 5 6 7	very much

2. How frequently do you engage in the following when speaking in tongues?

praise	very little	1 2 3 4 5 6 7	very much
prayer	very little	1 2 3 4 5 6 7	very much
edification of self	very little	1 2 3 4 5 6 7	very much
other, specify	very little	1 2 3 4 5 6 7	very much

3. Does your speaking in tongues sound similar to the speaking in tongues of the person who first led you into this experience?

	very little	1 2 3 4 5 6 7	very much

4. What is the purpose of speaking in tongues?

prayer	very little	1 2 3 4 5 6 7	very much
prophecy	very little	1 2 3 4 5 6 7	very much
worship	very little	1 2 3 4 5 6 7	very much
spiritual battle	very little	1 2 3 4 5 6 7	very much
other, specify	very little	1 2 3 4 5 6 7	very much

5. How frequently is speaking in tongues preceded by the following?

closed eyes	very little	1	2	3	4	5	6	7	very much
jerking	very little	1	2	3	4	5	6	7	very much
perspiration	very little	1	2	3	4	5	6	7	very much
tears	very little	1	2	3	4	5	6	7	very much
other, specify	very little	1	2	3	4	5	6	7	very much

6. How much have the following helped you to understand speaking in tongues?

famous preachers	very little	1	2	3	4	5	6	7	very much
church leaders	very little	1	2	3	4	5	6	7	very much
friends	very little	1	2	3	4	5	6	7	very much
conferences	very little	1	2	3	4	5	6	7	very much
books	very little	1	2	3	4	5	6	7	very much
magazines	very little	1	2	3	4	5	6	7	very much
audio tapes	very little	1	2	3	4	5	6	7	very much
video tapes	very little	1	2	3	4	5	6	7	very much
personal Bible study	very little	1	2	3	4	5	6	7	very much
other specify	very little	1	2	3	4	5	6	7	very much

PART 3. INSTRUCTIONS: Please answer each question by putting a circle around ONE of the responses 'yes', 'no' or '?' (where '?' = 'don't know').

1. Can the purpose of speaking in tongues change for the person concerned over time?   YES   ?   NO

2. Can the purpose of speaking in tongues differ for different groups?   YES   ?   NO

3. Is the interpretation of tongues directed from God to the congregation?   YES   ?   NO

4. Is the interpretation of tongues directed from the congregation to God?   YES   ?   NO

5. Would you say that any Christian could speak in tongues?   YES   ?   NO

6. Is tongues the only sign of baptism in the Holy Spirit?   YES   ?   NO

7. Is speaking in tongues necessary as the initial evidence of baptism in the Holy Spirit?   YES   ?   NO

8. Do you sometimes feel emotional when you speak in tongues?   YES   ?   NO

9. Can speaking in tongues be playful?   YES   ?   NO

10. Can speaking in tongues be serious?   YES   ?   NO

11. Can speaking in tongues sound like the noises made by infants?   YES   ?   NO

12. Should speaking in tongues be expected of church leaders?   YES   ?   NO

13. Does speaking in tongues bind people together?   YES   ?   NO

14. Can speaking in tongues be a healing experience?   YES   ?   NO

15. Does speaking in tongues convey feelings?   YES   ?   NO

16. Does speaking in tongues make you feel less isolated?   YES   ?   NO

17. Does speaking in tongues make you feel less reserved in public?   YES   ?   NO

18. Do you associate certain sounds in tongues as having specific meanings?   YES   ?   NO

19. If yes, do these meanings occur in your mind as you speak the sounds in tongues out aloud?   YES   ?   NO

20. Do you believe Christians are in daily conflict with demons?   YES   ?   NO

21. Do you believe healing will always occur if a person's faith is great enough?   YES   ?   NO

PART 4. INSTRUCTIONS: In this section please circle EITHER (a) OR (b). DON'T circle more than one option in any given line.

1. Which way of knowing do you *prefer* to trust?

EITHER	OR
(a) intellect	(b) intuition
(a) personal senses	(b) logic
(a) picture language	(b) literal expression
(a) detached observation	(b) individual participation
(a) mysticism	(b) reason

2. How do you *prefer* to think about God?

EITHER	OR
(a) one Being	(b) three Persons

3. How do you *prefer* to understand the Persons of the Trinity?

EITHER	OR
(a) equal	(b) unequal
(a) hierarchy	(b) community
(a) identical	(b) different
(a) eternal	(b) historical

PART 5. INSTRUCTIONS: In this section please circle EITHER (a) OR (b) OR (c). DON'T circle more than one option in any given line.

1. How do you *prefer* to understand God? A Being who is/wants:-

EITHER	OR	OR
(a) interested in me	(b) same as the universe	(c) out there somewhere
(a) fixed to creation	(b) recognizing my problems	(c) a supreme being
(a) watching from afar	(b) celebrating my joys	(c) bound in nature
(a) not above this world	(b) not involved at all	(c) meeting my needs
(a) space, time, history	(b) us to work it out for ourselves	(c) caring for me

2. Which Person do you *prefer* to worship?

EITHER	OR	OR
(a) God the Father	(b) Jesus Christ	(c) the Holy Spirit

3. Which Person do you *prefer* to pray to?

EITHER	OR	OR
(a) God the Father	(b) Jesus Christ	(c) the Holy Spirit

4. Which Person do you *prefer* to adore?

EITHER	OR	OR
(a) God the Father	(b) Jesus Christ	(c) the Holy Spirit

5. Which Person do you *prefer* to thank?

EITHER	OR	OR
(a) God the Father	(b) Jesus Christ	(c) the Holy Spirit

6. Which Person do you *prefer* to have fellowship with?

EITHER	OR	OR
(a) God the Father	(b) Jesus Christ	(c) the Holy Spirit

Glossary

The following list of terms has been constructed in order to assist the non-specialist reader who is unfamiliar with the range of terminology contained in this book. These definitions of terms should be regarded as working definitions enabling the reader to appreciate how I have used them within this study. I have restricted the list either to terms that I regard as important for practical theology or to ones that have not been defined in the text.

ACTION-REFLECTION
: The process of learning, investigation or intervention which proceeds by first seeking to understand the existing action or concrete situation through engagement before subsequently considering abstract possibilities for renewed action.

AFFECTIONS
: Abiding dispositions or concerns that characterize the person.

CRITICAL CORRELATION
: The activity of bringing two different disciplines together in order to allow the mutual critique of one upon the other without disciplinary distinctions being lost.

DIALECTIC
: The oscillation between two opposite or different positions.

DISCOURSE
: A particular way of speaking, writing or communication that assumes certain conventions.

EMPIRICAL THEOLOGY	Theology which is experience orientated usually through an investigation of the beliefs, values and practices of individuals, groups and communities by means of social science research methods.
EPISTEMOLOGY	Theories of knowledge; what we know about something.
ESCHATOLOGY	End of time ideas and thinking, usually conceptualized as part of a scheme.
HERMENEUTICS	Theories or strategies of interpretation regarding literary texts. This may be extended to societies and communities, hence 'social texts'.
HYPOTHESIS	An idea or conjecture regarding a description or explanation of something which posits a positive relationship of some kind.
INTER-DISCIPLINARY	An academic approach that seeks to use two different disciplines in a dialogical manner, without giving priority to one over the other.
INTRA-DISCIPLINARY	An academic approach that places one discipline in a position of privilege and uses other disciplines in a supportive or auxiliary role.
LIBERATION THEOLOGY	Theology that seeks to analyse contemporary situations in the light of oppression in order to help liberate those deemed to be oppressed by oppressors.
METANARRATIVE	A large-scale and universal theory, explanation or story, e.g. Marxism, Christianity and scientific progress.
METHODOLOGY	The conscious process or philosophical approach to doing something. In research it usually refers to the stages through which one moves in order to complete the exercise.

METHODS	The individual tools used in the investigation, e.g. participant observation, questionnaire survey, documentary analysis.
MISSIO DEI	The mission of God.
MISSIOLOGY	The theology of mission.
NULL HYPOTHESIS	The hypothesis that there is no relationship between two samples or two or more variables within a statistical sample, the opposite of a hypothesis.
ONTOLOGY	Speaking of the being of something in itself, the nature of the thing under discussion.
ORTHODOXY	Right praise and right theology.
ORTHOPATHY	Right affections before God and neighbour.
ORTHOPRAXY	Right action or activity.
POSTMODERNITY	The theory that western society has moved beyond the modern view dominated by scientific progress and absolute truth claims, instead there is a suspicion towards grand theories of meaning and truth, and a 'pick-and-mix' attitude towards beliefs and values.
PRACTICAL THEOLOGY	Theology which focuses on the concrete and lived experiences of contemporary people in church and society, and especially the action implications of such theology.
PRAXIS	Value-laden action or activity, conscious or unconscious, explicit or implicit, a mixture of beliefs and practices intertwined.
REFLEXIVITY	Self-awareness on behalf of the researcher regarding one's presuppositions, interests and concerns that influence the research process and outcome.
RELIABILITY	Used in relation to an instrument measuring beliefs or attitudes, it refers to the consistency of the instrument to measure what it intends to, a good instrument works under many different conditions.

VALIDITY   Used in relation to an instrument measuring
                                beliefs or attitudes, it refers to the
                                appropriateness of the instrument to measure
                                what it intends to, the right kind of
                                instrument for the task.

WORLDVIEW   A way of seeing the world, a set of
                                perspectives through which reality is viewed.

Bibliography

Albrecht, D. E., *Rites in the Spirit: A Ritual Approach to Pentecostal/ Charismatic Spirituality* (Sheffield: Sheffield Academic Press, JPTS 17, 1999).

Alpha Training Manual (London: Holy Trinity Brompton, 1993).

Alpha News, December 1995, March 1996, July 1996.

Anderson, A., 'Diversity in the Definition of "Pentecostal/Charismatic" and its Ecumenical Implications', paper presented at 31st Annual Meeting of the Society for Pentecostal Studies (SPS), Southeastern College, Lakeland, Florida, March 2002, pp. 731–47.

Anderson, R., *The Shape of Practical Theology: Empowering Ministry with Theological Praxis* (Downers Grove IL: Inter-Varsity Press, 2001).

Audi, R., *Epistemology: A Contemporary Introduction to the Theory of Knowledge* (London: Routledge, 1998, 2000²).

Archer, K. J., 'Pentecostal Hermeneutics: Retrospect and Prospect', *Journal of Pentecostal Theology* 8 (1996) pp. 63–81.

Baer Jr., R. A., 'Quaker Silence, Catholic Liturgy and Pentecostal Glossolalia: Some Functional Similarities' in W. E. Mills (ed.), *Speaking in Tongues: A Guide to Research on Glossolalia* (Grand Rapids MI: Eerdmans, 1986) pp. 313–27.

Baker, E., 'The Scientific Study of Religion? You must be Joking!', *Journal for the Scientific Study of Religion* 34.3 (1995) pp. 287–310.

Ballard, P., 'The Challenge of Sociology' in P. Ballard (ed.), *The Foundations of Pastoral Studies and Practical Theology* (Cardiff: The Board of Studies for Pastoral Studies, The Faculty of Theology, University College, Cardiff, 1986) pp. 86–94.

—— (ed.), *The Foundations of Pastoral Studies and Practical Theology* (Cardiff: The Board of Studies for Pastoral Studies, The Faculty of Theology, University College, Cardiff, 1986).

—— and Couture, P. (eds), *Globalisation and Difference: Practical Theology in a World Context* (Cardiff: Cardiff Academic Press, 1999).

Ballard, P., 'Practical Theology as an Academic Discipline', *Theology* 782 (1995) pp. 112–22.

—— and Pritchard, J., *Practical Theology in Action: Christian Thinking in the Service of Church and Society* (London: SPCK, 1996).

——, 'Where is British Practical Theology?', *International Journal of Practical Theology* 2 (1999) pp. 295–308.

Barnes, M. H. (ed.), *Theology and the Social Sciences* (Maryknoll NY: Orbis, 2001).

Baum, G. G., 'Remarks of a Theologian in Dialogue with Sociology' in M. H. Barnes (ed.), *Theology and the Social Sciences* (Maryknoll NY: Orbis, 2001) pp. 3–11.

Baxter, M. J., 'Whose Theology? Which Sociology? A Response to John Coleman' in M. H. Barnes (ed.), *Theology and the Social Sciences* (Maryknoll NY: Orbis, 2001) pp. 34–42.

Beckford, R., 'Back to my Roots: Speaking in Tongues for a New Ecclesia', *TransMission* (Bible Society, Summer 2000) pp. 12–13.

——, *Dread and Pentecostal: A Political Theology for the Black Church in Britain* (London: SPCK, 2000).

Benvenuti, S., 'Anointed, Gifted and Called: Pentecostal Women in Ministry', *PNEUMA: The Journal of the Society for Pentecostal Studies* 17.2 (1995) pp. 229–35.

Berg, B. L., *Qualitative Research Methods for the Social Sciences* (Boston: Allyn & Bacon, 1989).

Berger, P., *A Rumour of Angels* (London: Penguin, 1970).

——, *The Social Reality of Religion* (London: Penguin, 1967, 1973²).

Biggar, N., 'Should Pastoral Theology become Postmodern?', *Contact: The Interdisciplinary Journal of Pastoral Studies* 126 (1998) pp. 22–7.

Blaikie, N., *Approaches to Social Enquiry* (Cambridge: Polity Press, 1993, 1995²).

Bloesch, D. G., *A Theology of Word and Spirit: Authority and Method in Theology* (Downers Grove IL: Inter-Varsity Press, 1992).

Blumhofer, E. L., *Aimee Semple McPherson: Everybody's Sister* (Grand Rapids MI: Eerdmans, 1993, 1998²).

——, 'Reflections on the Source of Aimee Semple McPherson's Voice', *PNEUMA: The Journal of the Society of Pentecostal Studies* 17.1 (1995) pp. 21–4.

Bonnington, M., 'Patterns in Charismatic Spirituality: Worship as Dialectic, Sacrament and Story', *Anglicans for Renewal – Skepsis* 83 (2000) pp. 29–35.

Boone, R. J., 'Community and Worship: The Key Components of Pentecostal Christian Formation', *Journal of Pentecostal Theology* 8 (1996) pp. 129–42.

Boulard, F., *An Introduction to Religious Sociology* (London: Darton, Longman & Todd, 1960).

Le Bras, G., 'Religious Sociology and Science of Religions' in J. Brothers (ed.), *Readings in the Sociology of Religion* (London: Pergamon, 1967) pp. 129–49.

Browning, D., *A Fundamental Practical Theology: Descriptive and Strategic Proposals* (Minneapolis: Fortress, 1991, 1996[2]).

——, 'Toward a Fundamental and Strategic Practical Theology' in F. Schweitzer and J. A. van der Ven (eds), *Practical Theology – International Perspectives* (Frankfurt am Main: Peter Lang, 1999) pp. 53–74.

Brueggemann, W., *Theology of the Old Testament: Testimony, Dispute, Advocacy* (Minneapolis: Fortress, 1997).

Bruner, F. D., *A Theology of the Holy Spirit: The Pentecostal Experience and the New Testament Witness* (London: Hodder & Stoughton, 1970).

Bryman, A., *Quantity and Quality in Social Research* (London: Routledge, 1996[2]).

Calvin, J., *Institutes of the Christian Religion*, J. T. McNeill (ed.) and F. L. Battles (tr.) (Philadelphia: Westminster Press, 1960).

Carson, D. A. and Woodbridge, J. D. (eds), *Scripture and Truth* (Leicester: Inter-Varsity Press, 1983).

Cartledge, M. J., *Charismatic Glossolalia: An Empirical-Theological Study* (Aldershot: Ashgate, 2002).

——, 'Charismatic Prophecy', *Journal of Empirical Theology* 8.1 (1995) pp. 71–88.

——, 'Charismatic Prophecy: A Definition and Description', *Journal of Pentecostal Theology* 5 (1996) pp. 115–26.

——, 'Charismatic Women and Prophetic Activity', *The Spirit and Church* 3.1 (2001) pp. 97–111.

——, 'Empirical Theology: Inter- or Intra-disciplinary?', *Journal of Beliefs and Values* 20.1 (1999) pp. 98–104.

——, 'Empirical Theology: Towards an Evangelical-Charismatic Hermeneutic', *Journal of Pentecostal Theology* 9 (1996) p. 115–26.

——, 'The Future of Glossolalia: Fundamentalist or Experientialist?', *Religion* 28.3 (1998) pp. 233–44.

——, '*Interpreting Charismatic Experience* by David Middlemiss (London: SCM, 1996)', *Evangelical Quarterly* 71.1 (1999) pp. 85–8 (book review).

——, 'Interpreting Charismatic Experience: Hypnosis, Altered States of Consciousness and the Holy Spirit?', *Journal of Pentecostal Theology* 13 (1998) pp. 117–32.

Cartledge, M. J., 'The Nature and Function of New Testament Glossolalia', *Evangelical Quarterly* 72.2 (2000) pp. 135–50.

——, 'New Testament Prophecy and Charismatic Prophecy', *Themelios* 17.1 (1991) pp. 17–19.

——, 'A New *Via Media*: Charismatics and the Church of England in the Twenty-first Century', *Anvil* 17.4 (2000) pp. 271–83.

——, 'Practical Theology and Charismatic Spirituality: Dialectics in the Spirit', *Journal of Pentecostal Theology* 10.2 (2002) pp. 93–109.

——, 'Practical Theology and Empirical Identity', *European Journal of Theology* 7.1 (1998) pp. 37–44.

——, 'Prophecy in the Contemporary Church: A Theological Examination' (Master of Philosophy dissertation, Council for National Academic Awards, 1989).

——, 'The Role of Testimony in Worship', *Anglicans for Renewal – Skepsis* 87 (2001) pp. 27–31.

——, 'The Socialization of Glossolalia' in L. J. Francis (ed.), *Sociology, Theology and the Curriculum* (London: Cassell, 1999) pp. 125–34.

——, 'A Spur to Holistic Discipleship' in Hilborn D. (ed.), *'Toronto' in Perspective: Papers on the New Charismatic Wave of the Mid 1990s* (Carlisle: Evangelical Alliance/Paternoster, 2001) pp. 64–71.

——, *Testimony: Its Importance, Place and Potential* (Cambridge: Grove, Renewal 9, 2002).

——, 'Testimony to the Truth of Encounter: A Study of Pentecostal-Charismatic Epistemology', paper presented at 31st Annual Meeting of the Society for Pentecostal Studies (SPS), Southeastern College, Lakeland, Florida, March 2002, pp. 595–611.

——, 'Tongues of the Spirit: An Empirical-Theological Study of Charismatic Glossolalia' (PhD dissertation, University of Wales, 1999).

Chan, S., *Pentecostal Theology and the Christian Spiritual Tradition* (Sheffield: Sheffield Academic Press, JPTS 21, 2000).

Church of England (House of Bishops of the General Synod), *A Time to Heal: A Contribution Towards the Ministry of Healing* (London: Church House, 2000).

Coady, C. A. J., *Testimony: A Philosophical Study* (Oxford: Clarendon Press, 1992, 2000²).

Coenen, L., 'Witness' in C. Brown (ed.), *The New International Dictionary of the New Testament* Vol. 3 (Exeter: Paternoster, 1978) pp. 1038–47.

Coleman, J. A., 'Every Theology Implies a Sociology and Vice Versa' in M. H. Barnes (ed.), *Theology and the Social Sciences* (Maryknoll NY: Orbis, 2001) pp. 12–33.

Coolican, H., *Aspects of Psychology: Research Methods and Statistics* (London: Hodder & Stoughton, 1999).

Cotterell, P., *Prosperity Theology* (Leicester: Religious and Theological Studies Fellowship, 1993).

Coulson, J. E. and Johnson, R. W., 'Glossolalia and Internal–External Locus of Control', *Journal of Psychology and Theology* 5 (1977) pp. 312–17.

Cox, H., *Fire from Heaven: The Rise of Pentecostal Spirituality and the Reshaping of Religion in the Twenty-first Century* (London: Cassell, 1996).

Creswell, J. W., *Qualitative Inquiry and Research Design: Choosing among Five Traditions* (London: Sage, 1998).

——, *Research Design: Qualitative and Quantitative Approaches* (London: Sage, 1994).

Dancy, J. and Sosa, E. (eds), *A Companion to Epistemology* (Oxford: Blackwell, 1992, 1993²).

Davis, C. F., *The Evidential Force of Religious Experience* (Oxford: Oxford University Press, 1989, 1999²).

Davies, D., 'Social Groups, Liturgy and Glossolalia', *Churchman* 90 (1976) pp. 193–205.

Delanty, G., *Social Science: Beyond Constructivism and Realism* (Buckingham: Open University Press, 1997).

Dey, I., *Qualitative Data Analysis* (London: Routledge, 1993).

Dillistone, F. W., *The Power of Symbols* (London: SCM, 1986).

Dixon, P, *Signs of Revival* (Eastbourne: Kingsway, 1994).

Dreyer, J. S., 'The Researcher: Engaged Participant or Detached Observer? A Reflection on the Methodological Implications of the Dialectics of Belonging and Distanciation for Empirical Research in Practical Theology', *Journal of Empirical Theology* 11.2 (1998) pp. 5–22.

Ekstrand, T., *Max Weber in Theological Perspective* (Leuven: Peeters, 2000).

Ellington, S. A., 'History, Story, and Testimony: Locating Truth in a Pentecostal Hermeneutic', *PNEUMA: The Journal of the Society for Pentecostal Studies* 23.2 (2001) pp. 245–63.

——, 'The Costly Loss of Testimony', *Journal of Pentecostal Theology* 16 (2000) pp. 48–59.

Everts, J. M., 'Brokenness as the Centre of a Woman's Ministry', *PNEUMA: The Journal of the Society of Pentecostal Studies* 17.2 (1995) pp. 237–43.

Eysenck, H. J. and Eysenck, M. W., *Personality and Individual Differences: A Natural Science Approach* (New York: Plenum Press, 1985).

Flanagan, K., *The Enchantment of Sociology* (London: Macmillan, 1996).

Forrester, D. B., 'Theology in Fragments: Practical Theology and the Challenge of Post-modernity' in P. Ballard and P. Couture (eds), *Globalisation and Difference: Practical Theology in a World Context* (Cardiff: Cardiff Academic Press, 1999) pp. 129–33.

———, *Truthful Action: Explorations in Practical Theology* (Edinburgh: T&T Clark, 2000).

Fowler, J. W., 'The Emerging New Shape of Practical Theology' in F. Schweitzer and J. A. van der Ven (eds), *Practical Theology – International Perspectives* (Frankfurt am Main: Peter Lang, 1999) pp. 75–92.

Francis, L. J. and Jones, S. H., 'Personality and Charismatic Experience among Adult Christians', *Pastoral Psychology* 45.6 (1997) pp. 421–8.

——— and Kay, W. K., *Drift from the Churches: Attitude toward Christianity during Childhood and Adolescence* (Cardiff: University of Wales Press, 1996).

——— and Kay, W. K., 'The Personality Characteristics of Pentecostal Ministry Candidates', *Personality and Individual Differences* 18.5 (1995) pp. 581–94.

——— and Thomas, T. H., 'Are Charismatic Ministers Less Stable? A Study among Male Anglican Clergy', *Religious Review of Research* 39.1 (1997) pp. 61–9.

Frankenberry, N., 'American Pragmatism' in P. L. Quinn and C. Taliaferro (eds), *A Companion to Philosophy of Religion* (Oxford: Blackwell, 1997, 2000) pp. 121–8.

Garfinkel, H., *Studies in Ethnomethodology* (Cambridge: Polity Press, in association with Blackwell, Oxford, 1984, original publication 1967).

Gibson, H. B., 'Imaginative Involvement, Neuroticism and Charismatic Behaviour: A Note on the Use of the EPI Scales', *Contemporary Hypnosis* 8.2 (1991) pp. 109–11.

Gill, D. M., 'The Contemporary State of Women in Ministry in the Assemblies of God', *PNEUMA: The Journal of the Society for Pentecostal Studies* 17.1 (1995) pp. 33–6.

Gill, R., *Church Going and Christian Ethics* (Cambridge: Cambridge University Press, 1999).

———, *The Social Context of Theology* (London: Mowbray, 1975).

——— (ed.), *Theology and Sociology: A Reader* (London: Cassell, 1996).

Goldingay, J., 'Charismatic Spirituality: Some Theological Reflections', *Theology* 789 (1996) pp. 178–87.

———, *Models for Scripture* (Grand Rapids MI: Eerdmans, 1994).

——— (ed.), *Signs, Wonders and Healing: Seven Prominent Christians Debate Today's Issues* (Leicester: Inter-Varsity Press, 1989).

Goldman, A. I., *Knowledge in a Social World* (Oxford: Clarendon Press, 1999).

Gonsalvez, H. E., 'The Theology and Psychology of Glossolalia' (PhD dissertation, Northwestern University, Evanston IL, 1979).

Goodman, F. D., *Speaking in Tongues: A Cross-cultural Study of Glossolalia* (Chicago: University of Chicago Press, 1972).

Graham, E., 'Pastoral Theology: Therapy, Mission or Liberation?', *Scottish Journal of Theology* 52.4 (1999) pp. 430–54.

——, *Transforming Practice: Pastoral Theology in an Age of Uncertainty* (London: Mowbray, 1996).

Griffith Thomas, W. H., *The Catholic Faith* (London: Church Book Room Press, 1904, revised 1920, 1929, 1952).

Groothius, D., *Truth Decay: Defending Christianity against the Challenge of Postmodernism* (Leicester: Inter-Varsity Press, 2000).

Gumbel, N., *A Life Worth Living* (Eastbourne: Kingsway, 1994).

Haack, S., *Philosophy and Logics* (Cambridge: Cambridge University Press, 1978, 1995).

Hall, D. and Hall, I., *Practical Social Research: Project Work in the Community* (Basingstoke: Macmillan, 1996).

Hargreaves, M., 'Telling Stories: The Concept of Narrative and Biblical Authority', *Anvil* 13.2 (1996) pp. 127–39.

Hart, T., *Faith Thinking* (London: SPCK, 1995).

Hilborn D. (ed.), *'Toronto' in Perspective: Papers on the New Charismatic Wave of the Mid 1990s* (Carlisle: Evangelical Alliance/Paternoster, 2001).

Hine, V. H., 'Pentecostal Glossolalia: Toward a Functional Interpretation', *Journal of the Scientific Study of Religion* 8.2 (1969) pp. 211–26.

Hocken, P., *Streams of Renewal: The Origins and Early Development of the Charismatic Movement in Great Britain* (Carlisle: Paternoster, 1986, 1997[2]).

Hollenweger, W. J., *Pentecostalism: Origins and Developments Worldwide* (Peabody MA: Hendrickson, 1997).

Honderich, T. (ed.), *The Oxford Companion to Philosophy* (Oxford: Oxford University Press, 1995).

Hopkins, K. D., Hopkins, B. R. and Glass, G. V., *Basic Statistics for the Behavioural Sciences* (London: Allyn & Bacon, 1996).

Horwich, P., 'Truth, theories of' in J. Dancy and E. Sosa (eds), *A Companion to Epistemology* (Oxford: Blackwell, 1992, 1993[2]) pp. 509–15.

Hudson, D. N., 'Worship: Singing a New Song in a Strange Land' in K. Warrington (ed.), *Pentecostal Perspectives* (Carlisle: Paternoster, 1998) pp. 177–203.

Jackson, R., 'Prosperity Theology and the Faith Movement', *Themelios* 15 (1989) pp. 16–24.

Johns, C. B., *Pentecostal Formation: A Pedagogy among the Oppressed* (Sheffield: Sheffield Academic Press, JPTS 2, 1993).

Johns, J. D., 'Pentecostalism and the Postmodern Worldview', *Journal of Pentecostal Theology* 7 (1995) pp. 73–96.

—— and Johns, C. B., 'Yielding to the Spirit: A Pentecostal Approach to Group Bible Study', *Journal of Pentecostal Theology* 1 (1992) pp. 109–34 (pp. 125–7).

Kay, W. K., 'A Demonised Worldview: Dangers, Benefits and Explanations', *Journal of Empirical Theology* 11.1 (1998) pp. 17–29.

——, *Pentecostals in Britain* (Carlisle: Paternoster, 2000).

——, *Personality and Renewal* (Cambridge: Grove, Renewal 3, 2001).

—— and Francis, L. J. (eds), *Religion in Education* Vol. 3 (Leominster: Gracewing, 2000).

—— and Francis, L. J., 'The Seamless Robe: Interdisciplinary Enquiry in Religious Education', *British Journal of Religious Education* 7.2 (1985) pp. 64–7.

——, 'A Woman's Place is on her Knees: The Pastor's View of the Role of Women in the Assemblies of God', *Journal of the European Pentecostal Association* 18 (1998) pp. 64–75.

Kildahl, J. P., *The Psychology of Speaking in Tongues* (London: Hodder & Stoughton, 1972).

Kirkham, R. L., *Theories of Truth: A Critical Introduction* (Cambridge MA: Massachusetts Institute of Technology, 1992, 1995²).

Kitzenger. J, 'The Methodology of Focus Groups: The Importance of Interaction between Research and Participants', *Sociology of Health and Illness* 16.1 (1994) pp. 103–21.

Knight III, H. H., 'God's Faithfulness and God's Freedom: A Comparison of Contemporary Theologies of Healing', *Journal of Pentecostal Theology* 2 (1993) pp. 65–89.

Kolb, D. A., *Experiential Learning: Experience as the Source of Learning and Development* (Englewood Cliffs NJ: Prentice Hall, 1984).

Kydd, R. A. N., *Healing through the Centuries: Models for Understanding Healing* (Peabody MA: Hendrickson, 1998).

Land, S. J., *Pentecostal Spirituality: A Passion for the Kingdom* (Sheffield: Sheffield Academic Press, JPTS 1, 1993).

Larty, E., 'Practical Theology as a Theological Form' in D. Willows and J. Swinton (eds), *Spiritual Dimensions of Pastoral Care: Practical Theology in a Multidisciplinary Context* (London: Jessica Kingsley, 2000) pp. 72–7.

Leech, J., *Developing Prayer Ministry: A New Introduction for Churches* (Cambridge: Grove, Renewal 1, 2000).

Lewis, P. W., 'Towards a Pentecostal Epistemology: The Role of Experience in Pentecostal Hermeneutics', *The Spirit and Church* 2.1 (2000) pp. 95–125.

Lincoln, A. T., *Truth on Trial: The Lawsuit Motif in the Fourth Gospel* (Peabody MA: Hendrickson, 2000).

Lindbeck, G. A., *The Nature of Doctrine: Religion and Theology in a Postliberal Age* (London: SPCK, 1984).

Loder, J. E., 'The Place of Science in Practical Theology: The Human Factor', *International Journal of Practical Theology* 4.1 (2000) pp. 22–43.

Lovekin, A. A. and Malony, H. M., *Glossolalia: Behavioural Science Perspectives on Speaking in Tongues* (Oxford: Oxford University Press, 1985).

Louden, S. H. and Francis, L. J., 'Are Catholic Priests in England and Wales Attracted to the Charismatic Movement Less Stable?', *British Journal of Theological Education* 11.2 (2001) pp. 65–76.

Luscombe, P., *Groundwork of Science and Religion* (Peterborough: Epworth Press, 2000).

Lyall, D., 'Psychiatry in Pastoral Studies: An Interprofessional Encounter' in P. Ballard (ed.), *The Foundations of Pastoral Studies and Practical Theology* (Cardiff: The Board of Studies for Pastoral Studies, The Faculty of Theology, University College, Cardiff, 1986) pp. 102–9.

Macchia, F. D., 'Tongues as a Sign: Toward a Sacramental Understanding of Pentecostal Experience', *PNEUMA: The Journal of the Society for Pentecostal Studies* 15.1 (1993) pp. 61–76.

Marshall, B. D., *Trinity and Truth* (Cambridge: Cambridge University Press, 2000).

Marshall, I. H., 'Are Evangelicals Fundamentalists?', *Vox Evangelica* 22 (1992) pp. 7–24.

Martin, B., 'The Pentecostal Gender Paradox: A Cautionary Tale for the Sociology of Religion' in R. K. Fenn (ed.), *The Blackwell Companion to Sociology of Religion* (Oxford: Blackwell, 2001) pp. 52–66.

Martin, D., *Pentecostalism: The World their Parish* (Oxford: Blackwell, 2002).

Martin, D., *Reflections on Sociology and Theology* (Oxford: Clarendon Press, 1997).

Mather, A. R., 'The Theology of the Charismatic Movement in Britain from 1964 to the Present Day', University of Wales, Bangor, 1982.

May, T., *Social Research: Issues, Methods and Process* (Buckingham: Open University Press, 1993).

McGrath, A. E., *Christian Spirituality* (Oxford: Blackwell, 1999).

——, *The Foundations of Dialogue in Science and Religion* (Oxford: Blackwell, 1998).

McGrath, A. E., *A Scientific Theology Volume 1: Nature* (Edinburgh: T&T Clark, 2001).

McGuire, M. B., 'The Social Context of Prophecy: "Word-Gifts" of the Spirit among Catholic Pentecostals', *Review of Religious Research* 18 (1977) pp. 144–5.

McIntosh, M. A., *Mystical Theology* (Oxford: Blackwell, 1998).

Menzies, R. P., *Empowered for Witness: The Spirit in Luke–Acts* (Sheffield: Sheffield Academic Press, JPTS 6, 1994).

Middlemiss, D., *Interpreting Charismatic Experience* (London: SCM, 1996).

Milbank, J., *Theology and Social Theory: Beyond Secular Reason* (Oxford: Blackwell, 1990, 1993²).

Mitton, M., *The Heart of Toronto* (Cambridge: Grove, Spirituality 55, 1995).

Neanon, G. and Hair, J., 'Imaginative Involvement, Neuroticism and Charismatic Behaviour', *British Journal of Experimental and Clinical Hypnosis* 7.3 (1990) pp. 190–2.

Nicole, R., 'The Biblical Concept of Truth' in D. A. Carson and J. D. Woodbridge (eds), *Scripture and Truth* (Leicester: Inter-Varsity Press, 1983) pp. 287–98.

Norusis, M. J., *Guide to Data Analysis* (Upper Saddle River NJ: Prentice Hall, SPSS 8.0, 1998).

O'Connell Killen, P. and der Beer, J., *The Art of Theological Reflection* (New York: Crossroad, 2000).

Parker, S. E., *Led by the Spirit: Toward a Practical Theology of Pentecostal Discernment and Decision Making* (Sheffield: Sheffield Academic Press, JPTS 7, 1996).

Patterson, S., *Realist Christian Theology in a Postmodern Age* (Cambridge: Cambridge University Press, 1999).

Pattison, S., 'The Use of the Behavioural Sciences in Pastoral Studies' in P. Ballard (ed.), *The Foundations of Pastoral Studies and Practical Theology* (Cardiff: The Board of Studies for Pastoral Studies, The Faculty of Theology, University College, Cardiff, 1986) pp. 79–85.

Percy, M., 'Fundamentalism: A Problem for Phenomenology?', *Journal of Contemporary Religion* 10 (1995) pp. 83–91.

——, *Words, Wonders and Power: Understanding Contemporary Christian Fundamentalism and Revivalism* (London: SPCK, 1996).

Peterson, E. H., *The Message: The New Testament in Contemporary Language* (Colorado Springs CO: Navpress, 1993).

Phan, P. C., 'Method in Liberation Theologies', *Theological Studies* 61.1 (2000) pp. 40–63.

Poloma, M., *Assemblies of God at the Crossroads: Charisma and Institutional Dilemmas* (Knoxville: University of Tennessee Press, 1989).

Poloma, M., 'Charisma, Institutionalization and Social Change', *PNEUMA: The Journal of the Society for Pentecostal Studies* 17.2 (1995) pp. 245–52.

——, *The Toronto Report: A Preliminary Sociological Assessment of the Toronto Blessing* (Bradford-upon-Avon: Terra Nova, 1996).

Porter, S. E., 'Shaking the Biblical Foundations? The Biblical Basis for the Toronto Blessing' in Porter, S. E. and Richter, P. J. (eds), *The Toronto Blessing – or is it?* (London: Darton, Longman & Todd, 1995) pp. 38–65.

Powers, J. E., 'Recovering a Woman's Head with Prophetic Authority: A Pentecostal Interpretation of 1 Corinthians 11.3–16', *Journal of Pentecostal Theology* 10.1 (2001) pp. 11–37.

——, ' "Your Daughters Shall Prophesy": Pentecostal Hermeneutics and the Empowerment of Women' in M. W. Dempster, B. D. Klaus and D. Peterson (eds), *The Globalization of Pentecostalism: A Religion Made to Travel* (Carlisle: Regnum/Paternoster, 1999) pp. 313–37.

Poythress, V. S., 'Linguistic and Sociological Analyses of Modern Tongues-Speaking: Their Contribution and Limitations', *Westminster Theological Journal* 42 (1980) pp. 367–88.

Purves, A., 'The Trinitarian Basis for a Christian Practical Theology', *International Journal of Practical Theology* 2.2 (1998) pp. 222–39.

Quinn, P. L. and Taliaferro, C. (eds), *A Companion to Philosophy of Religion* (Oxford: Blackwell, 1997, 2000).

von Rad, G., *Wisdom in Israel* (London: SCM, 1972).

Richards, L., *Using Nvivo in Qualitative Research* (Bundoora, Victoria, Australia: QSR International Pty Ltd, 2000).

Ricoeur, P., *Essays on Biblical Interpretations* (London: SPCK, 1981).

Riley, J., *Getting the Most from your Data: A Handbook of Practical Ideas on how to Analyse Qualitative Data* (Bristol: Technical and Educational Services, 1990).

Roberts, R. C., *Spirituality and Human Emotion* (Grand Rapids MI: Eerdmans, 1982).

Roberts, R. H., *Religion, Theology and the Human Sciences* (Cambridge: Cambridge University Press, 2002).

Robson, C., *Real World Research* (Oxford: Blackwell, 2002[2]).

Roebuck, D. G. and Mundy, K. C., 'Women, Culture and Post-World War Two Pentecostalism' in T. L. Cross and E. B. Powery (eds), *The Spirit and the Mind: Essays in Informed Pentecostalism* (Lanham, MD: University Press of America, 2000) pp. 191–204.

Rorty, R., *Philosophy and the Mirror of Nature* (Oxford: Blackwell, 1980, 1989[2]).

Samarin, W. J., 'Glossolalia as Learned Behaviour', *Canadian Journal of Theology* 15 (1969) pp. 60–4.

——, 'Glossolalia as Regressive Speech', *Language and Speech* 16 (1973) pp. 77–89.

——, 'Language in Resocialization', *Practical Anthropology* 17 (1970) pp. 269–79.

——, 'Making Sense of Glossolalic Nonsense', *Social Research* 46.1 (1979) pp. 88–105.

——, 'Speaking in Tongues: A Cross-cultural Study of Glossolalia by Felicitas D. Goodman, Chicago: University Press of Chicago, 1972', *Language* 50.1 (1974) pp. 207–212.

——, *Tongues of Men and of Angels* (New York: Macmillan, 1972).

Sarbin, T. R. and Coe, W. C., *Hypnosis: A Social Psychological Analysis of Influence Communication* (New York: Holt, Rinehart & Winston, 1972).

Schweitzer, F. and van der Ven, J. A. (eds), *Practical Theology – International Perspectives* (Frankfurt am Main: Peter Lang, 1999).

Scotland, N., *Charismatics and the Next Millennium – Do they have a Future?* (London: Hodder & Stoughton, 1994).

Sequeira, D. L., 'Gifts of Tongues and Healing: The Performance of the Charismatic Renewal', *Text and Performance Quarterly* 14.2 (1994) pp. 126–43.

Shaull, R. and Cesar, W., *Pentecostalism and the Future of the Christian Church: Promises, Limitations, Challenges* (Grand Rapids MI: Eerdmans, 2000).

Shuman, J., 'Toward a Cultural-Linguistic Account of the Pentecostal Doctrine of the Baptism in the Spirit', *PNEUMA: The Journal of the Society for Pentecostal Studies* 19.2 (1997) pp. 207–23.

Silverman, D., *Interpreting Qualitative Data – Methods for Analysing Talk, Text and Interaction* (London: Sage, 1993).

——, *Qualitative Methodology and Sociology: Describing the Social World* (Aldershot: Gower, 1985).

Smail, T., Walker, A. and Wright, N., *Charismatic Renewal: The Search for a Theology* (London: SPCK, 1993).

——, 'The Cross and the Spirit: Towards a Theology of Renewal' in T. Smail, A. Walker and N. Wright (eds), *Charismatic Renewal: The Search for a Theology* (London: SPCK, 1993) pp. 49–70.

——, Walker, A. and Wright, N., '"Revelation Knowledge" and Knowledge of Revelation: The Faith Movement and the Question of Heresy', *Journal of Pentecostal Theology* 5 (1994) pp. 57–77.

Smith, J. K. A., 'The Closing of the Book: Pentecostals, Evangelicals, and the Sacred Writings', *Journal of Pentecostal Theology* 11 (1997) pp. 49–71.

Solivan, S., *The Spirit, Pathos and Liberation: Toward an Hispanic Pentecostal Theology* (Sheffield: Sheffield Academic Press, JPTS 14, 1998).

Spanos, N. P. and Chaves, J. F., *Hypnosis: The Cognitive-Behavioural Perspective* (New York: Prometheus, 1989).

—— and Hewitt, E. C., 'Glossolalia: A Test of the "Trance" and Psychopathology Hypotheses', *Journal of Abnormal Psychology* 88.4 (1979) pp. 427–34.

Springer, K. (ed.), *Riding the Third Wave: What Comes after Renewal?* (Basingstoke: Marshall Pickering, 1987).

Stanley, G., Bartlett, W. K. and Moyle, T., 'Some Characteristics of Charismatic Experience: Glossolalia in Australia' *Journal for the Scientifc Study of Religion* 17.3 (1978) pp. 269–77.

Stanley, S. C., 'Spirit Women: Alma and Aimee Reconciled?', *PURITY AND POWER: Revisioning Holiness and Pentecostal/Charismatic Movements for the Twenty-first Century* (27th Annual Meeting of the Society for Pentecostal Studies in special session with the Wesleyan Theological Society, 1998, vol. 2-Z) pp. 1–13.

Stringer, M. D., *On the Perception of Worship: The Ethnography of Worship in Four Christian Congregations in Manchester* (Birmingham: University of Birmingham Press, 1999).

Synan, V., 'The Role of Tongues as Initial Evidence' in M. W. Wilson (ed.), *Spirit and Renewal: Essays in Honour of J. Rodman Williams* (Sheffield: Sheffield Academic Press, JPTS 5, 1994) pp. 67–82.

Tappeiner, D., 'A Psychological Paradigm for the Interpretation of the Charismatic Phenomenon of Prophecy', *Journal of Psychology and Theology* 5 (1977) pp. 23–9.

Thiselton, A. C., *New Horizons in Hermeneutics: The Theory and Practice of Transforming Biblical Reading* (London: HarperCollins, 1992).

Thomas, J. C., *The Devil, Disease and Deliverance: Origins of Illness in New Testament Thought* (Sheffield: Sheffield Academic Press, JPTS 13, 1998).

——, 'Pentecostal Theology in the Twenty-first Century', *PNEUMA: The Journal of the Society for Pentecostal Studies* 20.1 (1998) pp. 3–19.

Tillich, P., *Systematic Theology* (Chicago: University of Chicago Press, 3 vols, 1951, 1957, 1963).

Tomlinson D., *The Post-Evangelical* (London: Triangle, 1995).

Torrance, T. F., *Theological Science* (Edinburgh: T&T Clark, 1969, 1996²).

Turner, M., *Power from on High: The Spirit in Israel's Restoration and Witness in Luke–Acts* (Sheffield: Sheffield Academic Press, JPTS 9, 1996).

——, *The Holy Spirit and Spiritual Gifts: Then and Now* (Carlisle: Paternoster, 1996).

Vanhoozer, K. J., *Is there a Meaning in this Text? The Bible, the Reader and the Morality of Literary Knowledge* (Leicester: Inter-Varsity Press, 1998).

——, 'The Voice and the Actor: A Dramatic Proposal about the Ministry and Minstrelsy of Theology' in J.G. Stackhouse (ed.), *Evangelical Futures: A Conversation on Theological Method* (Grand Rapids: Baker, Leicester: Inter-Varsity Press and Vancouver: Regent College, 2000) pp. 61–106.

Vaus, de, D. A., *Surveys in Social Research* (London: University College London Press, 1985, 1994²).

van der Ven, J. A., 'An Empirical Approach in Practical Theology' in F. Schweitzer and J. A. van der Ven, *Practical Theology – International Perspectives* (Frankfurt am Main: Peter Lang, 1999) pp. 323–39.

——, *God Reinvented? A Theological Search in Texts and Tables* (Leiden: Brill, 1998).

——, *Practical Theology: An Empirical Approach* (Kampen: Kok Pharos, 1993).

Wagstaff, G. F., *Hypnosis, Compliance and Belief* (Brighton: Harvester Press, 1981).

Walker, A., 'The Devil you Think you Know: Demonology and the Charismatic Movement' in T. Smail, A., Walker and N. Wright, *Charismatic Renewal: The Search for a Theology* (London: SPCK, 1993) pp. 86–105.

——, *Restoring the Kingdom: The Radical Christianity of the House Church Movement* (London: Hodder & Stoughton, 1985).

——, *Telling the Story: Gospel, Mission and Culture* (London: SPCK, 1996).

Warrington, K., 'Healing and Exorcism: The Path to Wholeness' in K. Warrington (ed.), *Pentecostal Perspectives* (Carlisle: Paternoster, 1998) pp. 146–76.

——, 'Major Aspects of Healing within British Pentecostalism', *Journal of the European Pentecostal Theological Association* 19 (1999) pp. 34–55.

—— (ed.), *Pentecostal Perspectives* (Carlisle: Paternoster, 1998).

Watts, F., Nye, R. and Savage, S., *Psychology for Christian Ministry* (London: Routledge, 2002).

Whitely, O. R., 'When You Speak in Tongues: Some Reflections on the Contemporary Search for Ecstasy', *Encounter* 35 (1974) pp. 81–94.

Williams, M. and May, T., *Introduction to the Philosophy of Social Research* (London: University College London Press, 1996).

Wimber, J., *Power Healing* (London: Hodder & Stoughton, 1986).

Wright, N., 'Charismatic Interpretations of the Demonic' in A. N. S. Lane (ed.), *The Unseen World: Christian Reflections on Angels, Demons and the Heavenly* (Carlisle: Paternoster, 1996) pp. 33–64.

Wright, N., 'The Theology and Methodology of Signs and Wonders''' in T. Smail, A. Walker and N. Wright, *Charismatic Renewal: The Search for a Theology* (London: SPCK, 1993) pp. 71–85.

Wright, N. T., *The New Testament and the People of God* (London: SPCK, 1993²).

Yin, R. K., *Applications of Case Study Research* (London: Sage, 1993).

——, *Case Study Research: Design and Methods* (London: Sage, 1989).

Yong, A., 'The Demise of Foundationalism and the Retention of Truth: What Evangelicals can Learn from C. S. Peirce', *Christian's Scholar's Review* 29.3 (2000) pp. 563–88.

——, '"Life in the Spirit": Pentecostal-Charismatic Life and the Dialectic of the Pentecostal Imagination', unpublished paper, 30th Meeting of Society for Pentecostal Studies, 16–18 March 2000, Northwest College, Kirkland, Washington, USA.

——, *Spirit-Word-Community: Theological Hermeneutics in Trinitarian Perspective* (Aldershot: Ashgate, 2002).

——, '"Tongues of Fire" in the Pentecostal Imagination: The Truth of Glossolalia in Light of R. C. Neville's Theory of Religious Symbolism', *Journal of Pentecostal Theology* 12 (1998) pp. 39–65.

Index

Made in the USA
Middletown, DE
13 August 2016